# Tales of
# Tofield

*Tales of Tofield* originally published in 1969
by The Tofield Historical Society

Edited by Grace A. Phillips

Layout and design by Momentum Productions • mpdesign@telus.net

Note for Librarians: a cataloguing record for this book that includes Dewey Decimal Classification and US Library of Congress numbers is available from the Library and Archives of Canada. The complete cataloguing record can be obtained from their online database at:
www.collectionscanada.ca/amicus/index-e.html
ISBN 1-4120-2872-8
Printed in Victoria, BC, Canada

# TRAFFORD

*Offices in Canada, USA, Ireland, UK and Spain*
This book was published *on-demand* in cooperation with Trafford Publishing. On-demand publishing is a unique process and service of making a book available for retail sale to the public taking advantage of on-demand manufacturing and Internet marketing. On-demand publishing includes promotions, retail sales, manufacturing, order fulfilment, accounting and collecting royalties on behalf of the author.
**Book sales for North America and international:**
Trafford Publishing, 6E–2333 Government St.,
Victoria, BC v8t 4p4 CANADA
phone 250 383 6864 (toll-free 1 888 232 4444)
fax 250 383 6804; email to orders@trafford.com
**Book sales in Europe:**
Trafford Publishing (uk) Ltd., Enterprise House, Wistaston Road Business Centre, Wistaston Road, Crewe, Cheshire cw2 7rp UNITED KINGDOM
phone 01270 251 396 (local rate 0845 230 9601)
facsimile 01270 254 983; orders.uk@trafford.com
**Order online at:**
www.trafford.com/robots/04-0701.html

10 9 8 7 6 5 4 3 2

# PREFACE

History offers something of very great practical value and citizens cannot afford to ignore it. Only when they have knowledge of the problems and successes and failures of other years are they in a position to plan wisely for the future.

And history can be charming as well as useful. It can be a companion as well as a guide. One of the good things to come from Canada's Centennial Year was a fresh appreciation of the nation's rich and exciting history. Westerners may be so bold as to conclude that the most fascinating part of Canadian history concerns their area, so recently occupied exclusively by Indians and fur traders. The achievements of one hundred years provide one of the greatest success stories in the western world.

Local or community history is a segment of the whole. Every district has a story of struggles and hardships and achievements. Best of all, it is a story of vigorous pioneers and great personalities. The record should be preserved. Happily, Centennial Year saw the preparation of many such local histories and the result will have lasting value.

The Tofield Historical Society, recognizing the community's rich heritage, has done well to gather the threads which will now appear as a lasting cultural fabric. Those whose imagination and effort went into the preparation of Tales of Tofield are to be congratulated and thanked.

Grant MacEwan
Lieutenant-Governor of Alberta

# DEDICATION

To:
>   —the pioneers of the Tofield area who with courage and
>   gallantry laid the foundations of our community
>   —the residents of contemporary Tofield who are building a
>   progressive community on those foundations
>
>   and most especially
>
>   —the youth of Tofield in whose hands the future lies,
>   —this book is lovingly dedicated.
>
>   —Tofield Historical Society

# FOREWORD

This book is the outcome of an idea conceived many years ago by interested citizens of Tofield. It is the story of the growth of this area over the last nine decades.

Eulogies are often looked at askance, but in this instance it is not possible to thank sufficiently all the people who have striven to make this book a reality.

The Tofield Historical Society would like to voice a special word of gratitude to: J. R. Francis for providing, through his photographs, a pictoral record of the past and for his untiring efforts in compiling and checking facts relevant to this book; to Grace Phillips for much research and for writing the articles which vividly preserve the past; Mrs. Daisy Young for the sketches introducing various sections of the book; typists, Mr. Floyd Irwin, Miss Elizabeth Rains, Mrs. Mildred Watson, Mrs. Fay Dodds, Mrs. Rita Halverson and Miss Joan Banack; Neil Phillips for proofreading and checking; Mrs. Esther Anderson for checking and assembling the sections of the book.

There are many others who have helped in the compilation of this book and to them all, I extend my warmest thanks and appreciation.

*Harold C. Schultz*

Harold C. Schultz
President
Tofield Historical Society

# MESSAGE FROM MAJOR FANE

I am honored in being given the opportunity to send greetings and express my good wishes to the Tofield Historical Society for its outstanding Centennial effort in providing a volume of local history of the town and district of Tofield, and I commend your Society most highly for its efforts in this connection. I am sure that, were it not for the records such as you are providing, the early history of our district would soon be forgotten, at least as soon as the descendants of our pioneers had answered their last call.

I would like to record the names of all the early pioneers in our area whom I remember well, but will not do so because someone would undoubtedly be missed. However, I do want to say that my family connection with the whole Beaverhill Lake area began when my father, the late Frank W. W. Fane, took up a homestead at the northeast corner of Beaverhill Lake in 1887 after his many years of service with the Royal North West Mounted Police. My late mother joined him when they were married in Lethbridge in 1890. I am their third child and only son. Hence my long association with the whole area surrounding Beaverhill Lake, and may I say that my father's original homestead is still the centre of my farm.

The Fane family and the Tofield family were always very close friends. This friendship between the surviving members of both families exists to this day. The late Dr. Tofield, after whom the town and district of Tofield were named, was a most outstanding citizen and through his untiring efforts to minister to all people became a legend in the whole area which he served as the only available doctor.

I remember him very well because he and Mrs. Tofield visited with my parents as frequently as possible in those early days which now seem so long ago. It is very important that the history of Tofield be recorded because Tofield is one of the earliest settlements in our part of Alberta. Tofield has been a very important place in our past and still continues to grow both in population and importance notwithstanding its proximity to Edmonton.

May Tofield long continue its present trend. The reason for Tofield's continued importance is the efforts of the publicspirited citizens who live there. Their tireless efforts on behalf of their community always in evidence, particularly so on July 1, 1967, at the Centennial Parade and Celebration held in Tofield that day.

My wife and I were greatly honored in being able to be present that day. For me, it has also been a privilege that, as Member of Parliament for the Federal Constituency of Vegreville since 1958, Tofield has been included in my district.

The support that I have received from the people of Tofield and District has always been outstanding and very highly appreciated.

Again, my congratulations to the town of Tofield and its surrounding district on their outstanding past and my very best wishes for continuing prosperity in the future.

Frank J. W. Fane
M.P. for Vegreville, Alberta

## THE YEAR TO REMEMBER
## A. W. GORDEY, M. L. A.

The Centennial year in Canada is, unquestionably, one of the greatest mile stones of our history since confederation. It is a year which should not be remembered by the people of Canada only as a point of interest in our progress and development; it should mean far more than that. Besides its historic importance, it should be a tine of sincere evaluation and appreciation of the many achievements of our people on all fields of progress throughout these years.

In such evaluation of our past, we find that we have a great historic wealth in this county; the hardships, determination, and dedications of our pioneers ; the glories of our men who fought on many battle fronts in time of stress and danger; the efforts and the vision of our great statesmen who molded the foundations of this nation and have piloted its course through many stormy waters; and the work and foresight of many dedicated men and women who have guided the destiny of our country in the past hundred years. This glorious historic past should be known, honoured and cherished by us, and by our succeeding generations.

# CONTENTS

SETTLEMENT

# AMISKWACHI

*(The Cree name for Beaver Lake is "Amiskwachi Sakyakn" Beaver Hills Lake)*
*Reprinted from the Vegreville Observer*

Hail, charming lake, that lies before my view,
A glitt'ring gem in Nature's glorious crown;
Thou'rt lonely now, and known but to the few;
But very soon shall see Old Sol look down
On thriving settlement and busy town;
And o'er thy surface many a pleasure boat
With living freight shall wander up and down
And as they with the gentle breezes float
Attuned to laugh and song shall be each fair one's throat.
For what is there that struggling mankind crave,
That will not here reward and honest toil?
An atmosphere the purest God e'er gave,
A bracing climate and fruitful soil
Await you here, all ye who sweat and moil
In European climes amidst the crowd;
While they for whom you waste life's precious oil
Pass by you scornfully, with haughty voice and loud.
Then come where Health and smiling Plenty stand
With outstretched hands to welcome you with joy,
No trampling armies here harass the land,
Nor steelgloved despotism you annoy;
Here may you honest labor well employ
Free from such stifling tyranny, and see
What shall your children's hearts exult with glee,
And in your own shall wake a newborn melody.
But now fair lake, I turn my eyes once more
Where Sol's departing beams, upon thy face,
Reflect the hills that skirt thy western shore
Or backward stand to give thee breathing space,
There many dales the sombre spruce doth space,

And in their gloomy depths you oft may hear
The lordly elk rush by at headlong pace.
The deep voiced moose, of antlered game the peer,
Has no Dunraven's gun to chill his blood with fear.
Yet, stay! What cautious figure do I see
Threading with stealthy steps the forest maze?
Ah, Monaywahsis! I'd forgotten thee,
For thou hast ended many a moose's days;
And though Dunraven's record may amaze,
It need not shame thee, for thine eye is true,
And well thy hunting deeds deserve my praise;
And I may praise thine honest nature too,
For I like thee, of thy race, are found, I ween but few.
But hush! What sound comes o'er thee now, Oh Lake?
A wailing cry as from a newmade grave!
Oh, weep," it says, "The Manitou did take,
Far to the Indian's heaven, the true brave!"
No human skill nor prayers his life could save!
He's gone, Oh Moose! No more thy trail he'll scan
For o'er him now the quivering aspens wave.
He died., as he had lived, a MAN,
Come forth and say aught else, all ye who dare or can.
The evening speeds. Oh, Lake! Thy face grows dark,
And shadows thicken over bluff and plain;
Far from the distance comes the coyote's bark
While waterfowl the echoes wake amain,
All giving presage of approaching rain;
And o'er the Indian's grave upon the lea,
The sobbing wind now sings a sad refrain,
But soon shall lash to foam thy waters free,
Till whitecapped breakers roar in durious revelry.
Written at Beaver Lake in 1884 by J.B. Steele

# THE ORIGIN OF TOFIELD'S NAME

In 1962, Mr. Stinson, the town secretary, received a query from Mr. F. Hewitt of Stewkley, England, inquiring as to the origin of the name of the town of Tofield.

Mr. Stinson replied to Mr. Hewitt, giving him the information requested and also informing him that Mrs. Edith Rogers, daughter of Dr. Tofield, for whom the town was named, was still a resident of Tofield.

Mr. Stinson again received a letter from Mrs. Hewitt. Enclosed with the letter were two clippings which explained how Mr. Hewitt had heard of Tofield. One clipping was a brief account of the death in May 1950, of the Tofield Siamese Twins, Beverly and Brenda Townsend, daughters of Mr. and Mrs. Bud Townsend. The birth of these little girls and the operation undertaken subsequently to separate them, attracted wide attention in many countries. The second clipping was the obituary notice for Mr. Francis J. C. Garford, also of Tofield.

Mr. Hewitt's letter was of historical interest to all residents of the Tofield area. It ran as follows:

Lumio, 1 Brunel Drive

Coombe Valley,

Weymouth, Dorset,

November 17, 1962

Dear Mr. Stinson:

Thank you for your letter of October 20, which my wife and I found most interesting and descriptive.

Although Dr. J. H. Tofield was presumably born in Yorkshire it is quite possible that his ancestors originated from Stewkley in Buckinghamshire, which was, and still is, looked upon as "home of the Tofields—in fact, one area of Stewkley still goes under the name of Tofield, and we would suggest that your town is the only other place in the world to bear that name.

Now Stewkly is a very old village which dates its known origin to about the year 1066. In that year, the English were defeated in battle by William, Duke of Normandy at the Battle of Hastings, in which action

King Harold, last of the Saxon kings, was killed.

Soon after this battle, the Duke of Normandy ascended the throne of England as King William I. Soon after ascending the throne King William ordered a survey to be made of the whole country in order that taxes might be levied upon the inhabitants to enable him to increase the revenue. Details of the survey were recorded in the Doomsday Book.

Stewkley was mentioned in the Doomsday Book as"Steuclai". which was a Saxon name. There appears to be no record of the meaning of the word "Steuc", but"lal" or "ley", means a "clearing in the forest".

As a result of this survey, the country was divided into a number of areas which were placed under control or jurisdiction of relatives or favorites of the king. A part of Buckinghamshire, including Stewclai, was placed under the king's cousin, Walter de Gifford.

Much of the history of Stewkley has been taken from the church records. The church, the Church of St. Michael, is reputed to have been built in or around 1150 A.D., and is in the Norman style and is said to be among the most ancient and best preserved Norman architecture remaining in the country.

It is understood that many of the old tombstones, most of which were in a state of decay, were removed from the church-yard over a hundred years ago, but among the old ones which still remain are a number belonging to the Tofield family.

It is possible that the Tocquefields or Tofields as they are now known, were of Saxon origin and were living in the forest settlement of Steuclai at the time of the Norman conquest of England.

We hope that the above information may be of interest to your friend, Mrs. Edith Rogers, and perhaps to the records of your town.

Frank F. Hewitt.

# PRE-PIONEER ERA OF TOFIELD AREA

While making repairs to the attic of his farm home, Harold Schultz discovered some copies of the "Tofield Standard" which were printed in 1907. The Standard was the forerunner of the Mercury and was published by R. N. Whillans. The papers found by Mr. Schultz contain much invaluable information about the pre—pioneer era of the Tofield district. The following article was apparently a letter written to the editor by the son of Phillip Tate, who was the H. B. Co. factor at Victoria.

"The destruction and wanton waste caused by prairie fires are incalculable. Beautiful groves, timber, wild fruit trees, the young wild animals, with thousands of duck eggs and prairie chicken eggs, are swallowed up by the indispensable friend and relentless foe. First, not having seen Beaver Lake or neighborhood since I was a boy in the early seventies, it was with a genuine feeling of regret that I noted the total absence of maple trees during a recent tour of your beautiful Lake so changed from those early days.

Acting on the advice of their friend and pastor, a band, of Christian Cree Indians, isolated themselves from the other bands and made for the then more wooded part of the country; that is north and north-west sides of the lake toward the hills. The fearful and much dreaded smallpox was prevalent among those tribes frequently on the open prairies, especially among the Blackfeet. It was well for this particular portion of Chief Bobtail's band, that they isolated themselves as already stated, escaping this frightful scourge.

The Indians were camped at the outlet of Beaver Lake, on the Beaver Creek. The winter's hunt had been very successful from every point of view. It must have been with feelings of unmixed gratitude these Indians here formed their camp instead of going into the fort at Victoria. Still fearing the smallpox, they decided to send for the Oukeyma or his agent to come to them and their furs. This suggestion was readily complied with.

At this time my father was in charge of the H.B. Co.'s fort at Victoria, and great was my joy when he told me I was to accompany him to visit the Indians in their camp near Beaver Lake.

It was a good and wise custom for friendship and policy, that each official of the H.B.Co. should have a "Quay-may"or namesake or a "Chewam" or brother, or uncle, or nephew, as the case might be, in every camp where one was recognized as the chief or head man.

On arriving in camp we were most heartily welcomed by my father's "Che-wan" Chief Bobtail, and his followers. There was nothing too good for us; all the known delicacies of the times were placed at our feet—moose noses, beaver tails, buffalo "boss", or bump, ducks, geese, eggs, and will you believe it—good maple sugar, made in their camp. Dainty maple syrup, in skin vessels, or properly speaking, bladders.

Neither was the supply limited and could I have accepted all offered to me I would certainly have had forty or fifty pounds.

As we had ridden on horseback in advance of the carts with the trading goods, they would not be in camp for several hours. Chief Bobtail suggested that my father should bring forth the swiftest "buffalo horse" and he would match him for a race. With a cheer our party promptly accepted the challenge, and immediately bets were made.

Pocket knives, silk handkerchiefs, coats, capotes belts, moose leather, buffalo robes, furs, marrow fat, lassos, whips, were freely laid one against the other. The big bet of the race was of course between the two heads of the respective parties. My father placed a single-barrel percussion gun, two pounds of tea done up in a cotton handkerchief, and two fathoms of rope tobacco on the ground, to be immediately balanced by three bladders of dried tongue, six large beaver tails, and six rogans full of maple sugar and a bundle of fur. The rules for entry and starting were few and to the point "Owners up" being the only one expressly stated. Accordingly the "Ou-key-mas" mounted their racers and rode to yonder willow bush about a mile off.

To turn the horses' heads and race like grim death was, for that bunch of shouting, yelling hunters, the thought and work of a moment.

The Indian rode well and his horse, which had seen service at the camps of the Big Knives, and had won laurels in all buffalo hunts, was no mean opponent.

From start to finish it was neck to neck; under the whip and lash the flyers ran in—a draw.

Immediately came the cry "the sons will take their fathers' places with their own ponies, and before I could realize the full meaning of the situation I was on the bare back of my pretty pony. He was a present from a friend, Mr. Hardisty, and had a good strain of the fiery breed in him, his grandsire having been imported via York factory and Lake Winnipeg.

If I had the disposal of the millions of a Rockefeller they would have been laid 100 to 1 on my daring little "Vermont". In a minute my cousin May-che-cha-kun" (The Coyote) dashed up on a prancing coal black pony. The preliminaries were quickly disposed of. I felt a "chill of premonition" as my favorite did not clear away at the first jump.

I sat immovable in my seat as did my cousin at my side.

I felt the breeze on my face and slender form, and I bent low over my horse's neck, only to note that The Coyote was almost lying flat over his mount. I tightend the grip of my little thighs as I drew them up, while The Coyote sat like a doubled up jack knife on his "Flying Crow".

Could it be possible that my "Vermont" had met his match? At Edmonton, Victoria, Fort Pitt, Carlton and Fort Ellice, aye, the whole North West, we had never seen the heels of anyone.

I prayed and prayed sincerely that the awful day be postponed, but still that black snake-like form in long sinewy bounds was at my side.

I urged, I coaxed; in despair, I commanded, and raising my hand with my open palm struck his sloping shoulders. As I did so, my pony seemed to come closer to the ground and while fairly flying through the air, I heard the swish, swish, right and left on the black flanks beside me and with a yell, which I often yet hear in my imagination as I watch the "home stretch" from the grandstand, my opponent flew past me and amid yells and cheers, and with my little heart like lead, I realized that The Coyote had shown us a clear pair of heels. I had lost, and lost to a better horse.

Leaping from my pony's back with my eyes full of tears, I remembered that The Coyote made a great brag of being a foot racer. He was two years my senior but I did not mind all this. In my haste for revenge I challenged him to run a race; he accepted.

If force of will power and a determination to win has any effect on an opponent, then it was impossible for my cousin "The Coyote" to do otherwise than he did by seeing the shape of my back.

The bets were divided up as originally intended—the Chief taking the gun, tea, and tobacco, while my father had the furs, tongues, and with his own hand Chief Bobtail handed me six rogans of maple sugar.

After leaving this camp we travelled towards the prairies and near the junction of Iron Creek and Battle River we again came to another large Indian camp and here again we were treated to maple sugar galore Now all is gone—Indians, maple sugar, and buffalo.

Speaking of this to my friend Mr.J. Stephenson, who had a ranch near Battle River, he tells me that there are still a few maple trees on the banks of the Battle but I never heard of any near Beaver Lake of late years.

Yours truly,

"Son of the Black Head"

*Editor's note: Robert Logan, whom we all know so well., was at the time of the incident narrated in the above story, clerk for the H.B. factor at Victoria, and no doubt Mr. Logan will remember the "Black Head" spoken of. It is also well worthy of note that the Red Head spoken of in one of our first stories of the Historical Beaver Lake was Mr. Hardisty, Hudson Bay Co. factor at Edmonton, and the Black Head was Mr. Phillip Tate, H. B. Co. factor at Victoria. These men were friends and came together to the west in the year 1874 by way of Fort Garry and across the prairies, suffering together all the hair-raising experiences of those early days.*

## THE DEVELOPMENT OF TOFIELD

The Town of Tofield had its beginning in 1906 when Morton and Adams built a General Store (carrying dry goods, groceries and hardware) close to the post office on the farm of George Cookson. Sr. the legal description of which was N.E. ¼ Sec.36, Tp. 5O, Range 19, W. of the 4th Meridian. (In 1967, the farm belongs to John Rempel.)

Before the spring of 1907, other businesses were begun. These included: W.C.Swift's lumber yard, R. 0. Bird's hardware, C.H. Cress and J. B. Harper's general store, Dr. McKinnon's drug store and office 0. H. Mahaffey's blacksmith shop. The Queen's Hotel just a frame shell when it survived moving from Townsite Number 1 to Townsite Number 2.

This move was made in anticipation of the arrival of the railway, the Grand Trunk Pacific. The first survey made by the G.T.P. crossed the "lake road" just north of where (1967) Art Hardy lives. The firm of Crafts and Lee of Edmonton bought the north half of Section 1, Tp. 5l, R.19 from Henry Wood and had it divided into town lots. The firm then offered free lots to anyone who would build houses on them. It is not known whether a time limit was placed on this offer, but it is known that the village moved from Townsite No. 1 to Townsite No. 2.

Mr. R. O. Bird is remembered for his habit, most unusual at that time, of going without a hat. Most men wore broad-brimmed hats of felt or straw but Mr. Bird was an individualist. Mr. Cress is remembered as being a sharp business man. Jim Francis recalls that as a small boy he took two dozen eggs to Mr. Cress' store; on being told, gruffly, the price, he asked Mr. Cress if he knew what Morton and Adams, rival storekeepers, were offering. Mr. Cress replied that he did not know and Jim was welcome to take his eggs to Morton and Adams if he preferred. So Jim did just that and made a cent a dozen on the eggs!

Tofield No. 2 sprung up north of Cookson Avenue, west of the site of the first brick school—at the north terminus of Dominion Street which goes past Oslunds. By the fall of 1908, there was a full row of houses along the west side of the street which ran through the location of the present school gym. Main street had two blocks of business places, fairly well filled in.

Alas for the site No. 2! When the G. T. P. made the final survey it came south of Site No. 2 (its final location) and the Craft-Lee town site gradually became deserted as all of the buildings on Main Street were moved to Townsite No. 3 whose Main Street ran perpendicularly to the railroad which reached Tofield in 1909.

During 1909, Tofield progressed from being the mere village which had been legally formed in 1907 and became incorporated as a town. The village had been administered by J. B. Harper, W. C. Swift and Joshua Noland., as councillors with A. J. H. McCauley as secretary. The mayor of the new Town of Tofield was J. 0. LeTourneau; the councillors were M. W. Ferguson who is still living in Tofield in 1967, R. E. Emery, A. F. Fugl, J. B. Harper, A. Maxwell and J. Lamoureax.

The legal description of the town in 1909 was: All of Section 1-51-19; the east 80 acres of all of S. E. 2-51-19; the east 80 acres of N. E. 2-51-19; 80 acres of S. W. 12-51-19; the south 80 acres of S. E. 12-51-19; S. W. 40 acres of S. W. 7-51-19; West 80 acres of N. W. 6-51-19; and S. W. 6-51-19; N. 80 acres of N. W. 36-50-19; North 80 acres of both N. E. and N. W. of 35-50-19. [all west of the 4th meridian]

The water supply for the town had never been very good and in 1910 the town decided to dig a deep well in hopes of finding a plentiful supply of water. At a depth of 500 feet, water was found in quantity but, unfortunately, it was salty and there were indications of natural gas in the same area. The discovery stirred up great interest. Deeper went the well.

At a depth of 1054 feet, gas was struck. This strike was reported in the Edmonton Journal of June 23, 1912 as follows: "Property values in Tofield have doubled and tripled as a natural gas strike is reported. Unofficial reports say the flow may reach 2,000,000 cubic feet. Townspeople say that Tofield is now another Medicine Hat since gas has been struck at 1054 feet." Another report stated, "To dramatize discovery of natural gas, Tofield residents have devised a street lighting system with gas flares ten feet high. Townspeople say that Tofield will become the Hamilton of the West."

Tofield had indeed been successful in striking gas but this discovery, important as it was, had not solved the problem of the salty water coming from the same source. The two flows had to be separated.

The driller, instead of pouring down straight cement which would have hardened to sufficient density to allow boring through it, mixed concrete and filled the well to the depth at which the water came in. In trying to bore through the concrete, the drill kept slipping to one side or the other. So this well had to be abandoned. The second well was drilled on the same lot. This too, was unsuccessful and still a third had to be dug.

During this time, the town council had gas flares burning all the way down Main Street to the station and the land boom was in full swing. New subdivisions were created. "Tofield Heights" was located in the S. W . ¼ of Section 6, Tp. 51, Rge. 18. This lay just east of town with the present (1967) Mennonite Church on its western boundary. "Euclid Park" was in the N. W. ¼of Sec. 6, Tp. 51, Rge. 19, just north of the Tofield Heights subdivision. "Tofield Rosedale" subdivision was planned for the N.1/2 of Sec.35, Tp. 51, Rge. 19, on the site of the present golf course and the home of Aino Jensen. The Sam Stauffer 1/2 section was subdivided and sixty acres of lots were sold on it.

The N.E. ¼ of Sec. 6, Tp. 51, Rge. 18, known as the "Baptist Place" was subdivided but was not placed on the market. John Rempel's quarter section, land now belonging to S. Pearson, and the east half of sec. 25, Tp. 50, Rge. 19 were all subdivided. West of town the town fathers subdivided the present Nickerson and Art Francis farms into town lots. The Jack Cookson farm was bought by the Council for $15,000. (This is the site,in 1967, of the Northwest Utilities Buildings.) This land, it was planned, would be Tofield's industrial area. J. G. Jobb built a foundry on the land occupied by C. Swanson's slaughter house. For six months it operated.

John Francis, visiting in Vancouver in 1912, saw in a window, advertisements for Tofield town lots. He wandered in, and on three walls of this office were glowing advertisements for his home town.

The Cookson place was depicted as having several large smokestacks to indicate a thriving industrial area. The fair grounds were shown with not only the truly existent race track but with an immense covered grandstand, as well as enormous cattle and horse barns to accommodate the prize stock and race horses.

John Francis, as a native of Tofield, was mightily interested and asked many questions — too many to please the gentleman in charge of the office who asked sourly, "Have you ever been in Tofield?" "Yes," answered John Francis, "three years ago when it didn't look anything like that."

When the gas well petered out, and the boom died down, many people found themselves poorer than before the town council faced a $90,000 deficit. This was in 1913; by 1967, the Council has the debt whittled down so that by 1975, they hope, the debt will be paid off and a "burning ceremony" can occur.

In 1913, when the boom had died down, real estate sales were at a standstill. Town taxes began to pile up on the lots which had been sold. Subdivisions were recreated into farm lands. Farmers now became the owners of recent subdivisions. The town faced a desperate debt-ridden situation. The 1920 assessment roll shows taxes still being paid on lots owned by Eastern Canada, the U. S. A., the British Isles, and some European countries. In 1916, the brick school had burned thus adding to the town debt as the replacement was completed. Vacant town houses were in many instances moved to farms.

The railroad and the coal mine payrolls helped to hold the town together. The railway payroll paid a station agent, an assistant agent, an expressman, a freight agent, three telegraph operators and a repair man as well as a switching crew of three or four, and a section crew. The coal mines operated all year round but business reached its peak in winter. In peak periods in winter, about 200 miners were paid by the three mines. The spending power generated by these payrolls kept the town business solvent. In 1923, Northwest Utilities exercised their franchise to instal gas into Tofield homes. A goodly number of employees of this company made (and still make) their homes in Tofield and their contribution to the economic life of the town was and is important.

In 1927, a curling rink housing 4 sheets of ice was built a block east of the Royal Alexandra Hotel. While many people helped, the name of John Chapman is prominent among those who built the rink. In 1960, the rink having become decrepit, plans were made to build a new one on the Exhibition Grounds. In 1967, this fine new rink has been in use for several years but is not yet finished upstairs.

In 1944 the Tofield Community League was organized by Herb Chandler. In 1946 this group built, largely by volunteer labor, the Memorial Hall. In March 1955 this hall was destroyed by fire but was rebuilt and opened in December of 1955 with Premier E. C. Manning conducting the opening ceremonies.

Until 1945, the town had to obtain permission from the Alberta Utilities Board in order to spend anything on local improvements. Finally money was obtained to replace with cement, the wooden sidewalks which had fallen into disrepair.

In 1954, water and sewage systems were installed in Tofield. Now many fine modern homes line the streets. A tree-planting program improved the appearance of the town. On Main Street, new buildings have replaced those lost in the centre of town. Mrs. Petra Stauffer, Centennial Queen, has been instrumental in development of a park on Main Street; so it has been nicknamed "Petra's Park."

In 1969, the population of Tofield is 1009. Its mayor is Dr. W. H. Freebury; Councillors are: Arnold Swift, Arny Klassen, William Christensen, Lloyd Cribb, Gabe Pittet and Conrad Patterson. Secretary of the town is Mrs. Rita Halverson.

## STAR TWINKLES ONLY ONCE

A copy of what is believed to be the first Tofield newspaper was received from Arnold Swift. It was the Tofield Star and Volume 1, No.1, published August 27th 1907, announced Tofield to be "A progressive Town with a Grand Future". Mr. W. A. Pratten was editor and manager and Mr. Pratten stated that the paper would be published weekly upon arrival from Winnipeg of the Tofield Printing Plant.

We have no further record of following issues of the Star so perhaps the obtaining of a printing plant for Tofield in those days was more difficult that Mr. Pratten surmised.

Among advertisers in this early issue we note C.E. Jamieson, druggist; Harper and Letourneau, furniture dealers; Mr. Sherlock, as manager of the A.T. Walker Lumber Company; Kennedy and Small, general merchants; Merchants Bank; Rot. Logan, merchant; Greenhill and Johnson., real estate; Ingram and Hayes, Pool Room; Canadian National Railways; A. W. Story, builder and contractor; Morton and Adams, butcher shop; A.W. Hunt Real Estate; L. Taylor, Milliner; Felix Paradis, blacksmith; Noland and Noland, livery; J. Gladue, livery; Swift and Emery, lumber; M. W. Ferguson, harness maker; Stonehocker Bros. real estate; C. H. Cress; general store; R. 0. Bird; Hardwood; O.M. McHaffey, blacksmith.

# THE TOFIELD "BLOWHARD"

*Editorial*
*(Appeared in Tofield Standard, 1909)*

"As it has lately been decided to hold the World's Fair in Tofield in the summer of 1909 we feel it is now a fitting time for a review of the history of Tofield's development as a city. When an old timer like the right Reverend Ralph Bradley, the convener of the Presbyterian Church in Canada (and whose esteemed father was at one time in charge of St. Andrew's Church in this city) is in a reminiscent mood [he] takes a walk a way from the jungle of wholesale houses on 1st Avenue to the beautiful residential part of the city, then tours in his automobile along the delightful drive by the lake shore; he looks back as in a dream, to the time when he chased coyotes and lynx on the vast prairie where now stands our grand Metropolis.

Not many years ago Tofield was but an infant in swaddling clothes, but even in her infancy she showed signs of a brilliant career. She learned to walk at a remarkable early age and toddled away from her parent, the dear old post office, when but a few months old. Having wandered across the prairie for some distance, she selected a spot suited to her fancy, but as her growth exceeded all expectations, she soon grew restive and desirous of extending her boundaries. Consequently having established a beautiful residential section, she, with one huge bound, extended her border to the G.T.P. where a magnificent station was erected. From this time forward the aggressive little town spread like a wild fire until it reached its present proportions. A fair idea of Tofield's size today, may be formed from the fact that if all buildings were placed together in a straight line—and not too close together—they would reach from Beaver Lake to Edmonton.

In some of the oldest and best of the wholesale houses on lst. Avenue, we see such names as Kennedy MaHaffey and Small, Letourneau and Harper, Jamieson and others. Some of these are long established headquarters of the Dominion.

While shopping by mail has been done more or less in all civilized countries, it has been left to C. H. Cress to bring this idea to its development. So successful has been the enterprise that Montgomery & Ward of Chicago, and T. Eaton of Toronto, are endeavoring to follow him—with a fair degree of success.

On 2nd Avenue a little to the east of Main Street is the Stock Exchange. Further north towards the residential center is the Tofield University, the President of which is Charles Shaw, a distinguished scholar whose father was at one time the Principal of the Tofield Public School in the early stage of its development.

Stanley Laidman, Judge of the Supreme Court,has settled permanently on Rosedale Avenue.

The Fire Department has reached a state of perfection with Lorne Lee as Chief of the Dept. The motor car is now giving birth to the airship which the manufacturer, Oliver Bird, turns out of his establishment daily.

The orchestra, begun in years past by the distinguished musician, C. Carter, is second to none on this continent.

The excellent social conditions in our fair city are such that the Dramatic Club was obligated to import villains from Ross Creek and Chipman as none could be found in Tofield.

Tofield has had many mayors but none better than W.C. Swift, who now holds the honoured position. In the City, a magnificent edifice may be seen portraits of the men who were founders of the Hub. Among them we see such names as Logan, Sherlock, McCauley, Tofield, Noland, Swift and others whose names have already been mentioned.

And still this indomitable city continues to rush forward. Its expansion is a growth, not a boom.Young as she is, Tofield, is unequaled in the Western Hemisphere."

The following is the text of an address given by Mr. A.J.H. McCauley, then mayor of Tofield, in October, 1922, as reported by W. Worton, editor of the Tofield Mercury at that time.

# EARLY DAYS AT TOFIELD

*Mayor McCauley Gives Interesting Address*

The subject, "Early Days at Tofield," on which I have been asked to speak to you is one that a person might write a book about. However, I will try to tell you briefly of some of the events that took place here.

For several hundred years this part of the Northwest was truly the happy hunting grounds of the Indians. The large lake at our door was called Beaver Hills Lake and the country for over twenty miles west of this lake was called Beaver Hills, owing to the large number of beaver being found here. Amisk Creek, a few miles East of Town, was given its name for the same reason, "Amisk" being the Cree word for beaver. Like the evergreenclad island you can see from Cooking Lake Station, these hills were covered with jackpine,spruce and tamarac, and the depressions between the hills with water. In this forest were to be found buffalo, bear, moose, deer, as well as beaver and on the lake swam geese, ducks, pelicans and all kinds of waterfowl by the thousands. During the first part of the nineties, fires destroyed this great forest.

As the fur trading companies kept pushing up the rivers from Hudson's Bay, in time trading posts were established on the banks of the North Saskatchewan at Edmonton, and at Victoria (Pakan).

Mr. William Rowland (now deceased), who told me stories of the buffalo hunting days, was during the sixties a chief trader for the Hudson's Bay Company. The Chief Factor sent him out periodically to trade with the Indians at Beaver Hill Lake. Mr. Rowland afterwards took up a homestead on the land where his sons William and John reside, part of which is now the property of the Tofield Cemetery.

The usual fighting ground of the Blackfoot and Cree Indians was along the Battle River for about twenty miles on either side, between Ponoka and Wainwright. The Blackfeet, whose camp was at Sarcee, just outside the present city of Calgary, were proving very troublesome to the Crees and had commenced to make raids around the South end of Beaver Hills Lake. Not wishing to lose this great hunting ground, the Crees, in 1860 or 1862, persuaded Chief Ketchamoot to come up with

27

four hundred braves from Fort Pitt. For several days this small army camped on the land where the golf links are and where Messrs. John W. Cookson, Alex Kellner, and James Muskett now live. After being joined by the Indians around Beaver Hills Lake and having secured a supply of food by killing twelve buffalo, they travelled South-west, passing through Camrose, and met the Blackfeet in battle south of Wetaskiwin.The Blackfeet were routed and the Crees captured a large amount of booty, including many ponies and twenty squaws. The chief took one and the others were given to his councillors and secretary-treasurer. The chief afterwards traded his Blackfoot squaw for a horse. Chief Ketchamoot spent his declining years here and was buried on the banks of the creek that bears his name --the first creek north of town. Ketchamoot school district, southwest of town, was also named after this celebrated chief.

In May,1868, the halfbreed buffalo hunters from Edmonton, St. Albert and Lac St. Anne to the west and to Victoria, White Fish Lake and Lac La Biche to the north met here, camping on the land now the farm of Mr. Peter McAllister, to make plans for hunting buffalo during the summer. It was necessary for the hunters to travel in large parties when hunting in the country to the south, for the Blackfeet were liable to mistake small parties for Cree Indians and kill them. Chief Factor Hardisty (who was later appointed first senator of Alberta) and Chief Factor Tate of Victoria, representing the Hudson's Bay Company, were here to attend this meeting and to trade with the Indians for furs. Rev. George McDougall--the pioneer Methodist missionary, who a few years later lost his life on the plains, was also at this meeting.

Two of the oldest settlers of this part, Messrs. Augustine and Jeremie Gladue, Sr. have killed many a buffalo in the buffalo hunts from here to the U.S. boundary. A favorite place for hunting the buffalo on horseback was just north of the farms of Messrs. George Wood, George Goeglein, E. Hardy, W. B. McNeil and Pete Gates, over the open country on the lake.

One way of getting a supply of buffalo meat, when stocks were running low, was to drive the buffalo into a buffalo pound. This pound was made by building a high fence with heavy logs in a circle having a diameter of about one hundred yards.In this pound was left a narrow opening from each side of which a brush fence extending outwards was built until the ends were over half a mile apart. Into this the buffalo were driven and after being shut in this circular pound were killed. In 1872, one of these pounds was built on the lands owned by Mr. Coombes and Mr. G. S. Sears and at another time one was built on the farms now occupied by Messrs. Thomas Cookson, Edmund Cookson, and Thomas Porter.

Mrs. Anderson, who lived ten miles north of Tofield with her father, Mr. Chas. Whitford (deceased) first saw Beaverhill lake in 1865. Mr. Whitford, who only camped here for a short time then, returned in 1873 and made his home for three years on the land later taken up by Roderick McKenzie and now owned by George McLaughlin. Mr. Whitford was the first man other than the Indians to make his home on the shore of Beaverhill Lake. Mrs. Anderson in company with other women followed many buffalo hunt and skinned many buffalo.

After 1870 it was noticed that the buffalo herds were getting smaller and by 1876 very few were left in the country. In 1874 the North-west Mounted Police were organized and sent out to the Western Prairies, a post being established at Fort Saskatchewan, about forty miles north-west of the lake. After peace was declared between the Blackfeet and Crees at Peace Hills, near where the city of Wetaskiwin now stands, freighting by carts from Winnipeg to Edmonton was regularly carried on. One of these trails ran at the north end of Beaverhill Lake, about sixteen miles north of Tofield. Over this trail in 1879 travellers drove from Winnipeg to Fort Saskatchewan, the trip taking three months.

During the eighties, settlers or squatters started to come in and take up claims along the West side of Beaver Lake. Mr. James Pruden with his sons Edward and Frank came in 1884 and Messrs. Robert Logan, John Logan, and William Lennie, George Norris, Joseph Norn, Augustine Gladue and Jeremy Gladue, Sr. in 1886. Mr. Robert Logan kept a trading post for over twenty years on his ranch, which was later bought by George A. Trent Messrs. J. O. Letourneau, J. Lafond, William Bloss , J. W. Cookson, George Cookson, Jr., George Wood, Thos. Herndon, and Wm. Hopgood came in 1891. Mr. G. Cookson, Sr.

and other members of his family followed the next year. Government surveyors came out in 1893 and surveyed the land around Beaver Hill Lake. Settlers were now given the right to secure homestead entries for the land they had squatted on.

The first post office on the west side of Beaver Lake was named Logan after Mr. Robert Logan and Mr. Roderick McKenzie was appointed the first postmaster, the post office being kept at Mr. McKenzie's place. Mails were received once a month. Previous to this the settlers had to go to Fort Saskatchewan or Edmonton for their mail. In 1897 a post office was secured at this end of the lake and was named Tofield after Dr.J. H. Tofield. Dr. Tofield came in 1893 and was the first medical man to settle in this district. Mr. G. Cookson, Sr., was appointed first postmaster at Tofield and he kept his office in a small shack which still stands on his farm, just east of town. The first year Mr. Cookson was Postmaster he sold $36.00 worth of stamps and received a salary of $12.00. The mail was then received once every two weeks.

In 1894, Mr. Peter B. Anderson came in with a large party of Norwegians and settled south of Tofield in the part of the district now called Bardo, and W. H. Neal and his son Harry took up the land on the south shore of the lake.

The first school was opened here in 1896 with Miss Harriet McCallum as teacher. The children were taught in a small house, which stood on the west side of the road, across from Mr. N. S. Smith's place. A few years before this, a school was opened near Logan post office, and the first teacher was Major William Stiff.

From this time on the district received many settlers and became known as one of the best mixed farming sections of Alberta. In 1906 the Grand Trunk Pacific Railway main line was surveyed through Tofield. During this year Messrs. Morton and Adams, Cress and Harper, W. C. Swift, R. 0. Bird and Jas. Mahaffey started business around the old post office.

Early in the year 1907 Messrs. Crafts, Lee and Gallinger, of Edmonton, surveyed the N.E. ¼ 1-51-19 W 4th M. adjoining the land located by the Grand Trunk Railway Company for their Tofield townsite, the south half of section 1-51-19-W4th M., and offered free lots to the people who would build on them. The Grand Trunk Pacific Railway Company having refused to survey their townsite until the following year, businessmen and others accepted this offer and moved their buildings, leaving the old post office by itself once more. Thirty business places, including a branch of the Merchants Bank of Canada, having been established here during the summer, steps were taken to apply for incorporation as a village. This application was granted and on September 9. 1907, Tofield was proclaimed a village. Messrs. J. B. Harper, W. C. Swift and Joshua Noland were elected as the first council and I was appointed Secretary-Treasurer.

The following year the Grand Trunk Pacific Railway Company surveyed their townsite and from then on business places and dwellings kept moving on down near the station. On June 30, 1909, the steel on the main line was laid into Tofield, which great event was fittingly celebrated on Dominion Day. In August of the same year construction on the Tofield-Calgary branch line of the Grand Trunk Pacific Railway commenced; the building of this line made Tofield an important railway point and assured its growth in the future. The first passenger train from Winnipeg to Edmonton passed through Tofield on August 13, 1909.

Incorporation as a Town was sought in October,1909. This was at once granted by the Government and the first town council elected was composed of: Mayor J.0. Letourneau; Councillors, Messrs. R.E. Emery, M. W. Ferguson, A.F. Fugl, J.B. Harper, A. Lamoureax and A.Maxwell. I was again appointed Secretary-Treasurer.

The events of which I have spoken cover fairly well I think the ground my subject calls for.

I will conclude by saying, today the young men of Tofield dream of future success in farming and other lines of business and of shooting geese around Beaver Hill Lake, but the old men dream of the Indian pow-wow with its accompanying "Hi-Yi" song and beat of the tomtom, of the trapping of beaver and the great buffalo hunts of the past.

On February 5, 1910, Premier Rutherford and others went to Camrose by train through Tofield to officially open the new railway to that point.

On March 31, 1909 we received the first issue of the "Tofield Standard", Tofield's first weekly newspaper printed and edited by the late R. N. Whillans.

# PRE-PIONEER ERA

*Pioneer Missionary Visited Beaverhill*

J. R. Francis, secretary of the Tofield Historical Society, discovered in an extract from the Journal of the Rev. Robert Rundle, quoted in "Messenger of the Great Spirit" (by Muriel Beaton Patterson), that this famous missionary visited the Beaverhill Lake area (now the Tofield area) in 1840.

On October 18, 1840, according to this record, Rev. Robert Rundle from England, via Norway House and the Saskatchewan River, arrived in Fort Edmonton where the Hudson's Bay factor., John Rowand, made him welcome. Immediately upon his arrival, Rundle held a church service, the first Protestant service ever held east of Fort Garry (Winnipeg).

"Soon after Rundle's arrival," Miss Patterson states, "John Rowand was going to visit the hunters' camp at Beaver Lake and suggested that Rundle accompany him. It was January, and cold, as western winters can be. On his return, Rundle recorded the journey as follows:

'We were drawn by four dogs driven by a half-breed. Weather was very severe and I was warmly clad; sealskin cap tied under chin, mocassins, pair of lamb's wool stockings, flannel shirt, woollen drawers to foot, thick trousers, leggings and black silk gaiters, waistcoat, pilot coat and shawl tied around the neck; and in the carriole, buffalo robe and blankets. It was a beautiful starlit night with faint glitterings of the aurora.

"The cold was intense and we stopped about 10 o'clock and lighted a fire: about 1:00 a.m. we came upon an encampment of two men belonging to the fort. Afterwards we proceeded until sunrise when we again halted on the Beaver Hills. The cold at this time was more severe than ever; a convincing proof of its intensity was afforded us by the very sluggish ascent of the smoke into the atmosphere. Indeed it might be said to scarcely ascend at all."

It is noted that Rowand and Rundle travelled at night to avoid snow-blindness.

Apparently the rigors of his trip to Beaver Hills did not deter Rundle, for next February (1841) he was off to Rocky Mountain House by carriole.

# LETTER TO THE EDITOR

McRae, Alberta
January 23, 1958
The Tofield Mercury
Tofield, Alberta
RE: History of Tofield and District
Dear Sir:

It is with a great deal of pleasure that I have had the opportunity to read your booklet issued on the occasion of Alberta's Golden Jubilee in the above matter. [A Concise History of Tofield and District Prepared by Tofield Jubilee Committee, July1st, 1955]

I have read your book with the purpose of obtaining authentic information in regard to the early history of the locality in which the story, Buffalo Days and Nights, refers in several places.

Peter Erasmus, guide, interpreter and traveller was hired as an interpreter to Rev. Woolsey, a Methodist missionary who was engaged in missionary work at Pigeon Lake and the vicinity of Edmonton.

He arrived in Alberta in the year 1855, from Fort Pitt where Reverend Woolsey met him by saddle horse. The years '55 or '56 and the winter of '57 and '58, Peter travelled with Woolsey on his trips, following the Pigeon Lake Crees.

In December of 1857, Rev. Woolsey accompanied the Crees on their winter quest for buffalo meat, getting sick near the Buffalo River where the Crees had a semi-permanent camp. Unable to stand the cold and privations in a canvas tent without a stove, he decided to move back to the Fort at Edmonton.

His guide and interpreter was delighted at his employer's decision which would give him an opportunity to share in the festivities of the Christmas holiday week that was a highlight of social life for the officials of the various forts that gathered there for a conference and planned their activities and needs for the following year's business.

The settlement of Lake St. Anne and the new settlement of St. Albert where a number of retired H.B.C. servants had taken up land and lived with their families furnished the women who were always invited to attend the dance in Edmonton on Christmas Eve.

Peter's progress back to Edmonton was slow as the Reverend Woolsey grew tired very quickly; the snow was heavy and he decided that if he made a direct route to the old trail, usually followed by the men of the Hudson Bay Post, hunting buffalo south of the Beaverhill Lake, that he would likely have a beaten trail back to the Fort., thus making it easier for the tired horse.

He managed to reach the south east shore of the Beaver Lake before it grew dark and was unable to find a sheltered spot to pitch their tent. He refers to the buffalo grass that grew luxuriantly along the south portion of the lake and was as good as grain for a tired horse.

Woolsey was then the first white man to see the Beaverhill Lake on December 22 of the year 1857 where they both camped overnight, and in Peter's own words, "I found my deductions to be correct in that I soon struck a well-beaten sleigh road, that was still undrifted and made the trail much easier for the horses. We made Edmonton early the next day, the day before Christmas, and believe me, I was happy to again join in the fun and good times that had become the one week of social life in a whole year of work."

1862—The battle under the leadership of Ketchamoot which won the Crees an initial victory was the means of rendering the whole area unsafe for any Cree for a number of years afterward as vengeance by the Blackfeet for their defeat under the Crees from Fort Pitt. This left the peaceful Indians of Pigeon Lake exposed to the depredations of these Blackfeet. They were forced to abandon their permanent homes at Pigeon Lake and were scattered in many areas north of the Saskatchewan river and among the Stoneys west of Rocky Mountain House.

Woolsey moved to Smoky Lake and started a mission there in 1862.

Trust this may be of interest to you. Please advise me if a copy of the booklet can be obtained for my files.

Yours truly, Henry Thompson."

# AN OLD TIMER,
# WILLIAM ROWLAND, IS GONE (1907)

The following is an interesting anecdote concerning the life of the late Mr. Rowland which appeared in the issue of The Tofield Standard on November 5th 1907. The article appeared originally as a letter to the editor signed by Etat Trebla. If you are good at decoding you will note immediately that this is the reverse spelling of "Albert Tate", a pioneer guide.

"At 6:30 p.m., last Saturday, William Rowland, Sr., one of the earliest pioneers of the Beaver Lake district succumbed to a severe attack of bronchial pneumonia. Mr. Rowland, although being an old man, was very hearty, until quite recently, when he felt a condition of general break-up coming. Only a few days ago a severe cold which developed seriously, culminated fatally. He was one of a very few in the Beaver Lake district who had reached the ripe old age of the eighties, he being 83 years of age. Just a week or so ago he received a visit from a brother whom he had not seen for over 18 years and who had lived northwest of Edmonton.

Having lived as he did many years in the west, in the early time when the H. B. Co. employees were the only white men in the country, Mr. Rowland always had a fund of stories at his tongue's end to tell about the remarkable things that happened in those days. Wonderful it must have been to him to watch the development which has taken place in the last decades in the march of progress.

The deceased leaves a sorrowing widow, two sons and two daughters to mourn his demise. The daughters are Mrs. E. Pruden and Mrs. J.Logan, and the sons, Messrs. Wm. Rowland, Jr., and John Rowland, all of whom live around Beaver Lake.

The funeral, which was one of the largest ever seen in the Beaver Lake district and which testified to the great respect the deceased held in the community, took place from the family residence, one mile west of Tofield, to St. James-the-Apostle cemetery at 1 p.m. last Tuesday. Rev. A.G.A. Rainier, curate in charge of the Anglican Church, of which the deceased was a member, conducting the obsequies.

The late Mr. Rowland was born in 1826 at Cumberland near Lake Winnipeg and spent most of his life in the west. In the early days he held an important position with the H. B. Co., traversing the north country between Fort Churchill on Hudson's Bay and Chipweyan in charge of shipments of the company.

Several brothers and sisters survived him. These are Fred and Alex Rowland, who live at Battleford, John who lives at St. Albert, Mrs. Kenneth McDonald and Mrs. John Sinclair of Edmonton and Mrs.Colin Fraser of Fort Chipewyan.

The old land marks are fast disappearing one by one. The connecting links of Kah-Yas long ago are getting fewer and fewer as each year claims its inevitable harvest.

At Beaver Lake lived one of the geniune "Old Timers" Willam Rowland, who for many years in 1860 to 1875, and even before that held the important post of special trader and interpreter to the great, war-like tribe of Blackfeet in the service of the mighty H.B. Co.

Living, as we do now, in peaceful and sunny Alberta with railroads, telephone and telegraphs at our command under the paternal care of the goverment, in other words, the R. N. W. M. P., we cannot realize how important an office was held by Mr. Rowland.

Not only between the great company and the Blackfeet nation did Mr. Rowland act as intermediary, but also between the hereditary enemies, the Crees and the Blackfeet. It was his duty, and a difficult one, to see that there was no open rupture between these enemies, at least within the horizon of the H. B.Co., immediate influence and forts, to so manage the periodic visits of these Indians that they did not encounter each other near the fort, and as far as possible, without the knowledge of the other tribes.

Mr. Rowland has seen some "mighty big feasts" around Edmonton fort during the days the trading was done. Could he be induced to tell a few of his experiences with some of the wild Indians, some of our curls would straighten out and the blood curdle in our veins.

The times and missionaries have changed and not the least noticeable is the reception accorded the aborigines, as they enter into the great trading emporim of the H. B. Co. on the corner of Jasper and Third Street, Edmonton.

I recall on one occasion when Mr. Rowland was trading with the Blackfeet an angry jealous husband, cool and deliberate, walked up to his wife, and taking her nose between his forefinger and thumb, with his scalping knife quickly snipped it off, and as he held the piece up so that all might see, rushed onto the young brave standing by and thrusting his hand over his mouth literally made him swallow the undelectable morsel! "You have eaten her, and now you can own her." he yelled.

All the buildings comprising the old fort at Edmonton were surrounded by a stockade 15 feet high. The Indian trading store was about twenty feet from the wall.

Immediately facing the store the stockades were doubled and trebled making it bullet proof. At each corner and commanding a full view of the stockade by the trading store, were bastions or sentry boxes, but very substantially built. They also were bullet proof. The port holes showed small cannon and glistening barrels of ever ready fire arms. A gallery ten feet from the ground ran along this stockade, connecting the bastions and overlooking the trading store.

In the stockade facing the store was a loop hole or hatchway on a level with the gallery, and about three feet square. Through this hole all the trading was done. The Indians remained on the outside of the bullet-proof enclosures with closed gates and glistening arms facing them.

An Indian wishing to trade rode up to this loop hole and threw his furs in, which were immediately counted and sorted, shouting out his requirements.

They were thrown out to him as unceremoniously as he had done his furs—always provided his furs were equal to the number of skins valued on the goods. And so the trading was continued for days and days until the Indians having no more buffalo robes to throw into the loop holes, once more took themselves off the plains.

Often there were occasions when the Indians, being headed by some of their great chiefs, were allowed to come into the fort enclosures and even visit the families.

The old time chiefs were chiefs not only in name. They had the power of life and death at their slightest call. Old Chief Mask-ke-pe-toon of the Crees and Chief Sapoo-mack-se-ca among the Blackfeet had and frequently were obligated to use their powers in maintaining their dignity. Both these chiefs were friendly to the whites but were "at daggers drawn" with each other as far back as the writer's memory goes.

In the end the Cree chief lost his life at the hands of a few unruly Blackfeet, while on his way to "patch up a Peace" and "smoke a pipe" with the head of the Blackfeet. Sapoo-mack-se-ca was horrified at the action of his treacherous subjects and dealt out summary justice to them.

Having called a great council he asked the bearers of the scalp of the Cree Chief to stand forth, which they proudly and promptly did, and as he received the scalp from them and with his own hands Chief Sapoomack-se-ca tomahawked both of the murderers.

These are the events which happened in the days when Mr. Wm. Rowland was a young man and held to be second to none in dealing with the meeting the Indians.

—"Etat Trebla"

# A SHORT HISTORY OF TOFIELD
# AS I REMEMBER IT

*George Cookson Jr.*
*Written approximately in 1920*

"Tofield got its name when the first school district was formed in 1895, and was named after Dr. J. H. Tofield, resident doctor at that time. The number of the school district was 376. The first trustees were J. W. Cookson, chairman, Dr. J. H. Tofield, John Lafond., George Cookson Sr., sec-treas. The first teacher was Miss Harriet McCallum, now Mrs. Tom Deby of Beaver Lake East. She was followed by Mr. Brown, Mr. D. Francis and Mr. Hendershott. The school was built of logs on the E. Gladue farm, close to the house where the Jeanettes are now living. Families attending school were: the Tofields, Lafonds, Letourneaus, Prudens Rowlands, Rickners, Gladues, and Hendersons. We had home-made desks which held four pupils at each desk.

At this time we were getting our mail every two weeks at the Logan P. 0. where Mr. R. McKenzie was postmaster. Afterwards (1897) we got up a petition to have a post office at Tofield and another at Northern (afterwards Bardo) which was granted. George Cookson Sr. was appointed postmaster for Tofield and Peter Jevning postmaster for Northern, with mail every two weeks. After a time we got a weekly mail and then a twice-weekly service. Albert Bruce and W. Rowland were mail carriers and brought the mail from Fort Saskatchewan.

The first regular church services were commenced in 1894 and were held at the home of Mr. George Cookson Sr. These were Presbyterian services conducted by a student minister, John Ferguson. In 1895, the Church of England under Rev. d'Easum started a service every two weeks, thus alternating with the Presbyterian service which gave us a service every week. This arrangement continued until we built the school when services were held there. Sunday School was then conducted by Mr. and Mrs. J. W. Cookson and Mr. and Mrs. D. Francis. Hours of service were: Sunday School 10:30 a.m., Church service 11:30 for the Presbyterians or 3 p.m. for the Church of England on alternating Sundays. After a few years, the Methodists commenced holding services with Rev. Hobbs as minister.

The village of Tofield was started in 1906 when the G. T. P. commenced running surveys for a transcontinental railway. The village was started on Mr. George Cookson's farm N. E. ¼ of 36-50-18, W.4. Morton and Adams built the first general store. Then followed a lumber yard operated by W. C. Swift, another general store operated and owned by Cress and Harper, a hardware store by R. 0. Bird, a drug store by C. Jamerson, furniture store by Harper and Letourneau, another drug store by Mr. McKinnon, a restaurant and butcher shop by Jim Mahaffey. The Notary Public was A. J. H. McCauley.

The school districts were reorganized and a village school built on S. E. corner of Sec. 36 with H. Martin as teacher. The village remained by S.½ of Sec. 1-51-19 for a townsite. Then Crafts, Lee and Gallinger of Edmonton North ½ of Sec. 1-51-19, had it surveyed into lots, and offered the storekeepers free lots if they would move their buildings to the Crafts, Lee and Gallinger townsite. The storekeepers took advantage of this offer and commenced moving their buildings to the Crafts, Lee and Gallinger townsite.

In the summer of 1907, the Presbyterian Church which had been built by the early settlers on Zion Hill north of William Thomson's farm was removed by tractor to a site just north of the present public school. It was moved again about 1910.

In the spring of 1909, the people of Tofield called a meeting to talk and try to secure a piece of land suitable for a cemetery and the present land was bought and surveyed into plots on May 17, 1909,—temporarily on account of Mrs. George Cookson's death– and surveyed later by qualified surveyor.

TRANSPORTATION &
COMMUNICATION

# ROADS WERE ESPECIALLY IMPORTANT TO THE DISTRICT'S ORIGINAL SETTLERS

*Roads in the Tofield Area*
*(Material for this article is taken from an account left by Mr. Jack Cookson.)*

Roads have always been vital to communications. The lack of them was one of the real hardships of the pioneer era.

The buffalo trails were probably the first, and not the worst roads, for they would follow the high, less heavily treed ground. Horseback riders could follow these with ease, but when the wagons containing settlers' effects must be brought in, these trails proved too narrow and too crooked. Sloughs, soft ground, creeks over which no bridges were yet built, steep hills—all proved major hazards in bringing in settlers' equipment.

In spite of the trouble involved, the pioneers did travel .... to Edmonton, to Wetaskiwin and for social gatherings.

As soon as the pioneers had their first major needs of food and shelter cared for they began to attack the problem of roads.

Mr. Jack Cookson has left us an account of how the first major roads were built.

To get to Edmonton, one could go around north of the hills by Fort Saskatchewan, which made the trip 65 miles long. Or one could go around south of the Beaver Hills by Hay Lakes which was 90 miles. Mr. Cookson says, "The first road was a shortcut from upper Ross Creek to the Nelson and Becker settlement, southeast of Fort Saskatchewan.

The next road was a trail from the Coombes place to Hastings Lake instigated by a man named Webster, assisted by Owens, Leggi, Walsh, Neal and others. It was difficult to travel, even in winter. The next trail was the Inkster Trail. Frank Oliver was our member in the Legislature of the N. W. T. and got an appropriation to help put a trail through from Cooking Lake to South Beaver Lake. Oliver promised Inkster the whole of $200.00 to take a wagon through to the lake in summer. He did it, but found numerous sloughs and went close to them to save chopping trees through the dense brush. The result was a crooked trail that Inkster got his wagon through and drew the $200.00. If there had been an inspection of the trail it would never have been approved because no one would have wanted to travel it more than once. Mr. Neal called it a "deathtrap". It came out at the Lake where Mr. Ed. Kallal lived on the north side of Ketchamoot Creek. (Now the home of the Stan Schacher family).

The next trail was the community trail built by volunteer help from Hunts to Cooking Lake. Everyone interested took hold. Lafond canvassed the merchants of South Edmonton and received donations of flour, tea, coffee, bacon and beans and even a keg of beer. A good job was done and all were proud of it. It became a much travelled road.

The next road was the baseline trail from Ross Creek to Edmonton, government built with a cutoff road for South Beaver Lake settlers. This cutoff trail struck the baseline road some ten miles from the lake. This road went past the John Phillips farm (now J. C. Warner's home) across the farm till recently occupied by T. R. Murray through Harold Weatherill's place north through the present forest reserve.

None of these roads could be travelled with heavy loads during wet times for there would be boggy spots but for light travel, they cut off a lot of mileage, for around the Beaver Hills, either north or south, it was some eighty miles to Edmonton.

As we travel over our modern blacktopped highways to Edmonton in less than an hour, we salute the pluck of the pioneers who first plodded their way through the Beaver Hills.

# THE POST OFFICE

When early settlers arrived in Beaverhill Lake area about 1886, Edmonton was the nearest post office so mail was brought out to this area whenever one of the settlers made a trip to Edmonton.

In the early 1890's the Logan post office of Tofield was started with Mr. Roderick McKenzie as postmaster. At that time the mail was brought from Edmonton to Fort Saskatchewan. From here it was picked up by the local mail carrier and transported to the Logan post office from whence it was collected by the owners every two weeks or so.

In 18971, George Cookson, Sr. became the first post master in the newlygranted Tofield Post Office. This first post office consisted of a small log shack with a sod roof which was overlaid with boards to protect it somewhat from the rain. Later, a shingled roof was constructed.

Billy Rowland was one of the first mail carriers . His task was made extremely difficult by the condition of the road at any time and during the "rainy years" 1899-1903, the roads were almost impassable due to the rainswollen creeks and sloughs spreading their areas.

When the Canadian Northern Railroad came through Chipman, the mail was routed from Chipman to Logan Post Office and from there to Tofield and onto Northern—later Bardo.

About the time the Canadian Government bought the Pueblo herd of buffalo in Montana, and decided to keep them in Elk Island Park, William Rowland had an unusual experience while on his mail route. The animals, after being shipped [to] Lamont were unloaded to be driven to Elk Island Park. From this drive, several animals escaped and proceeded to enjoy their freedom by roaming over the countryside. Mr. Rowland, driving with his load of mail for Logan, Tofield and Bardo met one of these large animals. He was not carrying a gun and thinking it would be wise to play it safe, he abandoned his rig and hid under a nearby bridge. The buffalo not being interested in the news of the day, calmly went on feeding. When the buffalo had passed by, grazing as they went, Mr. Rowland proceeded on his journey.

Mr. Cookson, Tofield's first postmaster, received the munificent sum of twelve dollars for his first year's service; he also sold thirtysix dollars' worth of stamps. Mr. Jevning of Bardo received seven dollars for his first year's work, but during his second year., his salary jumped to ten dollars with a commission on the sale of stamps. Undoubtedly, Mr. Cookson's salary was also increased by commissions on stamps as well as those on postal notes.

When Tofield was moved to the Craft, Lee and Gallinger property (near the present site of the school) C. H. Cress was appointed postmaster and held that position in 1907 and 1908. Mr. Cress was also the proprietor of a drygoods store and was, understandably, ruffled when asked to make out a money order for twenty or thirty dollars for the T. Eaton Co. in payment of an order for dry goods. Such parcels had to be picked up at Camrose as their large wooden containers were too large for the mail service to handle. One year, nobody received an Eaton's catalogue and while no investigation was made, people had their own ideas for the lack of "Eaton's bibles."

When the town moved to its present site, the post office again changed hands. This time, Mr. C. E. Jameison became postmaster. It was said he obtained the position because he was a good Liberal and the Liberals were in power. In 1911, the Dominion Government became Conservative and J. W. Somers became the Tofield postmaster. In 1918 Mr. A. A. Beirnes succeeded to Mr. Somers' position. About this time postmasters became civil servants and politics ceased to play a part in their appointment.

Following Mr. Beirnes came Mr. A. B. Clutterham as postmaster, a post which he filled from 1922–1949. Mr. Drew held the position after A. B. Clutterham's retirement until 1952 when the present postmaster, Norman E. Glover took over. Miss Edith Davison has been Mr. Glover's assistant up until the first part of 1968 when she married James Lancaster, and retired from the Post Office.

During the time that Tofield has had a post office the location of the building has changed many times. Beginning on the farm now owned by John Rempel, it moved to the north end of Main Street in townsite No. 2, to the north half of what was Brace's Store (later the O.K. Store), to the site of Bert Everitt's present store, to south of the present site of George McFadzean's drug store, to the small brick building south of the former Bank of Montreal (now owned by Conrad Patterson). The present post office was built in 1961 and continues to serve the public well. The staff in 1968 consisted of: Mr. N. Glover, Mrs. Evelyn Nolan (Assistant Postmaster), Mrs. Annie Hunley, Mrs. Joyce Hardy.

The rural routes started about 1912. Routes 1, 2, 3 and 4 were begun close together. Rural mailmen included: Thomas Herndon, Wallace Herndon, Bill Bailey, Gunder Thompson, D. G. McCarthy,

John Jones, Herman Tiedemann, Bill Hay. In 1967, the mailmen are Henry Heitman on Routes 1 and 2; Allen Herndon on Routes 3 and 4. In 1968, J. Graham Allan replaced Henry Heitman.

## TOFIELD TELEPHONES

In 1909, the first telephone office was established in Jamieson's drug store with Clara McHeffey as its first operator. She was followed in 1910 by Amanda Henderson (Mrs. Will Mitchell) who in turn was succeeded by Amy Morton (Mrs. Dobson) Jack Letourneau and Olive Letourneau. (Mrs. Spence). At this time, the switchboard was open from 8 a.m. to 8 p.m. on weekdays and from 8 a.m. to 4 p.m. on Sundays.

By 1915, the drug store had moved to what was later Bert Calvert's pool hall now the site of Watson's Ltd. and the switchboard moved with it. Mary Bethel (Mrs. John Wood) and Mildred Carter (Mrs. 0. P. Thomas) were the operators. The calls to the switchboard were shown by rotating balls the red side of the ball announcing that someone was calling "Central".

After the gasoline lamp used to provide light in the telephone office exploded and burned the place down, the office was moved to a location north of Swift's garage. By this time (1916) Tofield had continuous service; the operators concerned were: Beatrice Scott, Mary Nichol, Hazel Bowick, Mildred Bethel, Alma Bethel, Minnie Wood, Annie Hopgood, Jessie Hopgood. The telephone service men were: Ed Ruzua, Ray Herndon, Arthur Taylor, Gordon Hasler and W. 0. Glover.

The first rural 'phone line was in the Ingram district; W. Thomson's and the George Cooksons were the first two families able to talk on a rural line. There was also one 'barbed-wire" telephone between the R. C. Phillips and the W. Abernethy homes. Rural lines expanded rapidly until the depression era, during which time many farmers found it economically necessary to give up the government telephones and replace them with barbedwire phones. On these, neighbour could talk to neighbor and since at least one family in each area had retained the "highline" phone, messages could be relayed to and from the operator in Tofield.

During the middle and late '30's the mutual telephone companies as we know them came into being. These were: BardoGrand Forks; Beaver Lake; Beaverhill, Brookside; Ketchamoot Creek; Barnes; Lindbrook; Stirret; Tofield East; Tofield South; Willow Flats; Woodstead and Mac Lake Mutual Telephone Companies.

These phone companies served an area from Highway 16 to the Kingman area; east to Shonts and west to Ross Creek.

Mr. W. O. Glover, local plant inspector, retired in 1939 after which time all services were taken care of by inspectors from Edmonton.

During 1940, an exchange building was constructed which came into operation on July 9, a new switchboard and a soundproof booth were installed. In 1956, still another switchboard was installed and the process was repeated in 1959.

Miss Lorett Ross, now of St. Albert, was chief operator for many years. Under her, at various times worked Neva Wood (Mrs. P. Spangler); Ethel McClymont (Mrs. Freeman Hill); Esther Jacobs (Mrs. Anderson) Mary Nahrebeski; Ethel Scott (Mrs. Brown); Vivian Shaw (Mrs. Garbarz); Pat Burnett (Mrs. N. Glover); Lois Thompson (Mrs. Burnett); Goldie Jacobs; Hazel Young; Frances Hardy (Mrs. O. Reum); Emily Carlisle; Jean McGuire (Mrs Van Dewark); Edith Davison (Mrs. J. Lancaster); Betty Stinson (Mrs. Brooks).

After 1947 and until the exchange closed at the introduction of dial phones in 1964, Emily Carlisle was the chief operator. In addition to some of the foregoing operators, the following have worked under Emily Carlisle: Doris Oslund (Mrs. M. Schacker); Margaret McAllister (Mrs. Allan Pointer); Enid Blake; Ruth Torrie (Mrs. Good); Olga Shewchuk; Ella Campbell; Betty Townsend; Margaret Myers; Doreen Lee; Ivy May; Myrtle LaRocque; Yvonne Kendall; Ellen Ferguson (Mrs. Hoflin); Marianne Guenard; Joanne Boyles (Mrs. Lernowich);Mavis Mitchell (Mrs. McLeod); Vera Lukasiewich (Mrs.G.Warner;), Mary Stevenson; Mary Moore; Lena Boese; Mary Shemko (Mrs. J. Thiessen); Olivia Lukasiewich (Mrs. Lazarenko), Joan Herndon; Doreen Garbe; Verna Enns (Mrs. Epp); Jean Williams; Darlene LaRocque (Mrs. Williams);

Pat Stevenson, Louisa Vickner; Pat Brown.

In 1964 dial phones came to the Tofield area and the phone exchange was closed to be replaced by the present telephone building. Direct distance dialing came into effect in 1966.

# THE LAKE

If it could only talk, what stories Beaverhill Lake could tell! Once containing millions of fish, it is now only a sheet of water to look at, a source of water for stock, and a safe landing place for uncounted varieties of birds.

According to Mr. William Rowland, a onetime employee of Hudson's Bay Co., who homesteaded the land on which the Tofield Creamery now stands; "In 1885, the buffalo had to go to the springs in the centre of Beaverhill Lake for water." Between this time of low water and in 1902 when the record high water mark of the lake was established, a considerable amount of bush must have grown in what was once the lake because Mr. J. R. Francis can remember as a small boy the piles of driftwood of willow and poplar that piled up on the shore line of Beaverhill Lake.

Mr. Pete Lerbekmo has stated that between 1895 and 1897, when he and his father rowed over to "the point" trees four or five inches in diameter were standing in the water but were no longer alive and the great blue herons were nesting in the dry branches.

In the fall of 1899, a rainy cycle that lasted till 1903 replaced the dry years, and the lake is reported to have risen 18 feet. On taking soundings in the lake in 1965, J. R. Francis and D. W. Jacobs calculated that the lake would have had to rise 12 feet to achieve the 1902 level and 10 feet to reach even 1917 level.

"The point" situated towards the south end of the lake was commonly called "Francis Point." In 1903, it consisted of five islands; there were two channels between the islands deep enough for a boat to be rowed across.

Raspberries grew in abundance along the banks and people came from miles around to pick them.

From 1905 to 1910,the lake receded sufficiently to allow much of the once submerged land to be cultivated. Until the rainy fall of 1915, the water level remained fairly constant but from then till 1917, it rose steadily. This steady rise was the cause of a petition circulated among the farmers bordering the lake that the government lower the level of the lake. By the time the government had the necessary wheels of action in motion and a survey made to ascertain the cost to each landowner, nature had done the job. This was fortunate for the survey showed that a ditch 22 feet wide, 8 feet deep in places and 8 miles long would have been necessary to lower the water level by 3 feet artificially and the job would have taken three years. By 1922, the water level had returned to that of 1910. By 1929, the driest year recalled by the residents of the area, the lake had dropped 4 or 5 feet. The level remained much the same until 1950 51 when the lake came close to drying up completely.

In these two years, a certain gas company prepared to put a seismograph crew on the lake. First they obtained two AllisChalmer tractors equipped with steel rear wheels built 32 inches wide and of the usual height. The machinery was then mounted, front and rear, on these specially adapted tractors. The east side of the lake was selected as the initial site of the enterprise but success eluded the workers. The front wheels just slid in the mud and would not turn.

So a large steel barge 36' by 24' and 30" high was constructed and the machinery mounted on the barge so as to distribute its weight evenly. This worked from south to north along the east shore which is the deepest part of the lake. However, success was not to be theirs. One day when the wind was from the south east, the crew decided to strike out in a westerly direction, During the day they seemed to be successful but that night the wind dropped, and the water settled down leaving the machinerybearing barge stranded in the mud. All winter it remained in its muddy location; when spring came the crew thawed it out and removed it. In 1967 the water level is approximately that of 1930.

In 1914 there was no snow on the lake the latter part of February, and since its surface was smoothly frozen, three ice boats were constructed by local residents. Harry Rogers and Dawson Manners owned one of them.

When the lake froze in the winter a crack would form running parallel to the shore line. Sometimes the ice would pile up in a inverted V shape and at other times one sheet of ice would slide over the others. One particular Sunday afternoon, aided by a strong northwest wind, the trio of iceboats sailed east along the crack, well over to the east side of the lake and came back along the north side. When they began to look for a spot to cross the crack, it was not easily found. They spied a spot where the north sheet of ice slid over the south sheet. It looked like a fairly level crossing so they taxied around, and came at this gentler slope at about sixty miles per hour. After briefly "sailing through the air with the greatest of ease," they landed luckily-right-side-up. Stopping to observe what had launched their spectacular takeoff, they found they had climbed a sixfoot ridge and sailed through the air for seventyfive feet before they made their next contact with the ice. Dawson Manners' reaction to this experience was that, while he would not take a thousand dollars for the experience, he would not take ten thousand for a repetition of it.

In the spring of 1917, the ice had moved north on the lake and it looked as it that might be the last of it that winter. One morning, about 9 a.m. the wind freshened from the northwest and drove the ice before it across the lake. Hitting the north shore of the point, the ice was flung 80 rods inland in a pile 25 feet high and a mile and a half long. The easterly part of the floating ice missed the point and landed on the south shore of the lake.

During the years 1922–1931, Dr. William Rowan of the University of Alberta, accompanied by other naturalists used Francis Point as a site for collecting information about birds. Here, in a patch of bulrushes ten feet high growing in two feet of water, gulls built their nests among the flattened last-year's rushes. In a nest the size of two hands put together, the female gull would lay three brownish eggs. Dr. Rowan estimated that 40,000 gulls were hatched each spring in this area. Mr. Francis along with several others one day helped Dr. Rowan band 2,000 of the baby gulls which looked like turkey poults. They worked in two feet of water underlaid with plenty of mud.

In all, 239 species of birds were identified and collected on the Point. Even mice were plentiful; one morning the hundred mouse traps set out by Dr. Rowan the previous evening displayed over 40 different kinds of mice.

During the years, many a coyote has lost its life on or around the lake. Hounds have taken their toll and when the ice was sufficiently smooth, men with guns have used cars as a means of eliminating coyotes.

Dr. Bain once wanted a chance to chase coyotes on ice, so when Jim Francis reported ideally smooth ice, they started after the elusive coyote. The coyote enjoyed the run but eventually turned towards the shore. Dr. Bain's car had less traction than the coyote and spun completely around eleven times before straightening out. Disheartened, Dr. Bain sighed, "I guess that's it," and headed for home.

Many a winter trail across the frozen lake provided a welcome shortcut for the pioneer. Sometimes this trackless shortcut confused the traveller and lured him into travelling in a circle. Snowblindness was another hazard faced by the pioneers when they walked over the frozen expanse of the lake.

Sometime about 1909-10, six young men took this steamboat out for a ride on the lake. Part of their equipment for the trip consisted of a couple of bottles of liquor which they soon consumed. They were in high spirits and quite oblivious to the fact that their fuel supply was inadequate. They had embarked from the north west shore of the lake, and soon were speeded on their way by a brisk wind from the northwest whipping up the fourfoot waves which are so quickly aroused on a shallow lake. Now their coal supply gave out and they were at the mercy of the storm.

They were not what would be called a praying group but they earnestly sought Divine help as no other was available. One report has it that "some prayed and some tore up floorboards to use as fuel, each according to his belief." However, after a twohour, twelve mile voyage over the deep lake, the sailors drifted in to the east shore of the lake. They obtained a horsedrawn buggy from a nearby settler and drove back to Tofield to the relief of their families and friends who had feared the worst.

There were many fine bathing beaches along the south and north shores but summer resorts never developed from them. A few years ago, the Mundare Fish and Game Association developed a recreation area complete with slides, swings, barbeques, etc. This proved to be a success.

"Fish Stories" abound in the area surrounding the lake, but this is one with a different twist; the "big one" did not get away. Two early pioneers, Lafond and Letourneau, being short of feed for their pigs, built a fish trap in Ketchamoot Creek. From here, they secured fish by wagon loads and fed them to their porkers. This solved one problem but created another, for after the slaughtered, frozen fishfed pigs had been sold on the Edmonton market that market ceased to exist. After one experience of this fishflavored pork, the buyers would accept no more pork from Beaverhill Lake area until they had first fried and tasted it! Fish is fine as fish, but not as pork!

Thus since the days the Crees paddled over its glassy surface, Beaverhill Lake has been an integral part of the Tofield area and a factor in its development.

—*J. R. Francis*

Education

# EDUCATION IN TOFIELD
# HAS EARLY BEGINNING

Tofield has been in an official school district since 1909 but even before that, the local children were struggling with the three R's. According to an account left by Jack Cookson, "Mr. Robert Logan and Mr. Roderick MacKenzie started the first private school in 1890 and hired an old soldier, Major William Stiff to teach the children of the Pruden, Logan, MacKenzie, Gladue, Norn, and Rowland families many of whom had come here after the Riel Rebellion of 1885." Major Stiff was referred to in Tony Cashman's "More Edmonton Stories" as being "a fine hand with a fiddle." No doubt a useful accomplishment in a pioneer community.

Major Stiff was ingenious as well as accomplished. He had no watch, so he devised his own system of telling time. The school door faced south. When the sunlight came directly in the door, Major Stiff decided that the sun had reached its zenith and made a mark on the floor to indicate its position. Using the mark as a basis, he could tell the time quite accurately—on sunny days at least.

The school where Major Stiff operated his primitive sundial was later named MacKenzie in honour of Roderick MacKenzie on whose land it was built. It was given the very low school district number 234 N.W.T, indicating how few schools there were at that time.

In 1895, Mr. Daniel Francis who was one of the first High School teachers in Edmonton came to teach at MacKenzie. With his wife and large family he lived on the farm south of John Wood's present home. He drove back and forth on weekends and hauled hay for his stock in the evenings.

"In 1896," again according to Jack Cookson, "There was agitation for a government school in the Tofield area. This was petitioned for and granted and the school was started in a rented log building owned by Billie Rowland." This was situated on the south east corner of Don Shaw's present farm. A board of trustees was elected consisting of J.0. Letourneau, J. Lafond and J. Cookson. The secretary was Dr. J.H. Tofield and George Cookson Jr. was the treasurer.

The number of the school district so formed was 376 N.W.T, again a very low number. Miss Harriet McCallum, though "not a certificated teacher," was the first teacher in the Tofield School District and continued her duties for twelve months.

In 1897, $800 was borrowed to build a school which was erected on the corner of the Gladue farm next to the road. This was a log building too, and was later used as a Methodist Church. It stood for many years behind the present United Church.

Again according to Jack Cookson: "Our first certificated teacher was R. Brown from Ontario. He was a real live coal and gogetter. He was most instrumental in getting a Post Office for Tofield. A public meeting had been called to discuss a post office to serve both Bardo and Tofield. Mr. Brown went to this meeting and strongly advocated petitioning for two post offices, one for Bardo and one for Tofield. This was agreed upon and the petition was granted. From this it can be seen that then, as well as now, a teacher's duties are many and varied.

Mr. Brown is somewhat a figure of mystery. He became ill and, for $2.00, Mr. Jack Cookson took him to an Edmonton hospital. Here he was admitted but soon left the hospital without permission and "was never seen again even by his relatives," according to Jack Cookson's diary.

In 1897, the people of the Bardo community organized Anderson School District which was given the number 434. This school was named in honour of Reverend Bersvend Anderson, the spiritual leader of the Bardo district. In 1898, school was opened with Mr. Harry Erwin in charge of the little log school.

It is proof of Tofield's pioneer status that all three of the schools established before 1900 belonged to the first 500 schools in Alberta.

In 1903 a new frame school was built on the George Cookson Sr. land. Mr. Martin, brother-in-law to Mrs. George Cookson Jr., was in charge. It was painted yellow, heated by a woodburning stove and had the usual three windows on each side. This modern school was used for five years and then, in 1908, was moved to the Ingram District. To the wrath of many Tofield residents, its low S.D. number went with it and Tofield's number was now 1939. In 1966 the original number was restored, due to the efforts of J.R. Francis and H. A. Pike, Superintendent of Schools.

There is a page of the school register for the month of January of 1898 in the possession of Mrs. Jack Appleby. It shows the teacher to be Mr. Daniel Francis. The children actually in school are listed, with their attendance marked and, for some reason not clear to us, the preschool district children are also listed. It may have been a school census.

The names of the children registered in school are Elizabeth and Jerome Gladue; Isabel, Lillie and John Lafond; Peter Rowland; Florence, May and Edith Tofield; Tealy, Fannie, Lily and Oma Rickner; Oliver Letourneau; Roscoe and Charles Junt; Gertrude, John and Mary Francis; Eddie Cookson; Perly and Marvin Rickner, Mamie Gallagher; Flora and William Pruden; Maggie, Betsie, and Alice Gladue.

The preschool children listed are: Charles, Edith and James Rowland; John, Ned, Harriet and Archie Pruden; Venah Rickner; Harry, George and Mabel Francis, Amanda and Lily Henderson, Jack Letourneau, Clara Gladue.

One room was not now large enough for the increased enrolment so the pupils were divided into two groups. The junior division was taught by Miss Reith and the senior room was in the charge of Mr. J. Younie.

The primary room was a small storeyandahalf building with a leanto. It had been built originally by A.J.H McCauley to store oats for the railway construction workers' horses. Later it was moved to the site of the present schoolyard, next door to the Hopgood house. It was part of the Art Torrie home and Mrs. Torrie said, that before the house was stuccoed, the original three windows to a side were still plainly visible.

Mrs. O. P. Thomas (nee Mildred Carter) says of Miss Reith, "She boarded various places but many of us have the picture memory of her coming from Jack Cookson's on snowshoes which she handled with ease. She came as directly as the crow flies. She was an excellent teacher, interested chiefly in the Arts. Holidays were spent in travel and in collecting articles which she might use to bring the other parts of the world to her pupils. Some years later she exchanged classrooms with Miss Marion Reid of South Africa. Later she taught in Oliver School in Edmonton."

Mr. James A. Younie taught the classes from grade IV upward in a room above the R.O. Bird Hardware which was near, if not on, the site of the former Boston Café. It was a very spooky place, according to Mrs. Thomas. Pupils climbed long steep stairs only to traverse a corridor which was lined with coffins. One wonders if these unusual accessories for a school room had a sobering effect on the pupils or if the reverse would be true.

The first school on the present site was of brick veneer construction, had four classrooms and boasted a belfry complete with the traditional school bell. Mrs. Mildred Thomas has some amusing anecdotes concerning one of the early principals, Mr. Frederick Hamilton Butcher. Of him, she says, "Frederick Hamilton Butcher left a vivid memory in his students of the time he disregarded the danger of skating on the thin ice on Beaverhill Lake. He went through the thin ice leaving little showing above the ice except his "Christie Stiff" hat. A human chain of kids fished him out. He dogtrotted all the way to town, "no doubt to the accompaniment of illsuppressed giggles."

Also, Mrs. Thomas writes, "Mr. Butcher was well endowed with certificates and had come to Tofield after considerable training at West Point. This training inspired him to give vigorous training to the high school students, boys and girls alike. He was a stickler for perfection and snapped out his commands, expecting military precision. "This line is wobbly. Straighten it. Stand up straight. Hands down by the seam of your pants." Since girls at that time did not wear jeans, "a positive mirth quake followed. During the time it took for his four shades of pink to subside, we had no drill."

Mr. Butcher was followed in 1914 by Mr. C.E. Poppleston. The school board minutes refer to him as "Principal Poppleston" which makes a nice alliterative title. Principal Poppleston was a man of undoubted talent, but, according to the records he seemed to have had great difficulty in getting along with the school board, the pupils and his teaching staff. According to Mrs. Thomas, and to the school records, he trained choruses to enter the, then very young, Alberta School Musical Festival, arranged for the pupils' transportation to the scene of the festival in Edmonton and found billets for those who had no relatives in Edmonton He also encouraged the organization of Cadets, securing the services of Rev. Leversedge as instructor; he sponsored basketball, he instituted public presentation of prizes for high standings in class; he promoted debating and Tofield High once journeyed to Vegreville to engage in verbal jousting with Vegreville High.

Jim Francis recalls that Principal Poppleston wore a moustache which once came to grief with a little help from Jim. It seems that Mr. Poppleston requested Jim to tie the valve of a football bladder which he had just inflated by mouth. Jim complied willingly. The fact that the string used to tie the valve securely was just as securely tied around Principal Poppleston's moustache was no doubt accidental. Much of the moustache was no longer secure when it and the football bladder separated.

The school population at this time was 170; a new building had been built for primary pupils (a small frame school south of the present school); the SecretaryTreasurer, Mr. McCauley received $75.00 per annum; the janitor, Mr. Powell, received $600 per annum; children were required to be vaccinated; $6500 [sic] was budgeted for the year's school expenses; the school board consisted of: N.S. Smith, chairman; H.W. Cookson, T.W. Jacobs and W.P. Rowe.

In 1916, Mr. Niddrie followed Mr. Poppleston. School opened in August with an enrollment of 146. To the dismay of the school board, if not of the children, the school burned down early in October. Mr. E. Rogers had turned in the alarm at 3:30 a.m. and a half hour later in spite of the efforts of the volunteer fire brigade, the school was only a memory; $7300. was realized from the insurance.

The school board was galvanized into action. They offered the Queen's Hotel $50. per month for the use of some rooms for the remainder of the year. An architect, Mr. A. M. Jeffers of Edmonton was commissioned to draw up plans for a new building to be erected on the site of the previous school. $8000 was borrowed to build the new school.

In November, 1917, the new building was opened. It was of brick construction, containing 4 classrooms, a principal's office, and a laboratory. It was heated by a coal furnace. Mr. Sheane, the new principal was in charge of the arrangements for the official opening.

Previous inspectors had been Mr. Hill (later librarian of Edmonton Public Library); Col. McGregor; Mr. Stickler who lived where Mr. and Mrs. Bruce Warner now live (then owned by J.C. Phillips) and now in 1918 the inspector was Mr. Williams. In his report, Mr. Williams stated that "the staff compares favourably with those in city schools."

Those were the years when Chautauqua was a popular entertainment. For a week, performances were given twice a day by a travelling group of entertainers in a huge tent. Everyone for miles around went to the Chautauqua. The school children and teachers presumably wanted to go too. So we see several hours being changed to accommodate them. School was to begin at 8 o'clock and close at 3 o'clock during Chautauqua week according to the school board minutes of June 4, 1918.

In 1919,1 Mr. J.W. Chapman replaced A.J.H. McCauley as secretary and the minutes state that the board was instructed to reengage Miss Irene Hawley (later Mrs. T,R. Murray) for another term. Mr. McCauley was not retiring; he now became chairman of the board for a period to be followed by Mr. E.P. Rowe.

The records of the meeting of August 7, 1923 state "Moved by Mr. Worton that the secretary be authorized to execute an agreement with the Northwest Utilities Ltd. whereby the latter be empowered to lay gas pipes to the school." Until now, coal oil lamps and coal furnaces had been used.

Baseball has always been a favourite game in Tofield. The high school boys had a good team in 1927. It was a high school team only in the sense that the players were all the students; they provided their own equipment, their uniforms were made at home and father or some other public spirited citizen, provided transportation when needed. In 1927, this team journeyed in Frank Marden's touring car, with Hank Thompson driving, to Vegreville to participate in the May 24th Sports Day. To their delight, they captured first prize. The boys who played on the team that year were : Bill Worton, Syd Worton, Ed Hill, Bob Whyte, Kenneth Ball, Neil Phillips, Joe Kallal, Murray McHeffey, Ray Martin, and Boyd Stauffer. The school received assistance from local organizations.

"Mrs. Ward, Mrs. Abbott and Mrs. Baptist, representing the W.I. were present and discussed with the board the matter of the Institute cooperating with the board in the matter of fencing and improving the school grounds." according to the official minutes of the school board meeting of April 8, 1928. At the next meeting fence was ordered and arrangements made to erect it.

*For the following information we are indebted Mrs. J. W. Robinson.*

In 1926, a school fair was planned for Tofield as part of the Alberta Government sponsored School Fair programme and in 1927 the first Tofield School Fair was held. Mr. J.W. Robinson was president of the School Fair Committee for many years. Mr. Russel, principal of the school was keenly interested in the project.

The Alberta Goverment supplied seeds for vegetables and flowers. The children planted these seeds and cared for the resulting plants in their home gardens. In the fall, prizes were awarded for the best exhibit in each class. Cooking, canning, sewing and knitting were all exhibited. School work was displayed in various classes, woodwork prizes were competed for and competitions in sports were held. There were also prizes awarded for singing, reciting and P.T. demonstrations. In 1927 the judges were Inspectors Russel and Robinson for school work; Mr. Heckburt and Miss Story from Vermilion School of Agriculture for garden products and domestic science classes; Mrs. Pincott, Mrs. J.W. Robinson and Mrs. Rowe for singing.

Later classes in livestock and poultry were added for the special benefit of the country children. Exhibits were on view as soon as the judging was over and great excitement prevailed when results were made known.

Each pupil's prizes were carefully listed and points awarded according to the value of the prize. The boy and girl with the highest individual scores won a week's tuition at the Vermilion School of Agriculture the following summer. The number of points for each school was also carefully computed and certificates of merit awarded to the school having the highest rating in the educational field and in the agricultural field. These awards were eagerly sought. Schools participating were: Ketchamoot, Bardo, McKenzie, Lakeshore, Ingram, Woodlawn, Amisk Creek and Tofield.

About 1930, school festivals were sponsored by the Provincial Government and the schools of Tofield and district took part enthusiastically. Competitions from grades 1 to 12 were held in solos, duets, chorus work, action songs, folk dancing, dramatics and recitations. The festivals which Tofield attended were held in Camrose as it was the centre of the inspectorate. The schools north of town were in the Lamont inspectorate and the festival rotated among the towns in that area. Certificates of merit were awarded to the participants by judges of such renown as Mr. Vernon Barford and Mrs. Elizabeth SterlingHaynes. The school receiving the highest number of points was awarded a special certificate. In the evening of the day of the festival a concert was presented which consisted of the winning items of the day.

Both School Fairs and School Festivals were a lot of work but the results were very worthwhile. The whole community worked in various ways helping to train the children, making costumes, arranging for transportation and acting as chaperones during the big day itself.

About the same time track meets began. First a local meet was held for the purpose of eliminating and then the winners journeyed to the central meet for further competition.

By 1927, teachers' salaries had risen somewhat, for we find in the minutes of the Sept. 6, 1927 that "Mrs. R. Davison (trustee) moved that the board approve of the engaging of Mr. R.V. McCullough as Principal at a salary of $1900. per annum and Miss Marion Argue at $1000. per annum be approved. Mr. J.W. Chapman moved that Mr. A.B. Evenson's salary be raised to $1250, in view of him having to teach high school subjects."

For many years Mr. Fred McHeffey was janitor at the school. In addition to his duties as janitor he was required to supervise the pupils' behaviour during the noon hour.

Mr. J.T. Bullock, B.A., became principal of the Tofield School in 1928. He specialized in the teaching of English; hunting and woodwork were his hobbies, he could coach any game from marbles to rugby. He was Church Warden of Holy Trinity Anglican Church and active in the social welfare work of the church. Mrs. Bullock also had her B.A. degree and did private tutoring in high school mathematics. She too, was active in church work.

During Mr. Bullock's regime, additional classrooms were constructed in the basement and gas heaters and lamps installed. The parents of rural pupils were given permission to construct a stable on the school grounds to accommodate the horses which conveyed the country children to school.

Following Mr. Bullock, in 1934 came Mr. O. Paul Thomas as principal. Mr. Thomas had a special interest in Tofield since his wife was the former Mildred Carter, one of Tofield's early telephone operators. Mr. Thomas was interested in music and trained choruses for the music festivals. He was an ardent curler. In 1934, the staff consisted of: Mr. Thomas, Mrs. McIntyre, Mr. Broughton, Miss Stewart (now Mrs. Everitt), Mrs. Wingrove and Miss Forester.

In 1937, Mr. W. McDonnell became assistant principal. Mr. Larry McLeah joined the staff the same year, other members of which were Miss Stewart, Miss Wingrove, Miss McCrea (now Mrs. S.J. Sears).

Mr. McDonnell, later principal of Camrose High School, has these memories of the spring of 1938. " Mr. Thomas left in the spring to work for the Department of Meteorology. I inherited his chorus which was preparing for the musical festival at Camrose (accompanist, Mrs. Stinson) and a few days later the roof blew off,

I stood in the east room upstairs and watched the stovepipe suddenly disappear straight up." (This was due to a violent wind storm and the roof literally blew off the old brick building. Until the roof was repaired to last another 20 years, high school was held in the old town hall, later demolished.) The lower rooms of the brick school were still usable. Mr. Ralph Zuar and Mr. Bev. Facey, now superintendent of Strathcona County, filled in the remainder of the spring term after Mr. Thomas' departure.

Mr. Larry Broughton became principal in 1938. He had great musical talent and was generous in sharing it. He trained choruses for the music festival and was choir leader in the United Church. He was also the moving spirit behind the Tofield Handicrafts Fair at which event antiques and handicrafts of all types were displayed.

In 1940, Mr. W. McDonnell became principal. In the spring this year the Divisional Festival was held in Tofield and a great deal of work organizing it fell upon the local staff, especially, Mr. Larry Broughton.

Mr. McDonnell remembers his championship girls' softball team on which Velma Stevenson was pitcher and Audrey Swinton was catcher. Some of the backstops put up on the school softball diamonds for the teams of those years are still in use, he tells us. Also he says he and A.B. Clutterham and Jack Beirnes "got a golf course laid out one time. There were four games of golf played on it." During this period, the school fair was still very important. Mr. J.W. Robinson was also keenly interested, says Mr. McDonnell. He also recalls that Edith Robinson (daughter of Mr. and Mrs. J.W. Robinson and now Mrs. W. Brickman), "graduated from Grade XII after twelve years' attendance with an almost unbelievable record of no absences and no lates." Salaries in 1937 were: Principal $1,400., High School Assistant $1,000., other staff $855. Other high school teachers here in Mr. McDonnell's regime were Selmer Olsenberg, Wilbert Stevens, Isobel Deane.

Larry McLeah of the Tofield Staff was director of a play in the winter of 1937-38.It featured Harold Schultz, Gwen Firth, Esther Pyle, Bill Worton, Hazel Patterson, Marj. Stewart, Joy and "Mac" McDonnell and Jack Whyte.

One of "Mac's" most vivid memories of school affairs in Tofield is the tremendous amount of leadership in A.T.A. affairs given by Arkle Richardson, then teaching at Lindbrook. Mr. Richardson was later on the Tofield High School Staff, after teaching many years in the senior room at Lindbrook School, where Mrs. Richardson taught the primary room.

In 1944, Mr. A.H. Elliott came as principal of Tofield and remained here for nine years. He was a popular teacher and an outstanding citizen of the town. He coached high school baseball and hockey teams; he was an excellent player as well as coach.He inspired, and played in a high school orchestra, other members of which were, Bob Torrie, Joan Fraser and Leonard Lawson. Mr. Elliott was also a member of the United Church choir, a Sunday School teacher, and a member of the Masonic Lodge. Mrs. Elliott was also active in church and community work.

During these years the pattern of school organization was changing. In 1938 the Holden School Division absorbed the small country districts whose affairs now were administered from Holden.The inspector now became superintendent, Mr.McLean, followed by Mr. E.M. Erickson and then H.A. Pike, who remained until 1966, as superintendent of schools in the County of Beaver. Mr. Marvin Bruce became Superintendent in 1966.

The town of Tofield did not join the Holden S.D. until 1947. About this time, it became the provincial government's policy to centralize the schools. The small country schools gradually closed and the children were taken to Tofield. Since this greatly increased the school population, greater classroom accommodation was needed. The MacKenzie, Amisk Creek, and Palmer Schools were moved into town; a one room school was built in 1951. The Elementary Wing was built in 1957, as well as the gymnasium-auditorium and a circular building containing nine classrooms, was built in 1959.

The old brick school was abandoned in 1957. In the 1958 winter it was gutted by fire of an unknown origin and, as a safety measure, the remaining walls were pulled down.

During these transition years, mention should be made of devoted service by Mr. Charlie Sears who was the trustee from this area. Since the inception of the county system in 1958, Mr. Harold Weatherill is our representative on the council of the County of Beaver. Mr. Weatherill, takes a keen interest in school affairs. Mr Sears replaced Mr. Weatherill in 1967 when the latter resigned.

Following Mr. Elliott, who left Tofield to become Superintendent of Schools at Oyen, Mr. Claude May was promoted from viceprincipal to principal. The viceprincipal then became Mrs. L.M. Graham who had been on staff for some time.

In 1959, fifty years after Tofield School District was formed there was a school population of 500 pupils Seven buses brought the children to the central school Only two rural schools remained open and there was discussion of closing them. There were twenty classrooms, as well as the shop and home economics rooms. The Superintendent of Schools, Mr. H.A. Pike moved to Tofield and the new position of Assistant Superintendent was filled by Mr. Marvin Bruce formerly of the Tofield staff.

The High School staff in the Golden Jubilee Year consisted of: Mr. R.H. Harris, B.A... Principal; Mr. Marvin Bruce, B.Ed., VicePrincipal; Mr. Cal Annis, B.A.; and Mr. Ronald Rix., B.Sc.

The Junior High School staff consisted of: Mr. Jack Lampitt; Mrs. Howard Brown; Mrs. Conrad Patterson; Mrs. W. Fraser, Assistant to the Principal; Mrs. C. Noble.

The teachers of the Elementary grades were: Mrs. Dahl; Mr. D. Kauffman; Mrs. E. Wideman; Miss M. Turner; Mrs. Art Torrie; Miss Betty Brown; Mrs. Bert Everitt; Mrs. Neil Phillips; Mrs. M. McCormick; Miss Joyce Stauffer; Mrs. Reg. Callard; Miss Freda Warkentin. Home Economics classes were taught by Miss Ethel Brown, B.Sc., and shop taught by Mr. Earl Hardy, M.L.A.

In the Golden Jubilee year of education in Tofield some innovations were made in school activities. In addition to the Christmas Concert produced by grades 6 to 9, Mr. Annis' drama class produced a play early in the winter. His physical education class gave a tumbling display to complete the evening. In February, Mr. Harris scheduled a day of parentteacher interviews. This was well attended having the highest percentage of parent attendance of any town in the County. The High School girls' basketball team were the champions of the county, under the expert coaching of Mr. Bruce.

Mr. R.H. Harris resigned as principal in 1964 and Mr. C.F. Annis became principal with Mr. J.C. Lampitt as VicePrincipal. During preceding years the library had outgrown its original location in the round wing so in 1965 a new library, biology laboratory, and typing room were added to Tofield School. Miss Komarnisky became the first commercial teacher in the new typing room, Mrs. Edna Bowick set up the new library as she had done for the previous one in the Round Wing.

In 1966, Mr. Annis became School Superintendent and Mr. K.R.

Eastlick became principal, Mr. H.A. Pike was replaced by Mr. M.S. Bruce as Superintendent of Schools. In 1967, Mr. Bruce, Mrs. Bruce and their two daughters moved to Tofield.

In 1967, Miss Roberta Cumming who had taught French and English for several years left the staff for a position in Eastern Canada and Mrs. Edna Bowick left for the County of Strathcona.

In September, 1967, the staff of the Tofield School consists of: Mr. K.R. Eastlick, Principal; Mr. J.C. Lampitt, VicePrincipal; Mrs. Mollie Conn; Mr. Lloyd Cribb; Mr. Harold Ferguson; Mr. Dick Thiessen; Mr. Ronald Taylor; Mr. Gian Pohar; Mr. Robert Lyslo (half time); Miss Gail Lauber, Librarian; Mr. Floyd Irwin, Commercial; Mr. Leo Rurka, Physical Education; Mrs. Grace Phillips; Mr. Paul Koziol; Mr. Howard Meger; Mr. David Balzer; Mr. Robert Hohol; Miss Patricia Hoveland; Miss Margaret Mitchell; Mrs. Florence Ingram; Mrs. Doreen Cribb; Mrs. Helen Tiedemann; Miss Sylvia Melezko; Mrs. Marjorie Everitt; Mrs. Marjorie Astley; Mrs. Eleanor Campbell; Mrs. Jean Sears; Mrs. Daisy Young and Mrs. Carol Rurka.

The school secretary is Mrs. Faye Dodds. Staff Sergeant Coates of the P.P.C.L.I. comes twice a week to teach band music. Students receive home economics and industrial arts courses in Ryley. Nine buses bring the nearly six hundred students to school. Mr. and Mrs. W.E. Lindsay are the chief caretakers.

The High School published a Centennial yearbook in 1967 which will be a valued pictorial record of the Tofield of this era.

Though the Tofield School has enormously increased in size and enrollment since 1909, its educational aims remain the same—to train our youth so they may fully develop their potential abilities to live happy useful lives.

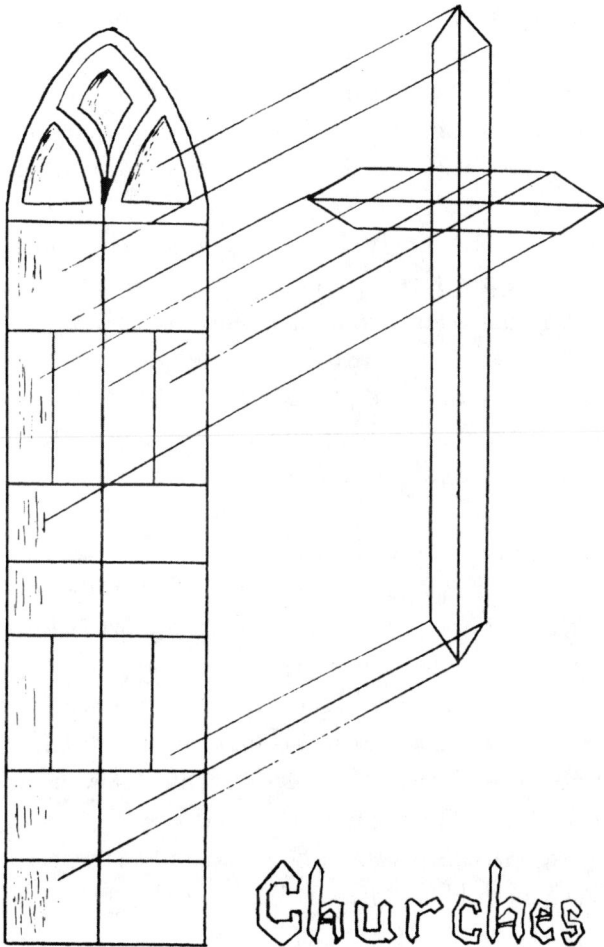

Churches

# ST. FRANCIS OF ASSISI CATHOLIC CHURCH

*Much of the information for this article was obtained from the account "Tofield and the Catholic Church" written by Mr. J.J. McDevitt.*

Mr. Augustus Gladue donated a piece of land for the building of a Catholic Church some time prior to 1906. This site was located in the old town and so became unsuitable with the removal of everyone to the new town site. During this period, visiting missionaries said Mass on their infrequent visits. Father Gaboret of Beaumont was one such missionary.

During the winter of 1915 a priest was seen trudging around on foot. This was Fr. Koolen, assistant to Fr. Steinmetz at Viking. He announced that Mass would be said regularly in Tofield. The building used was a former real estate building on the west side of Main street opposite the then Variety theatre (now the site of George Arnett's garage.) Mass was well attended. There were 4 Letourneaus, 2 Hannans, two or three Yakabuskis, Mrs. Forman and her daughter, Mr. and Mrs.Joe Welch, Charles Kallal, J.J. McDevitt, Steve Sullivan, also two brothers working on the G.T.P. station.

Fr. Koolen was pleased at the turnout and promised to come once a month in the future. Fr. Koolen was also the priest for the Calder area in Edmonton. Train transportation was very convenient and he never failed to be present to hold services. Mass was held in the Variety theatre until 1911. In that year it was held "in the little house, second house east of the Red and White store, which was the residence of Charles J. Kallal who had just been married."

Shortly after this, the Catholic church obtained the use of the "little blue building" north of the present Bank of Montreal and there they remained until 1920.

During the years of World War I Fr. Koolen continued his loyal and conscientious ministry, often walking out into the country to see someone who needed him. The influenza epidemic depleted attendance at Church and on one Sunday, Peter Yakabuski was the only parishioner able to be present.

In Feb. 1919 Fr. Cochet arrived to take over Fr. Koolen's work. Under his guidance the present property for the church was obtained.

This, 1919, was the illfamed "hard winter." Snow was heavy and attendance at Mass was low. At one mass, Fr. Cochet informed the two men present that he had purchased a small dwelling in the upper or old town for $350.00 and that he had arranged with Mr. William Bowick to move it down to the church property where it would be made over into a small church. After Mass Fr. Cochet and his parishioners went to see the building even though the snow was so deep that they had to walk single file.

Soon the building was moved to its appointed spot, sitting high on its abutment of old railway ties so that a foundation could be placed under it when the snow melted. Mr. Muskett, a good carpenter who farmed east of town, took a contract for most of the work. Steve Sullivan came in and did the finishing work and also built a nice little altar.

The little church, finished and ready, was the scene of its first Mass on July 19, 1920. After the opening of the church attendance increased. His Grace, Archbishop O'Leary, arrived for his first visit in the fall of 1921, attended by his secretary, Fr. McGuigan (now Cardinal McGuigan) and Fathers Cochet and Gaorst.

Mr. H. Hannan, hotel proprietor, served the banquet for the occasion. He had invited the Mayor, councillors, the school board, the three Protestant ministers, the town and Municipal secretaries, the Alberta Provincial Policeman, as well as members of St.Francis Church. Archbishop O'Leary spoke with wit and humor at the banquet and again that night to an audience in the Variety theatre.

From this time, services were held regularly and in 1927, Fr. Quirk arrived to take charge of the parish. He started plans for a new church. Work on the new building was started in June 1927 and completed in the fall. His Grace, Archbishop O'Leary came in November and blessed the new church, which is still in use.

Fr. Quirk left around the end of the year (1927) and was followed by Fr. McLeod. In 1932 Tofield and its missions passed into the charge of the Redemptorist Fathers who looked after it until 1938. Priests who served the area during this period were: Fathers B.W. Malone, Scollion,

McElligott, C. Moreau, J. C. Naphin. In 1938 Fr. N. Smeltzer was appointed and was succeeded in 1945 by Fr. B. Gorman who remained until 1948. In 1948 Fr. Gorman was succeeded by Fr. E. F. Purcell, who remained until September, 1961. Fr. E. McCarty was appointed at that time and remained until September 1964 when he was succeeded by Fr. L. Scriven.

The parish of Tofield now consists of the town of Tofield and the surrounding area as well as the mission of Ministik which was opened in 1952 because bad roads leading to the Hastings Lake church caused difficulties.

A new Rectory was built at Tofield in 1954. In 1949 the Catholic church at Ryley was recovered and blessed and officially opened in September of the year. Approximately two years later the hall at Ryley was opened. Fr. C. Van Acht of Catholic Immigration helped out for about a year. Beginning in 1955 Fr. P. McCorkell was the first full time assistant, remaining about a year; then Fr. E. Crough helped out on weekends for about the same length of time. In 1958 Fr. J. Leszczynsky came to help.

During the past years the Catholic population of Tofield has remained relatively stable so that in 1968 there were 45 families making up the parish of a Catholic church possible in this area.

## THE AMISK CREEK LUTHERAN CHURCH

*The following material has been made available by Mrs. Berg,*
*Mrs. Flaaten and Mrs. Conrad Patterson.*

In all places where Scandinavian pioneer life endured its bitter struggles, a deep yearning was felt for a house of worship.

This yearning was strong in the hearts of the pioneers of the Amisk Creek district. They lived in the steadfast hope of having a church, no matter how small. With this thought in mind, the Ladies' Aid worked untiringly for the fund which would provide the House of Worship they longed for.

In the spring of 1914, their hopes became a reality as the decision to build a church was made. That summer, the Pederson brothers of Round Hill were given the contract. With the money the Ladies' Aid had gathered, the subscriptions from the congregation, and other generous donations, the building fund totalled $1,075. Mr. Alfred Patterson donated the land for the church and the cemetery.

On the completion of the church in the fall, it was incorporated on December 31, 1914, under the name of the Norwegian Lutheran Church of Amisk Creek.

In 1928, through the efforts of the Ladies' Aid and members of the congregation, a full basement was put under the church. In 1938, a kitchen was added and in 1955, power was installed. The congregation had eight families, a number that remained fairly constant for many years. Fiftyfive children and adults received baptism; thirty were confirmed.

Finally in 1964, the congregation, consisting now of five families and a bachelor, could no longer function and the little church, the focal point of the community for so long, closed its doors after a Fiftieth Anniversary service had been held to bid farewell to an era.

# THE BAPTIST CHURCH

The Baptist Church of Tofield was begun in 1942 with meetings at the Ole Sware home under the leadership of Pastor P. Peterson of the Kingman Baptist Church. In December 1942, at a meeting in the home of Mr. and Mrs. A. Herndon, the congregation was formally organized and plans were made for the building of a church. The present church was built in 1943. (The covered skating rink was purchased from the town; the lumber was used in the construction of the church.) Volunteer labor had the church ready for worship in December 1943.

In 1944, the Rev. D. M. Anderson, Swedish Baptist field missionary, came to dedicate the church. A missionary program has been a chief concern of the church. Young people who have gone out as ministers and missionaries include: Hazel Runs (Winder) to India; Muriel Anderson

(Williams) to British Columbia; Mervin Williams to Sweden; Grant Quillams, Berean College, Calgary; Garry Francis, Rosebud, Alberta; Sydney Takema, Port Moodie, B.C.

The Miquelon Bible Camp is a project of the Baptist Church; it serves young people from eight years through the teens.

After Rev. Peterson came the following ministers: Mr. F. Krup (194546); Mr. D. Brotsky (194849); Mr. Webber (194950); Mr. H. Montgomery (195152); Mr. L. Gardner (195355); Mr. Allan Ironside (195556); Mr. Merv. Williams (1957); Mr. Duane Norton (195860); Mr. Ernest Kennedy (196162); Mr. E. Love (196364); Mr. D. McLean (196465); Mr. L. Smith, at present.

The present program includes Sunday School, two church services, young people's work, weekly prayer meeting, and the Ladies' Monthly Mission Circle.

## THE BARDO LUTHERAN CHURCH

The settlement of the Bardo community in central Alberta, Canada, began in 1894, following an investigation by interested parties the previous year.

Most of the original Norse settlers of this community who immigrated here in the midnineties came from Crookston, Minnesota or the country near by. However, a few years later, a great number of settlers came direct from Bardo, Norway.

The reasons for settling in Central Alberta were many and varied but the most important was the availability of free land of good quality for a colony.

The first four settlers arrived in May, 1894. They were: Martin Finseth, P.B. Anderson, John Lerbekmo, and Nels Jevning. During the summer and fall, their families arrived and with them came the aged Pastor, Bersvent Anderson, who had been asked to come along and be their minister. Thus, on the first Sunday after his arrival on November 3, 1894, he conducted the first Norwegian Lutheran service in the Canadian Northwest.

During the first winter, services were held from house to house. A regular congregational meeting was called for May 23, 1895, at the Nels Jevning home at which time, all who wished to become members signed a charter forming the Norden Lutheran Church. These charter members were: Bersvend Anderson, Peter B. Anderson and family, Martin Finseth and family, Nels S. Mosland, George Bruass, Nels Jevning and family, Simon P. Simonson and family, Peter Oas, Johan Jevning, Pedar S. Moen and family, Halver Haugen and family, Olaf M. Jevning, Lars Johnson and family, Tollef Carlson and family, Pedar Jevning and family, and Johannes Johnson and family. From this group, Martin Finseth was elected as the first chairman and P.B. Anderson as the first secretary.

After the school was built in 1898, it became the centre for all services and other meetings. A site for the cemetery was chosen diagonally across the road from the old school and therefore lay more than a mile north of where the future church was to be built.

Members of the congregation longed for the time when they could worship in a church of their own. Some wanted to build the church in the north part of the community; others preferred the south. However, when Asbjorn Moen donated a site in the central part of the community, the first church was built there. The men cut and sawed the logs into lumber; finishing lumber was hauled from Camrose. The Ladies' Aid helped to install the furnace and other fixtures and also made it possible to hire a contractor to help with the building. The Thimble Club provided an organ and Bersvend Anderson made the first altar. The church was dedicated on August 6, 1908.

At the annual meeting in the fall of 1968, the name "Norden" was changed to "Bardo". At this same meeting missionary Rev. H.N. Ronning of China, who had settled in the Bardo district with his family, joined the congregation. Although he never served as its minister, he often preached in the church and he used his influence for much good.

In 1921, the church was struck by lightning and burned down. No insurance was carried and only the interior furnishings were saved. Now the congregation had to meet in the school house again. With the help of the Ladies' Aid and personal gifts, the Church Fund reached $2,500.00 within three months. A little over a year after the fire, the first service was held in the new church.

When the church was dedicated in 1926 the men, women, young people, and children rejoiced as they viewed the results of their labor—the completion of the second church in their midst.

The congregation continued to worship and flourish in the little church nestled beside the creek. Various modern conveniences were added to the building and the people were happy and blessed with the ministry of God's gospel. Then, with dramatic suddenness, on August 27, 1965, everything came to an end when lightning again struck-the church was burned to the ground. Residents of the area quickly arrived on the scene and saved most of the furnishings. These were brought to the Bardo Community Centre where services were held for some time.

An important decision now faced the congregation as to the site of the new church. Should they rebuild on the former site or in the town of Tofield, a distance of eight miles? On September 14, at a meeting of the congregation, a vote was taken and a clear majority was in favor of rebuilding on the Tofield site. It was felt that, by moving into town, the church would have a greater outreach in spreading the gospel of Jesus Christ.

On May 28, the groundbreaking ceremonies were held and on June 12, the excavation for the basement was begun. In just a little over five months, through the cooperation of building superintendent, Mr. Ed Hoffman, carpenters, Mr. Sam Mostowich and Mr. Olaf Haugen, and the tremendous response of voluntary help, the church was ready to be opened.

Dedication ceremonies took place from Friday 17 to Wednesday, November 22, 1967. The theme of the dedication services was "Build Temples External" 2Tim. 2: 1526.

The officers of the Bardo Evangelical Lutheran Church of Tofield at the time of its dedication were:

| | |
|---|---|
| President | Mr. Lester Severson |
| Vice-President | Mr. Phillip Anderson |
| Secretary | Mr. Leonard Stauffer |
| Treasurer | Mrs. Agnes Haukedal |
| Deacons | Mr. Sam Cinnamon, Mr. Don Litwin, |

|  | Mr. Andy Heiberg |
| Trustees | Mr. LeRoy Finseth, Mr. Leif Foshaug, Mr. Eystein Heiberg |
| Building Committee | Andy Heiberg, Mary Finseth, Sam Cinnamon, Lester Severson, Phillip Anderson, Evelyn Foshaug,Glen Reil LeRoy Finseth, Olaf Stokkan, and Axel Kindley |

Lutheran Church Women

| President | Mrs. Bernice Heiberg |
| VicePresident | Mrs. Borghild Rude |
| Secretary | Mrs. Olive Foshaug |
| Treasurer | Mrs. Evelyn Foshaug |
| Education | Mrs. Mary Finseth |
| Stewardship | Mrs. Norma Anderson |
| Memorial | Mrs. Agnes Haukedal |

# HOLY TRINITY ANGLICAN CHURCH

Canon Newton who arrived in Edmonton in the fall of 1875 visited the Tofield area occasionally between then and 1890. In 1892, Mr. d'Easum was assigned to this area for three years. In 1892 logs were cut for the construction of a church but were destroyed by fire. A second lot were cut and a church called St. James was built in 1893 on land donated by Robert Logan.

Bishop Pinkham visited the parish in 1894, celebrating communion both at St. James and in the home of George Cookson, Sr. Late in 1895, Rev. Robert Connell arrived. On January 20, 1806, the parish of St. James the ApostleNewtonLogan was formed by Bishop Pinkham of Calgary. The first entry in the parish register, still [in] existence, is dated January 19, 1896. Bishop Pinkham held a confirmation service at St. James on September 11, 1898.

Tofield at that time was a mission of St. James Church. The first resident Anglican minister in Tofield was the Rev. Rainier who came in 1907.

On May 24, 1912, Bishop Pinkham formed the parish of Holy Trinity. On July 18, he dedicated the Holy Trinity Church.

A service was held in Deville in December., 1912,and in 1913, it was made a separate parish, St. Hilda's. To it was added North Cooking Lake.

Services were held at Bathgate, Deville, Ardrossan, North and South Cooking Lake, and St. James.

Rev. J.P. Mason ministered from 1912 to 1914; Rev. Leversedge, 1914–1917; Rev. Nugent Wilson, 1917–1919. Student ministers served the parish for a number of years, supervised by Archdeacon Hawcroft and Archdeacon Cornish.

From 1931 to 1938., Rev. Albert Wallis (now Canon Wallis) was in charge; he was followed by Rev. T.W. Teape

in 1939. After his departure, student ministers again served the parish until Rev. E.N.P. Orme came in 1946 to be replaced by Rev. V.P. Cole (now Canon) from 1950 to 1957. Rev. Brian Brown was in charge 1957 to 1959, followed by Rev. Mundy. Rev. W.L. Hammett was the minister until he retired in 1967.

A new rectory was built during Rev. Hammett's tenure, replacing the one purchased in 1946 (the former Dr. Law house.)

Since Rev. Hammett's retirement, Holy Trinity has been served from St. Matthew's parish, Viking.

## MENNONITE BRETHREN CHURCH

*The following account was written in 1959 by Rev. Peter Warkentin in answer to the request of the Golden Jubilee for a history of the Mennonite Brethren in the Tofield area.*

"After the revolution in Russia in 1917, our beloved homeland became foreign to us. Then God, in His mercy, led the Canadian government to open the door to us scattered and homeless Mennonites. In February, 1928, a group of these homeless refugees found their new home in this country, eleven miles northeast of Tofield. How thankful they were to

God and the Canadian government for this, their new homeland, and they resolved to stay true to God and the faith of their fathers.

On March 4, 1928, a congregation of fourteen members joined and named themselves, "The Mennonite Brethren Church" as it had been in the old country. The group 's first minister was Rev. Abram Froese. At first, they had their services in the various farm homes but the congregation soon outgrew this accommodation as more people joined this group as they moved into the districts around Tofield. From 1937 to 1940 they held their services alternately in the Lindbrook and Woodlawn schools. In 1940, they built their own church six miles west of Tofield and two miles south of Lindbrook However, in several years, the building was no longer adequate, so an extension 14' by 241' was added. Still the congregation increased as several large families came from southern Alberta to the Tofield area. Again the church was too small so in 1955, a full basement was put under the church and used for Sunday School classes.

Once more the congregation outgrew its building and the necessity of a new church was plain. This time it was decided to build the church in Tofield and in 1963, the large new church was erected in the southeast part of Tofield between Highway 14 and the C.N.R. tracks.

In 1968, the congregation consisted of 93 members served by three ministers, Rev. George Quiring, Rev. P. H. Warkentin and Rev. David Balzer. For the past few years, the congregation has been led by Rev. George Quiring.

# HISTORY OF THE SALEM MENNONITE CHURCH

When farming opportunities in the various states and in Ontario began to close in for many people, they looked to Alberta. The Tofield district was investigated and it was discovered that there were people located here for over 15 years who were happy even though it was real pioneer living for them with no railroads or modern roads or highways. Practically no bridges existed and only trails were evidence of people surviving the hardships and still living. Evidently the prospect that this district had a bright future and would be a drawing card for attracting people, convinced a real estate firm to use its energies in even far away lands. They impressed folks of its benefits and advantages over the older and crowded places in which they were living and that there were better opportunities for them, such as, for instance Sunny Alberta could provide.

Saskatchewan was investigated and some land investment was obtained, but Tofield district was the most favored as is evident by our forefathers locating mainly in this district. The firm that interested the first settlers was Crafts, Lee and Gallinger. This Gallinger, was the late well known Claude Gallinger who throughout the years built up a place with buildings and raised stock second to none which gives ample proof to their claims that Tofield was a desirable place to settle. Local men in Nebraska, (Tom Blackburn and the late O.C. Blackburn., who later made large investments) became agents of this firm and tried to interest people in Alberta as early as 1907. Whole sections of land could be bought in one block though no fences or buildings had been constructed as the land was still prairie and bush.

Daniel Bender and family arrived about the year 1908 and settled in Camrose, but left again. Later the same year Chris Sutter came and was a tenant of T. Blackburn on the land now known as the farm of the late V. L. Roth. Other early settlers here were the Peter Reil, John L. Stauffer and Valentine Roth families. Elmer Mauer, Joe and Sam Stauffer came in the spring of 1910. That same fall, Bishop N.E. Roth with his family as well as the Ben Lauber family moved here in September. All these persons were charter members of the Salem Mennonite Congregation.

The Jacob Swartzendrubers, and Simon Stalters came in late 1910. Benjamin Stauffers, Dave Yoders, William S. Stutzman (who later erected a modern Service Station in Tofield) and Jake Yoder came in 1911.

Jake Yoder and Barbara Stauffer were the first couple of this group of settlers to get married in Alberta.

M. D. Stutzman and family came in August of 1911. The Joseph E. Kauffman, Henry Yoder and Levi Yoder families came in 1912. J.R. Stauffers and Jacob Brennemans arrived in 1913. Also Moses

Burkholder and family moved here from Oregon.

Another early settler here was Peter Ginger and his family who attended services at Salem though they were not members. Their attendance was greatly appreciated.

People did not come to church in cars or trucks; they came in democrats, wagons, rode horseback and walked. Gates needed to be opened many times because of lack of roads. It was quite an improvement when the brush was cleared away to be able to get through. One Sunday morning in 1915 this was heard, and the following happened, "But look" "Sure enough" "Well what do you know about that"—"Will Stutzman is coming to church with a Ford and a new one too."

Now the mosquitos were challenged. No more pails hanging on the Democrats with smudges for some relief from the swarm clouds that filled the sky on occasions About the next Sunday Peter Ginger appeared with a car of the same make and model and since there were no styles to choose from. Will's first advice to Pete was "Don't be afraid to hit the mudholes. Put her up to 15 miles an hour; they are not made of glass."

Other families followed during the years and in 1918 the Mayton Mennonite Congregation from Mayton, Alberta, consisting of John Lehman, Will Wideman, Abe Wideman, Sr., and Abe Wideman Jr., Ivy Wideman, Milton Sitler, and their family moved to the Tofield district. Later on the William Boettgers came to live here also. In the fall of 1918 Aaron King moved here.

In 1924 and 1926 a group of Mennonites from Russia came west to Canada to settle after their belongings and land had been confiscated. The Canadian Pacific Railroad brought them to Canada with the promise of payment later. Many came to this district and lived in our homes over the winters of both these years.

Bible School during these years was held during the winter consisting of a six weeks' course. This was largely attended by our young people and others in the district as well. Later this type of Bible School was discontinued owing to many going away to get this training at longer term Bible schools and Institutes.

Summer Bible Schools have proved a blessing and benefit and

earlier were attended by many of the Denominations as well as those from homes who had no interest in spiritual things with up to 226 children attending for two weeks. This work is still carried on with Bible Study and children engaged in singing.

School houses were used as meeting places until April 9, 1911 when the first church was dedicated. The original building was 24'x 32' and was erected at a cost of $800. This was enlarged in 1915 to 24'x 48' at a cost of $500. Again it was enlarged in 1926 to 38' x 48' at a cost of $4,000. This was finally torn down in 1954, after the present building was completed with an overall size of 48'x82' at a cost of approximately $50,000, plus an approximate $15,000 worth of donated labor. This building was dedicated in August, 1954. Sufficient room even for the foreseeable future was considered in this building project. A building fund has been established through the years so as not to interfere with the many missionary calls in the needy fields in the world.

During these early years most of the young people stayed on the farm. Later a few were teachers, nurses, XRay technicians, mechanics, secretaries, office workers, salesmen, many teachers, pharmacists, doctors and still others are taking advanced Bible Training.

When a family or group of families suffered a loss by fire or similar disaster, everyone went to help this unfortunate friend or brother. Now with such a diversity of occupations this was more difficult, so it was decided in 1956 to organize a Mennonite Disaster Service in this community. This organization is ready to serve on short notice and in cases of disaster such as tornadoes, earthquakes, floods and fires. This service reaches much farther than our own immediate community. As a part of the larger organization of Mennonite Disaster Service(Canada and U.S.A.) we have opportunities to alleviate suffering and to help build communities in many parts of the world. MDS takes charge of work along with the Red Cross in whatever can be done for others in the Name of Christ.

*This article was contributed by Bishop John Stauffer.*

# THE TOFIELD MENNONITE CHURCH

In 1924, the first immigrants of the General Conference sect arrived in Tofield. They were received by members of the Salem Mennonite Church. However, they did not stay long but left for other parts of Alberta or other provinces of Canada.

In 1925, another group arrived who were also welcomed by the Salem Mennonites. Many of these also left but a few found jobs on farms and remained. In 1928, several families bought farms north of Tofield. Among these were H. Schroeder, Sr., John Heidebrecht, John Rempel and Peter Dyck. In October, 1929, D.A. Heidebrecht an ordained minister, arrived from the Old Country. Occasional church services had been held, but now plans were made to hold regular services in the homes of members until a suitable place for worship could be found.

During the drought years of 1933-1934, many more families arrived from the Chinook and Delia areas to rent or buy farms. The first church group was finally organized on January 21, 1934. A house was purchased east of town for $350. Services were held in it until it became inadequate for the congregation. The house which still stands in the churchyard, was later used to house two Sunday School classes and the library.

On June 15, 1936, the church was named the Schoenseer Church. Rev. D.A. Heidebrecht was the leading minister. The pressing need for more rooms soon prompted the building of a new church, 30' by 50', with full basement for classrooms.

On July 25, 1937, the new church was dedicated with Bishop W. Martens of Coaldale officiating. In 1939 the new church was incorporated as a self sustaining church with other churches in the Alberta Conference. In 1943, Rev. D.A. Heidebrecht was ordained as bishop. Other members were ordained as ministers.

As soon as regular church services started, Sunday School classes were organized. Only two classes were held in the beginning, but as membership increased, more classes were added. The children presented programs for Christmas, Mothers' Day, Children's Day, when, weather permitting, a special outdoor program was held

A choir of the young people of the district was also organized. This choir has favored the congregation with several numbers almost every Sunday.

During the years 1940–1945, more families arrived from Peace River and Lacombe to make their homes in Tofield. In 1950, the church again became too small and had to be lengthened by 20′ to take care of the overgrowing population.

On February 25, 1957, the congregation was saddened by the passing of its bishop, D.A. Heidebrecht.

In recent years, improvements to the church have included electricity, a gas furnace, running water, piano and public address system.

On January 11, 1960, the name of the church was changed. The original name of "Schoenseer" had commemorated the original site of the church on the Caspian Sea (beautiful sea). Now, however, the difficulty of pronouncing and spelling this German word led to the choice of the name more realistic and more meaningful to the congregation. The church was henceforth to be called "The Tofield Mennonite Church."

The Rev. John Neufeld was ordained as bishop on August 6, 1961.

In 1969, the church membership stands at 140.

The church officers for 1969 are:

| | |
|---|---|
| Bishop | Rev. J. Neufeld |
| Leading minister | A. Baergen |
| Assistant | Rev. A. Heidebrecht |
| Secretary | G.J. Baergen |
| Treasurer | P. Wiens |
| Groups | |
| Senior Ladies' Aid | Mrs. D. Regehr |
| Junior Ladies' Aid | Mrs. Katie Baergen |
| Sunday School Leaders | |
| Superintendent | D. Boese |
| Assistant | O. Epp |
| Secretary | G. Schroeder |

There are 111 attendants at Sunday School. These are taught by 21 teachers and substitute teachers.

Activities

| | |
|---|---|
| Young people | J.B. Baergen |
| Wayfarers | Mrs. Anne Ewert |
| Choir | H. Schroeder |
| Sunday School | D. Boese |
| Library | Agnes Rempel |

# THE TOFIELD UNITED CHURCH

The growth of the United Church in Tofield parallels that of the community and the province. In 1868, the Methodist missionary, Rev. George McDougall, visited this area to minister to the Indians; by 1895, the area was sufficiently settled to require the services of two student ministers. Mr. Henry Sterling was the Presbyterian student and Mr. Whiteside was the Methodist student. Following these came Mr. Guy McGallop, Mr. Hodge and Mr. Ferguson. The Methodists and Presbyterians held services on alternate Sundays in the log schoolhouse one-half mile north of the present school.

Daniel Francis, assisted by Mr. and Mrs. Jack Cookson, inaugurated the first Sunday School.

In 1904, the Presbyterian congregation built a church,, called St. Andrew's on the hill overlooking the Amisk Creek valley. This hill was called Mt. Zion. The Methodists then took over the log schoolhouse for their own. In 1908 and 1909, these churches were both moved to Tofield which was then situated north of the site of the present school. Following the arrival of the railway Tofield itself moved to its present location and the churches followed suit. The Presbyterian church, now the Masonic Hall, was moved to its present site and the log church to the lot which is now the site of the Tofield United Church.

During this period, the Presbyterian ministers were Rev. Little, 1901; Rev. Rothnay, 1902; Rev. Pow; 1903; Mr. Thornaloe, Rev. Cameron, Rev. Robinson, Rev. Robert Whillans, a pioneer of the Ketchamoot district; Mr.Beet, Rev. Bradley, 1906–1908; Rev. Gold, 1908–1913;Rev.Stewart, 1913–1918, Rev. Firth, 1918–1921, and Rev. Watt, 1921–1922.

The Methodist ministers of this period were: Rev. Finlay, 1901 who served from Vegreville; Rev. Longley, 1902; Rev. Cox 1903; Rev. Shaw, 1905; Rev. Tough, 1905–1906; Rev. Laidman, 1906–1908; Rev. H. Munton, 1908–1910 Rev. Nicholsin, 1910–1912; Rev. Wiggins, 1912-1916; Rev.Bowen, 1916-1918; Rev. Simpson, 1918–1921; Rev. Barnes, 1921–1922.

The first Ladies' Aid was formed in 1904 with Mrs. Jack Cookson as president. The first organist was Mr. A. J. H. McCauley.

The people south of town formed the Ketchamoot congregation and as early as 1895, services were held in the Sears, Mitchell and Owen homes with Rev. Sterling, Rev. Whillans or Rev. Whiteside in charge. Later, these people attended services in Mt. Zion Presbyterian Church. The Ketchamoot Ladies' Aid was formed in 1903, with Mrs. Hugh Mitchell as its first president. After the building of the Ketchamoot school in 1906, services were held there. The Sunday School was organized with Mrs. L. Carlisle as Superintendent and Mrs. Ellen Sears as organist.

In the Lakeshore district, services were held in the Henry Woods home by the Rev. Laidman in 1907. In 1911, Sunday School was organized with Mr. Kendall as superintendent. The affairs of the congregation were administered from Tofield. In 1924 the Ladies' Aid was formed with Mrs. Zoe Phillips as its first president. In 1930 a separate Lakeshore congregation was officially organized.

After the formation of the United Church of Canada in 1925, the ministers serving the Tofield Lakeshore-Ketchamoot, charge were Rev. A.G. Watt, 1922-1927; Rev. J.T. Gordon, 1927-1933; Rev. D.K. Allan, 19331945; Rev. H.B. Ricker, 1945-1951; Rev.J.Wood, 1951-1953; Rev. K. Iwaasa, 1953-1956; Rev. S. Bell, 1956-1960; Rev. G.B. McNeil,, 1960-1962; Rev. W. McDannold, 1962-1968. Rev. S. Bessey came in 1968.

The present United Church, built under the supervision of J.R. Francis and J.W.Robinson., was opened in May, 1955. Volunteer labor, including that from other congregations, was the means of building the church.

# THE UNITED CHURCH SUNDAY SCHOOL

The Sunday School was headed by W.C. Swift as superintendent for 17 years. In 1947, H. Lovell took this office. He was followed by J.R. Francis in 1949 who was in turn succeeded by Mrs. Hazel Patterson and by the present superintendent, Thomas Jacobs.

Superintendents of the Junior Department of the Sunday School have been: Mrs. Firth until 1938; Mrs. Patterson for the next twenty years; Mrs. J. Ingram and, at the present, Mrs. Dorothy Clark.

The church officers in 1968 were:

Clerk of the Session.1 W.A. Swift; Members of the Session, Mrs. J. Richardson., Mrs. G. Allan, G.Abernethy,T.W. Jacobs, R. Rudzcki, C. Sears, R. Whillans. The Board of Stewards consists of: H. Seller., J. Lampitt, J.Francis, W.A. Swift,V.Walker, R. Goeglein, S. Sears, J. Ingram, J. Wall.

# THE COOKSON ORGAN

This is the story of an inanimate object-an organ. It shared the rigorous pioneer experience of the early settlers, sank into obscurity for a time, but in 1958 again became the centre of attraction.

It was brought from Winnipeg to Edmonton, before 1890, packed in a Red River Cart. One might wonder if the horrible squeaking of the allwooden Red River carts did not cause excruciating agony to the musical soul of the organ.

The organ was destined for the first Anglican mission in Edmonton and no doubt its acquisition was a joy to the congregation.

Some time prior to 1900, the organ was acquired from the Mission by Miss Annie Cookson (later Mrs. Matthew McCauley) and brought by her to the Cookson home in Tofield about 1900. Miss Cookson's father, George Cookson Sr., was one of Tofield's earliest settlers and his home had become a centre of religious activities in the Tofield area. The organ was a most welcome addition to the church services held in the Cookson home. These services, as well as weekly prayer meetings, were conducted by the Rev. Robert Whillans. George Cookson Sr. was an accomplished organist and spent many happy hours at the organ.

Social gatherings too, were enlivened by music from this organ. In the early diaries of both George Cookson Sr. and Mrs. Cookson, mention is made of Jack and George Jr., singing "0 Dem Golden Slippers" at various social functions both at home and in public. Following the death of his wife in 1909, George Cookson Sr., went to live with his son and daughter-in-law Jack and Jessie Cookson. To his son Edmund, who had lived at the parental home until now, was given the organ.

Edmund married Olive Isabel Ingram and a family of a son and two daughters were born before his premature death from appendicitis. The older daughter, Mrs. Hugh Bruce of Lindbrook was custodian of her grandfather's organ until 1947 when, after consultation with the members of the original Cookson family, she donated it to the Northern Alberta Old Timers' Association on behalf of the Cookson family. The late James McCool, then Secretary of the Old Timers' Association, accepted it on their behalf.

During the Christmas season of 1958, the old organ was repaired and put into such good condition that it could again give forth Christmas carols.

Mrs. George Cookson while visiting her daughter, Mrs. Art Lampitt in Edmonton, received a hurried phone call from her son, Inspector of Detectives Cookson advising her to turn on her radio. Hastening to do this she was overjoyed to hear the familiar tones of the Cookson organ playing the still older carols of Christmas.

## THE TOFIELD BAND

*The material for this article was obtained from Mr J. L. Abbott and Mr. and Mrs. Bill Spilsted.*

Music has always played a big part in the life of Tofield. The pioneers had neither movies, radio, nor television, so had to provide their own entertainment.

In 1908, the first village band was organized. It was sponsored by the village council: in the minutes of the council, there is a notation that a hall had been rented for band practice and $50.00 had been donated towards the cost of the necessary instruments. The leader of this band was Mr. C. Davidson and the members were Mr. W. C. Swift, Mr. H. K. Adams, Mr. R. O. Bird, Mr. Harriman, Mr. Abbott, Mr. McMullen and Mr. Herb Diamond.

According to Mr. Abbott, when the Village of Tofield became the Town of Tofield in 1909, the Town Band played "a few selections in front of the old Queen's Hotel in honour of the occasion." The Mayor of the newlyconstituted town, J. O. Letourneau and the councillors, Mark Ferguson, R. E. Emery, A. F. Fugl, J. B. Harper, A. Maxwell and A. Lamoreaux were the honoured ones.

In 1913 a new band was organized and some of the former members rejoined together with a few new ones. Mr. Abbott was the leader; some of the new members were George Brace, Russ Graham and Ernie Rogers. This band used to play for the soldiers to march and parade on the parade ground where the United Church now stands.

Later, the indefatigable Mr. Abbott organized a Tuxis Boy's Band. He was conductor and apparently found the task arduous for he said, "The boys didn't know a note from a mule's ear, so we had to start from scratch by learning to blow the instruments. But before this band broke up, we had given several concerts in aid of some charity."

The Tuxis Boy's Band was composed of: the Kask brothers, the Cole twins, Arthur Smith, Gordon Jobb, Harold Lewis, Barney Kendall, Teddy Paradis, Clifford Lee, Bill Swift, Oscar Brook and B. K. Hingly.

In the early 1940's a band was organized by Mr. Herb Chandler, a fine and enthusiastic musician. When, after a few years, he left Tofield, Mr. Rex Boyles became band leader. This band continued for several years. It is worthy of note that at one time there were three generations of the Jacobs' family playing the band: D. W. 'Mudge," his son, Thomas, and his grandson, Kenneth.

The July 1 parade was always led by the band; band concerts were given and band music was contributed to other entertainments. In the 1960's, however, lack of members forced the group to disband.

In the early 1960's, instruction in band music was begun in the school. Captain of the P.P.C.L.I was the first instructor. He was followed by Staff Sergeant Coates. The present instructor is Mr. Bus. Under these instructors, the band has grown steadily both in numbers and in proficiency.

# THE TOFIELD UNITED CHURCH CHOIR

*The following information was compiled by Mrs. J. E. Stinson and Mr. J. R. Francis.*

In the very early days of Tofield, when the Presbyterian and Methodist Churches had united services, J. R. Francis said that while there was no regular choir, many duets and quartets were sung at the services.

One quartet that he remembers very well was composed of Mr. and Mrs. R.W. Whillans, Mr. Jack Cookson and Mrs. Daniel Francis. After the service, they received an unexpected comment on their musical ability when Billy Rowland came up to them and said, "Say, you folks sure got mixed up in that song but you came out even at the end."

When separate Methodist and Presbyterian congregations were formed in 1907, each church had its own choir. Some of the members of the choirs in those days were: Mr. and Mrs. J.B. Harper, Mr. and Mrs. C.H. Cress, Jack and George Cookson, Mrs. P. Lee, Harold Martin, Mr. and Mrs. R.W. Whillans, Ethel Noland, Sid and Jack Carter, Mrs. McConnell, Lily, Oma, Fanny and Venah Rickner, Fred Casey, Charlie Chillman, Mr. Paul, Mrs. Newbigging, Margaret and May Gladsby, Hazel Mallory, Mr and Mrs. H. Ward, Mrs. Daniel Francis, R.E. Emery, Mr. Latimer, Mrs. J.W. Morton, Miss L. Hammond, Mr. and Mrs. Roland Murray and Miss Ila Murray.

Until 1907, Miss Gertie Francis was the organist for the church services. After that date, while Miss Francis continued in the Methodist Church, Mr. A. J.H. McCauley became the organist for the Presbyterian Church. After 1912, Charlie Carter replaced Miss Francis in the Methodist Church; Mr. McCauley continued in the Presbyterian Church for many years.

In 1935, Mrs. J.E. Stinson became organist for the United Church and Mr. Larry Broughton took over the leadership of the choir. Among the choir members of that time were: Jack and George Cookson, W.C. Swift, Mrs. Firth, Mrs. Torrie, Mr. and Mrs. L.W. Smith. Cantatas were sung at Christmas and Easter.

When the Smiths and Larry Broughton left Tofield the choir dwindled until it was not carried on regularly.

A few years later, Mr. Herb Chandler, who was also active in the band and the Community League, took over the leadership of the choir and it flourished again. But when, in turn, Mr. Chandler left Tofield, the choir again diminished. Mr. Roland Murray, a fine musician, was the choir leader for several years when it sang on special occasions.

In 1955, when the present church was opened, a new choir was formed under the leadership of Mrs. Seller, a fine musician with a wonderful voice and a talent for leadership. This choir consisted of members from the former congregation of Ketchamoot, Lakeshore and

Tofield, now united into one congregation.

Mrs. Seller continued as leader until illness forced her to retire in 1959. Mrs. Stinson then took over the task of directing the choir and has continued until the present, while filling the post of organist as well. The choir has been enhanced by the presence of several groups of High School girls who have sung in the choir until they went away to further their education elsewhere. Members of the choir in 1968 are: Mrs. Lil Schultz, Mrs. Doris Oslund, Mr. and Mrs. John Wall, Mrs. Daisy Young, Mrs. Betsy-Ann Gallinger, Mrs. Faye Dodds, Miss Beth Ingram, Miss Vicki Wall, Mr. George Abernethy, Mr. James Ingram. Until his death early in 1968, Mr. Keith Appleby was a valued member the choir.

## UNITED CHURCH JUNIOR CHOIR

This choir began in 1936 under the leadership of Mrs. J.E. Stinson, after a group of Sunday School pupils had practised a special number for Rally Day. The average number of members was twentyfour. They sang at church services the first Sunday of the month, wearing white gowns and winecoloured ties. They prepared music for special occasions.

In 1951, Mrs. George McFadzean became the leader of this choir. Eventually, there were so many members that the choir had to be divided into two sections. They sang at special services, at Christmas Carol Festivals, at music recitals and at concerts. In 1958 and 1959, they took part in the Junior Choir Festival held in Convocation Hall at the University of Alberta. This choir continued until the late 1960's.

## THE COMMUNITY
## CHRISTMAS CAROL FESTIVAL

Since 1955, the Tofield Community League has sponsored the annual Christmas Carol Festival. This has been a very important event of the Christmas season. All the local choirs as well as choruses from the Tofield and Ryley schools participate. Community singing of the beloved Christmas carols has been led by Mrs. Seller, Mr. Henry Schroeder, Mr. Paul Voegtlin and Mr. Terry Granger. The following is an excerpt from the Christmas issue of the Tofield Mercury in 1958:

There wasn't even standing room for the overflow crowd who attended the Carol Festival on Wednesday evening. The items were introduced by Rev. Sydney Bell and Mrs. Seller led in the community singing. Local choirs taking part in the festival were the Bardo Lutheran Church Choir, the St. Francis of Assisi Junior choir, Schonseer Mennonite Choir, the Mennonite Brethren Senior Choir, United Church Senior Choir, and the Salem Mennonite Choir.

## OTHER ORCHESTRAS

During several decades, the Tiedemann orchestra has played for country dances. First, Fred, August, and Ed formed the orchestra; then Chris, Ben, Ella, Bill, and Emil. The second and third generation, Ed's son, Bert, and grandson, Donald, as well as Ben's son, Kent, have played in the Tiedemann orchestra.

The Lawson boys, Wayne and Leonard have also made a name for themselves with their orchestra.

Just recently, The Aino Jensen Orchestra has been in demand for local dances.

## MUSIC INSTRUCTION

Music lessons have been given over the years in Tofield. Some of the teachers of piano have been: Mrs. Firth, Mrs. Stinson (who first presented the annual music recital), Miss Lydia Boese, Miss Enns, Miss Barbara Phillips, Mrs. Calvin Annis, Mr. L. Brodeur (who came out from Edmonton), Miss Glenda Patterson, Mrs. Madeleine McCormick, Miss Hilda Riedeger, Mrs. Andy Heiberg.

# HOLY TRINITY ANGLICAN CHURCH CHOIR

Mrs. Webb, Sr. was organist from 1912 to 1914; she was followed by Mr. Poppleston, 19141917. A mixed choir served the congregation. Mrs. Webb and Mrs. J. W. Robinson were organists, followed in 19311938 by Mrs. D.G. McCarthy. Rev. Wallis was choir leader; cantatas and concerts were presented under his leadership as was also the case when L.A. Broughton led the choir. During the regime of Rev. Orme, a junior choir was formed which sang over C.F.R.N. At this time Mrs. Evans, Mrs. Garford and Mrs. Robinson alternated as organists. Mrs. Brian Brown, Mrs. Marie Eaglesham and Miss Elizabeth Crispin have also served as organists. Mrs. Reg Crispin is the present organist.

# THE BARDO CHOIR

The first Bardo Choir was organized in 1899. It consisted of Mr. Peter Jevning, Mr. Martin, Ragna and Magda Jevning, Petrina Strand, Mr. P. B. Anderson and Ingeborg Jevning. The choir leader was Mr. P.B. Anderson.

By 1900, Mr. Bower, teacher of the Bardo school, had organized a choir of his students, assisted by Delia Bartness and Jennie Lerbekmo. These young people sang the sacred cantata, "Under the Palms" under the direction of Mr. Bower.

Rev. O.K. Blomlie, pastor 1923 to 1926, took over the direction of the Bardo choir during this period; cantatas and anthems were presented. Since that time, the choir has been led by various people, some of whom have been: Alice Broughton, George Hendrickson, and Monrad Finseth.

The Bardo Male Chorus was organized in 1930 under the direction of Albin Anderson. This was an enthusiastic group of singers under an enthusiastic leader and they did a great deal of singing for a number of years. Their music consisted of both sacred and secular numbers.

One of the highlights of the existence of the Bardo Male Chorus was its tour of the Grande Prairie country in 1941 when they gave concerts in the various communities in the north country.

After 1942, Alice Broughton directed this chorus for a couple of years. Since then, it has been reorganized at intervals under various leaders. In later years, a number of members have passed away or have left the community so the chorus is no longer functioning. Their singing has left pleasant memories in the Community.

In 1951, a parish choir of fifty singers was organized with members from Bardo, Kingman, and Round Hill.

This choir flourished about three years and presented concerts and cantatas at Christmas and Easter.

Under the direction of Mrs. Lester Severson, this parish choir continues to contribute to the musical life of the Tofield area.

## PIONEER DANCE ORCHESTRAS

The Spilsteds and Mr. Abbott said that one of the first musical teams in Tofield was Mr. and Mrs. Barker. Mrs. Barker was a harpist as well as a pianist and had secured her musical education in Vienna, Austria. The Barkers and Mr. Abbott formed the first Tofield orchestra. After the Barkers left a Miss Henderson, a teacher, played the piano, Mr. Rattray, the violin and Mr. Abbott, his trumpet. Later, Mr. and Mrs. Pincott were added to the orchestra.

Then a new orchestra was formed with Bill Spilsted on the violin, Bob Robinson on the clarinet, Bert Calvert on the traps and drums, Lem Abbott on the cornet and Harold Bone at the piano. This orchestra was much in demand for the dances which invariably followed the hockey matches in which Tofield's Silver Seven participated. Other members of the orchestra were Warren Hopper and Mr. Roberge. When the Variety theatre was in its youth as a dance hall, this orchestra supplied the music.

Bill and Carmen Spilsted recalled the house dances with nostalgia. Since there were few public places available for dancing, houses and schools were used. The place didn't matter too much; enough people to dance and someone to play for them were the only requirements of a successful dance and all pioneer dances were successful.

Bill and Carmen would hurry through their chores on the day of a dance and set out by horse and buggy or horse and cutter according to the season, Bill with his violin and Carmen with her banjo. On the cold winter trips, Carmen always carried an umbrella yes, an umbrella! She had found that it made an effective windbreak, a function that was much appreciated. Not that they would have let the weather intimidate them with a dance in the offing.

Dances began at sundown and lasted until sunup. Square dances, schottisches, polkas and waltzes were the order of the day. The "caller" for the square dances was frequently Frank Steinbach, brother-in-law of Frank Shupe and Mrs. Hosler.

Everyone danced with vigour and pleasure through the long winter night. Children too young to dance were put down on a convenient bed; teenagers danced with their elders; every dance was a family affair. They were held from as far north as the Bill Bloss (Ron Goeglein) place to the southern areas of Miquelon and Kingman. The Spilsteds were happy to play for them anywhere.

INDUSTRY

# THE COAL MINES OF TOFIELD

In 1913, Tofield had three coal mines; the Dobell Mine, the Tofield Coal Company Mine and the Pioneer Mine. The Dobell mine and that of the Tofield Coal Company were strip mines with seams of coal six to seven feet deep. The Pioneer Mine, owned by Jim McDevitt, was an underground mine on the land now farmed by J. W. Thompson. Since the Pioneer had no railway facilities, wagons came in groups so that the combined efforts of the teams could be utilized to haul the loaded wagons up the hills. Wagons came from as far as fifty miles away for coal.

In 1916 McDevitt built a dock (loading platform) on the Industrial Site, (The railway was on the property of J. W. Robinson) and hauled the coal two miles.

The Dobell mine had the railroad and had a small Marion Steam Shovel and a rail track of twenty four inch gauge. Koppel steel cars would strip mine hundreds of yards a day. The coal was loaded by wheel barrows. Eight to ten cars were loaded during the fall and winter. In the early 1930's, the Tofield Coal Company bought the Dobell mine.

The Tofield Coal Company was the largest of the three mines. Mr. J. W. Robinson who worked for the Tofield Coal Company for many years says,

"I have a picture of the mine tipple in 1907. At that time, the mine was of the underground type. When I came in 1913, it was a strip mine. In 1912, the management imported a dirtmoving machine called the Lubrecher. It was selfpropelled and had a number of buckets similar to the ones used in a grain elevator which loaded the dirt on a conveyor belt and dumped it where the coal had been taken out in the previous year. They also had a steam drag line called the Ledgerwood which followed behind the Lubrecher.

The Lubrecher,, which cost $40,000, was made in Germany. Bill Morton was the engineer; he had a First Class British Board of Trade Certificate. He came with the machine to erect it and remained to become manager of the mine. Bill Morton's father, whom I knew, was Chief Boiler Inspector for Tyneside, England.

In August, 1916, I started to work for the Tofield Coal Company where I was in charge of the pumps—two steam pumps which could deliver two hundred gallons per minute and a portable gasolinedriven centrifugal pump.

In the spring of 1917, Bill Morton and I completely overhauled the Lubrecher and I was supposed to be the engineer in charge of it. However in May, Mr. Morton bought a small shipyard in Quebec. The new superintendent brought his own engineer so I never had the pleasure of running the machine.

Later on in 1917, the Tofield Coal Company rented a steam shovel from Huff's Gravel Pit, west of Edmonton. We hauled the clay out of the pit with a steam hoist and another hoist hauled it up the dump. They hauled the clay from the shovel with a team of horses; this was a slow process.

In 1918, they converted the hoists into steam derricks. A long boom swung the dirt quite some distance from the coal face. The other derrick was used to load coal into the cars.

Also in 1918, the Tofield Coal Company bought a Marion steam shovel and the three Davenport Donkey locomotives and later bought a Number 14 Davenport.

In 1924, another steam shovel (called a Bucyrus) was bought along with several Donkey locomotives. Finally, in 1930, they had nine Donkeys. In 1942, No. 6 and No.7 Donkeys were sold to the Coal Valley Company where I was working during the year. The small shovel would move 20,000 yards and the big shovel 25,000 yards per day.

The largest shipment in one day was 38 cars. From September to New Years', thirty cars a day were shipped. From then on, the demand slackened. At one time, three travellers (salesmen) were on the road selling Headlight Coal—the trade name used by the Tofield Coal Company.

Finally, the Tofield Coal Company got the stripping done by contract and disposed of the engines and shovels. After the discovery of oil at Leduc, the coal trade gradually died out. The mine was closed in 1957.

At the peak of its output, the mine shipped over 200,000 tons a year and employed over 100 men.

Mr. Claude Gallinger was in charge and was manager from 1918 till the mine closed down. Mr. Gallinger was not just a manager. He would cut all the brush ahead of the shovels and if they were short of men, he would join the work gang. I have seen him working on the dump and at one time, he was brakeman for me for a few days.

"In 1939, had an accident which terminated my employment at the mine. Looking back on my years at the mine, in spite of the hard work and occasional trouble with the engines, I remember those years as a wonderful experience."

—J.W.Robinson

# THE TOFIELD FOUNDRY

*The material for this article was made available by Mr. J. W. Robinson.*

The Tofield Foundry was built during the 1912 gas boom, on land which was part of the late J.W. Cookson's homestead, on the corner north of the main C.N.R. track near the Gas Company's valve station. It was a large twostorey building with dozens of windows. The walls and roof were of galvanized iron. The top storey was used as a patternmaking shop and for charging the furnace. The first floor was a moulding and machine shop which had shafting and several metal working machines including a large lathe which was powered by a gasoline engine. They had a large horizontal steam engine to be installed later, which was finally sold for scrap. Laborers received twenty cents an hour and the machinist received forty cents an hour.

The foundry was under the supervision of Mr. Jobb and had some connection with the Medicine Hat Foundry. It operated for a short time. They had a patternmaker and moulder and a machinist. They made several items of machinery for the machine shop, including a hoist to hoist the iron ingots to the furnace. When the foundry was dismantled, the Brick Company bought the hoist for their brick machine and they made some small rollers and bearings for the brick plant. The C.N.R. had a spur track to the foundry.

There was a grain elevator nearby owned by a German company. In the early thirties the elevator burned down. One morning when Mr. Robinson was doing chores at 5 a.m., he noticed smoke coming out of the elevator roof and turned in the alarm. Exactly five minutes later the fire brigade was on the scene under Mr. Pete Leberkmo [Lerbekmo], the fire chief, but the building could not be saved.

In 1928, the C.N.R. had a colonizing plan to bring in settlers. These Dutch families arrived in two colonist cars in which they lived on the spur track for ten days or two weeks until they found accommodation. They had thirty-three children ranging from babies to teenagers who swelled the school population so much that an extra room had to be built at the school in the basement. They were clean, goodliving citizens and grand singers. One family lived in Dr. Tofield's house (now occupied by Mr. Ray Henriksen of Calgary Power). A few worked at the mine, others on farms. A number took up farms at Neerlandia and did well. Others worked in the city.

# LIVESTOCK

The raising of livestock has always been a very important part of life in the Tofield district. As far back as 1900, it was not uncommon to see herds of more than a hundred cattle; several of the early settlers had herds of this size. Not only cattle, but horses, too, were kept in large numbers; Charley and Eugene King at one time had two hundred head of horses. At this time, there were large areas of open land because much of the area granted to the C. P. R. by the Canadian Government had been bought by speculators but left unfenced. This open land with its covering of "prairie wool" provided excellent conditions for horses to run out all winter and remain in good condition.

In these days, the country was referred to as "open range" which meant that crops, rather than animals, must be raised behind fences. A

legal fence was a threestrand barbedwire affair; the bottom wire was 18"
off the ground, the other two strands were 16" apart. The crop grown
in this enclosure was not to be planted closer than eight feet from each
fence.

But as settlement increased, the law was changed to meet changing
conditions. Now it was the stock which must be fenced in; this was the
herd law. When the open range was no longer available to cattle owners,
the size of the herds began to decline.

Even during the era of the open range, the cattle had hardships to
endure, perhaps the chief of which were the mosquitoes which plagued
them all summer long. Towards evening, cattle owners would light
smudges; the cattle, grateful for the relief afforded by these smudges
would crowd close, hating to leave the first one started even though the
herdsman lit several more.

Some of the big cattle raisers, hearing of the Barr Colonists' arrival
in Lloydminster in 1903, gathered about sixty head of cattle and drove
them to Lloydminster to sell to the immigrants. This venture was quite
successful.

On their way home from Lloydminster, the cattlemen met a young
English fellow from the Barr Colony walking along the road followed
by a cow. Stopping to talk to him, they found that this lad had walked
to Calgary and back, just to accompany another young Englishman
who had decided to return to England and was boarding the train at
Calgary.

In answer to questions, the lad explained the presence of the cow.
He said that he had been the consumer for the cow's production. He
had milked her into the threepound lard pail he was carrying and this
milk had been his only food since he had started for home. His cow had
served him in other ways as well. When a stream had to be crossed the
lad would turn the cow's head towards the water, tap her on the back
and, after she entered the water., grasp her tail. Across they would go!
In 1903 they would have had some fairsized streams to cross on their
long journey. But they made it!

Previous to the arrival of the railway, stock from the Tofield area
had to be driven to Edmonton to reach a market. When the railway

came to Tofield in 1909, the method of marketing stock changed. The stock was sold to local buyers and brought to town on regular shipping days. Or an owner could ship a carload of his own.

In 19289, Ed Hicks, while working for Imperial Oil agent, George Agnew, had an idea and in a Mercury of that year, a notice appeared saying that he had made a deal with the Beaver Lake Stock Association to truck their stock to Edmonton. In the Sept. 9, 1931, issue of the Mercury Ed informed the public that he had purchased a truck and could be hired for all kinds of hauling, including stock at 35¢ per cwt. Trucking soon became the favoured method of shipping stock and since the stockyards were used less and less, they were finally dismantled.

Among the first breeders of purebred cattle were: T. R. Henderson of the Dobell Coal Co. and Stuart Hall both of whom raised Shorthorns. Later, Claude Gallinger became famous for his Killearn herd. The Mercury in the spring of 1931 records Gallinger's purchase of a Shorthorn bull at the Edmonton Spring Sales. He bought the females for his herd by type as well as by breed so developed a herd of a distinctive type. He imported bulls from Scotland to improve his herd and when, in 1944, he had his first sale of twoyearold bulls, buyers from all over the continent attended. Killearn breeding became famous. One report in the Mercury stated that Killearn bulls had won nineteen top honours in State Fairs in the U. S. A.

In 1932, Earl Moore and son John came to the Tofield district and brought with them a herd of polled Herefords. In 1967 John Moore is still carrying on the work begun by his father.

In the fall of 1940, C. J. Kallal and Sons bought their first registered Herefords which became the nucleus of their famous herd. They have been highly successful in the Edmonton and Calgary bull sales and have won many awards from shows in Western Canada as well as at the Toronto Royal.

Other Tofield breeders have built up excellent herds of purebred Herefords. Among these are found: E. Geoglein and Sons., M. C. Wood, C. J. Moos, Joe Brown and Sons. Stanley Brown with his herd of Polled Angus has also brought honours to the Tofield district.

All of these breeders have won ribbons for prize animals as well as adequate financial return for their efforts. In doing so they have won favourable publicity for Tofield but they have made other contributions to the district of even greater value. The results of their pure breed livestock breeding programs are evident in the improved quality of local livestock attained through sale of good bulls and heifers in this area. One has only to attend a 4H Calf Club Achievement Day to note the improvement in the quality of the calves over the last twenty years.

So, in 1967, the scene has changed. Where once vast herds of buffalo roamed, feeding on the "prairie wool" and wallowing in shallow ponds, now herds of sleek cattle feast on tame grasses behind retaining fences.

ORGANIZATIONS

# HISTORY OF THE TOFIELD UNION LADIES' AID

*This information was compiled by Mrs. Ethel Wood, from the original minute book of the Union Ladies' Aid*

The minute book of the Tofield Union Ladies' Aid, now in the United Church Archives in Edmonton states that on Thursday, January 28, 1904, a meeting was held to organize a union ladies' aid society to raise funds for the Tofield Union Meeting House. The ladies present were: Mrs. J. W. Cookson; Mrs. L.H. Harriman; Miss Ada Cookson (who were elected president, vicepresident and secretary, respectively); Mrs. J. 0. Letourneau; Mrs. C. Harriman; Mrs. M. McCauley; Mrs. Rickner; Lily Rickner; Oma Rickner; Mrs. William Wood; Mrs. J.C. Phillips; Miss A. Story; Mrs. Harry Neal; Miss May Williams; Mrs. Felix Paradis; Miss Lena Whillans; Miss Clara Thorsley and Mrs. George Cookson.

Annual membership fee was set at 25 cents. At their first regular meeting at Mrs. Rickner's in February, it was decided to offer to buy the old Tofield school "for the purpose of retaining it as a Union Meeting House to be used by all denominations, the offer to be made at the school meeting."

Their next meeting at Mrs. Harriman's saw arrangements made for holding their first "social" on March 29 at 7:30 with admissions of 15 cents for adults, 10 cents for children from 9 to 14 years. The financial return from this enterprise was $9.50. This included the returns from a sale of cakes.

In the minutes of the May meeting we find it written that "we should spend our time at our meetings on sewing or useful needlework." That day, too, plans were completed for the first Ladies' Aid Booth on the sports grounds on July 1, where they planned to "serve meals and light refreshments." Provisions except fruit, were to be purchased in Edmonton on credit.

Some of the money from this effort was spent on cups, saucers, and spoons for use at socials, and for materials to be made into bazaar articles and to renovate the old school house. The building was plastered with mud, both inside and out, and whitewashed inside by Mr. Louis Pruden for $7.00 and afterwards scrubbed and cleaned by Miss G. Francis for $2.00. Lunches at socials were served in paper bags. The members of the Ladies' Aid found it necessary, as the ladies of the Community League still do, on show nights, to puncture each bag in advance to forestall a noisy evening.

Prices for some of the materials purchased by the Aid were: White cotton at 15 cents a yard; Turkey red cotton at 12 ½ cents a yard, 6 spools of thread for 25 cents. The bazaar articles were sold on credit, a months time being allowed for payment.

In October that year, the ladies bought a pig from Mrs. J. Cookson for $2.00. The pig was sold in 1905 for $7.50, having been kept with the Cookson pigs till ready for market.

The candy left over from July 1 booth was given to the children the following Christmas; two dozen chairs and a table were ordered for the meeting house as well as wool for comforters and yarn for knitting.

In January, 1905, they ordered half a cord of firewood to be sawed, cut ready for use and delivered by Jim Francis for $1.75.

The audit of the books for the first year showed total receipts of $173.20 with expenditures of $100.40. Each of the student ministers of the Presbyterian and Methodist churches received $4.00 from the Aid.

Nina Wood was the first regular caretaker of the meeting house. She was followed by Venah Rickner. Both were paid at the rate of 15 cents per week for building the fire, sweeping, dusting and tidying up.

The biggest expenditure in 1905 was for an organ. One member made a cover for it; another made a feather duster for cleaning the instrument.

The members of this pioneer Ladies' Aid applied the commandment to "love thy neighbour." When Jeremy Gladue's house was destroyed by fire, he was given a donation towards replacement. Another time, a girl was hired and paid to help a sick mother.

By 1906, various denominations were beginning to establish churches in the district. The Methodist parsonage and the Presbyterian manse each received $50 for furnishings from the Ladies Aid.

In 1907, $400 was donated to each of the above churches, Mr.

A.J.H. McCauley's audit of the books for that year showed that the Ladies' Aid had raised $500.62

When the churches decided to separate, the ladies decided to divide the goods and possessions equally between the two churches e.g. the curtains to one church, the icecream freezer to the other, and so on. From then on each church was large enough to have its own group of women workers.

## THE BANK OF MONTREAL IN TOFIELD

The Merchant' Bank established a branch in Tofield in 1907 near the site of the present school. When the town moved, in 1908 to its present site, the bank moved from its rented frame building to its newly built structure on Main Street. This building still stands across the street from the Royal Alexandra Hotel. On the second floor were four rooms used as quarters for the staff. In a booklet published in 1913 by the"Industrial League of Tofield" there is an excellent picture of this pioneer bank.

The bank began with a staff of two to serve a population of two hundred. Mr. R.I. Stinson was the first manager in 1907. He was succeeded in 1908 by N.C. Legge. Other managers have been: C.H. Rowe; 1913, IV. C. King, 1917; H.A. Doak, 1921; J.A. Constantine, 1925; C.H.Rowe again in 1928; L.W. Smith, 1931; A.E. Allan, 1936;D.R. McKay, 1946; E.O. Pederson, 1947; H. Seller, 1954.

A branch of the Dominion Bank opened in 1922 closed a year later.

In 1936, the Bank of Montreal was moved to its present site, though it was housed in the building now used as the Legion Hall.

On June 6, 1955, the present premises of the bank were opened. The staff was made up of: Horace Seller manager, Ernie George, Margaret Sware, Joan Fraser Sophie Haugen and Malissa Nomeland.

In April, 1957, the bank celebrated its fiftieth anniversary in Tofield. The staff then consisted of:Horace Seller, John Weir, Margaret Sware, Verna Baergen, Irma Thiessen, Isabel Dunki and Dolores Wideman.

In 1959, Horace Seller's staff were: Steve Falabrenza, Lloyd Horn, Inez Kauffman, Sylvia Wideman, Isabel Dunki and Patsy Roth.

In 1967, Canada's Centennial year,the Tofield bank celebrated its sixtieth year in Tofield as well as the 150th anniversary of the Bank of Montreal in Canada.

A commemorative historical plaque, was placed on the original bank building (now owned by Conrad Patterson). The ceremony was attended by the members of the Tofield town council, members of the Chamber of Commerce and Mr. Harold Weatherill, representing the County of Beaver. The ceremony was enhanced by the presence of Mark Ferguson, one of the original councillors of Tofield and one of the first customers of the bank, in 1909.

At this time the bank staff, in addition to manager Horace Seller included Gordon Penny, Dean Niemetz, Margaret Jensen, Diane Ferguson, Dolores Lehman, Barbara McGinitie and Shari Ast.

In July 1967, Margaret (Sware) Jensen took over the post of second officer of the branch. The remainder of the staff consisted of: Diane Ferguson, Dolores Lehman, Gloria Hoover, Fern Stauffer, Isla Hjelter and Bob Knull.

In 1968, an addition to the premises of the Bank of Montreal was constructed to accomodate the growing business of the Bank.

# THE TOFIELD AGRICULTURAL SOCIETY

The Tofield Agricultural Society originated in 1909 and continued until 1923, sponsoring an Agricultural Fair each year. The booklet "Tofield, the Heart of the Beaver Lake District," published by the Tofield Board of Trade in 1910, states: "The Agricultural Society will hold its annual exhibition this year on September 27", thus indicating the existence of a Fair in 1909. The minutes of the Town Council dated September 13, 1910 note that "the Agricultural Society requests the loan of one of the town fire engines." (At that time, the town had two fire engines stationed at J. Gladue's livery barn).

The two livery barns of Tofield played an important part in

the Agricultural Fair. Mr. Gladue's barn on Lot 19, Block 14 where Watson's have (in 1967) their West lumber yard and Mr. Josh Noland's barn across the avenue on Lots 1,2,3, Block 13, housed the livestock exhibits. Grains, grasses, vegetables, cookery and fancy work exhibits were on display in the building Mr. W. C. Swift had contracted to display Massey–Harris machinery just east of the present (1967) Calgary Power office.

There were no loading chutes in the barns so it was not surprising that it took five men and a boy to load the 600-lb winning Berkshire sow when it was time for her to return to the Olsen farm. Someone (probably the boy) twisted her tail to speed up her progress; the resulting noise would drown out any brass band.

Several early residents were responsible for the inception and administration of the Agricultural Society Wm. Thompson, the first president and R. W. Whillans, the first secretary were assisted by J. L. Gray, Jack Cookson, R.E. Emery, George Didon, John McGinitie, D. Francis, Billy Wood, Sam Bethel, Sam Stirrett, Jack Willis, John Morton., Mrs. Morton and Pete Lee.

Soon, the Agricultural Society needed room to expand. The town minutes of February 3, 1910, note, " R. W. Whillans was present on behalf of the Agricultural Society, seeking a piece of land to hold Tofield's Fair on.

In 1911, the present Exhibition grounds were set aside and town and country worked together to improve the site of the Fair. A long, narrow building was constructed about where the west sheet of curling ice is now; this housed the ladies' fancy work, cooking, vegetables and grains. To the north was a shed for horses and pens were made for sheep and pigs. Cattle were exhibited much as they are in the present calf club shows.

A halfmile race course was constructed for the trotting horses pulling their sulkies as well as for the racehorses. A judges' stand, large enough to hold six or seven men, completed the racetrack equipment.

When the Fairs were first instituted they were divided by the Dep't of Agriculture into classes A,B,and C. Edmonton and Calgary Fairs ranked as Class A; those in Vermilion, Vegreville and Camrose as

Class B; Tofield, Holden and Ryley were in Class C. The Government of Alberta provided two-thirds of the prize money the remaining third was raised by the local directors who canvassed the district. Later, the grant was cut to 50% which meant more work for the directors; they had to secure bigger contributions from the community.

Some prominent exhibitors were: J. S. Gray and John McGinitie for their vegetables; Mrs. John Morton and Mrs. Peter Lee for fancy work; Mrs. Jack Cookson, Mrs Gray, R.N. Whillans, D. Francis, E. Hardy, and Mr. Goeglein Sr. for poultry; J. McGinitie, D. Francis , Sam Bethel, George Quam, Tofield Coal Co., T. Noland ,J.B. Warner for livestock.

The Fairs continued successfully until 1922 when the Government reduced its financial support to one third of the prize money. The increasing use of the automobile also contributed to the demise of the fairs as people could now travel further and more easily; local events were no longer the only available attraction.

The rivalry between the Clyde and Percheron horse breeders also contributed to the downfall of the already declining Fairs.

The Government used to supply the judges for the livestock. One year, the horse judge from the U.S.A. was a short stout man whose body seemed much too heavy for his legs to support. He had a decided preference for a special kind of horse; if the horse was a black or an irongrey, he was sure to be awarded the prize money. But tastes differ and the next year the judge was a tall bony Scotsman who preferred a fine team of bays with white faces and white stockings. When a team answering this description appeared, a prize was surely in the offing!

When the Fair was no longer held, one of the exhibition buildings was cut up and hauled up to the school to make a barn for the horses driven by school children. About twenty horses were stabled there at one time.

The other exhibition building seemed to disintegrate as the town boys discovered that the ten-foot planks of which it was composed made excellent material for rafts!

So passed an era in local history!

# TOFIELD LIBRARY

As early as November 30, 1909 the town records show that "a petition was received from 20 rate-payers praying that a library be established in town." In 1910 the minutes of the town council state: "The secretary (A.J.H. McCauley) was instructed to write to Dr. J.E. Hammond advising that those who signed the petition forlibrary appoint a committee to write to Mr. Andrew Carnegie for full information regarding the conditions he would require in the event of a library grant being given by him." Somewhat later, a form to be filled out if the town wished a library grant was received from Mr. Carnegie, but apparently no grant was received.

Mrs. Crawford Baptist, who has always been an avid reader as well as a community worker, said "The first public library to be established in Tofield was due to the efforts of the Women's Institute when in 1916 each member agreed to donate one good book as the nucleus of a library."

At that time the W.I. meetings were held at the homes of the members and, a little later, in the upstairs rooms of the present Red and White Store. They had dreams of establishing a W.I. rest room for local and district women. This would also house the library.

A committee was appointed to take charge of the venture. It was responsible for the books for soliciting donations and for supervising the material. At that time Mrs. Jacobs (mother of Mr. D.W. Jacobs) was president and members of the early executive were: Mrs. Ward Somers, Mrs. Herb Ward and Mrs. Raymond Pincott.

Mrs. Pincott will be remembered in Tofield as a member of the famous Palmatier family of entertainers. She was known and beloved as a concert violinist and even better known as a comedienne. She was a real acquisition to Tofield and had a vital interest in the Library. When her sister in Edmonton died, her large and valuable collection of books was offered for sale. Mr. Pincott (who was Mayor of Tofield in 1919 and 1920) informed the W.I. of the opportunity of buying these books. While the W.I. was considering ways and means, Mr. Pincott bought the whole collection and presented it to the W.I. so the Tofield Public

Library got an enormous boost.

Grateful members willingly took charge. Rows of bookcases were built and established in the Institute rest rooms, which had been purchased by the W.I. The building served for many years as a meeting place and recreation centre for town and country women. It has only recently been demolished to make way for the Lion's Club Museum.

Mrs. Gilbert McCarthy, among others, will always be remembered for devoted management of the library which under her capable administration grew to the two thousand volume mark.

Mrs. Baptist was also librarian at that time.

"Later," to quote Mrs. Baptist again, "other interest and exploits diverted the Institute members and the organization quietly died out.The rest room was taken over by the Holden School Division and used for a Home Economics room.The library was shifted from one place to another."

The following information was supplied by Mrs. W.H. Freebury.

"In 1944, the library was housed in the town hall (on the site of the present drug store) and the librarian was still Mrs. Gilbert McCarthy, who was on duty every Saturday afternoon.When Mrs. McCarthy was forced by illness to sever her long association with the library, the work was carried on by Mrs. Ray Coatta until the new town hall was built in 1951.

The library books were then sorted. Those suitable for youth reading were given to the Tofield High School and the remainder were stored in the Old Methodist Church building until the new Community Hall was built and the use of the meeting room was donated to the library by the Community League.

For some years there were various book clubs formed among ardent readers of the town and country. Books were passed among members at two-week intervals. In 1954 one of these book clubs became the forerunner of our library.When Mrs. Marguerite Anderson, the organizer of this club left Tofield, she bequeathed her record books and information regarding the libraries supplied by the Department of Extension to Mrs. W.H. Freebury who then took over the task of organizing the library.

The Tofield Community League supplies the meeting room of the Community Hall, rent free, as its contribution to the library. The Town of Tofield donates a sum yearly. The table and chairs were purchased by the Jubilee Committee of 1955 with the proceeds of the booklet "A Concise History of Tofield."

On October 19, 1964, as a result of a petition received by the Town of Tofield, a bylaw was passed establishing the Tofield Municipal Library. The advantages of changing the status from the Tofield Library were that a larger grant could be obtained from the Provincial Government and that the financing policy setting and administration of the Library are the responsibility of a Library Board and not the Library Staff as was the case under the Tofield Library. The first library Board appointed consisted of Mr. E. Watson, Chairman; Mrs. Joan Dunham, Treasurer; Mrs. Rita Halverson, Secretary; Mayor Dr. W.H. Freebury' and Mr. D.L. Jefferson, representatives from the Town Council; Mr. D.E. Hardy and Mrs. Hazel Patterson. The Tofield Municipal Library is under the custodianship of Mrs. Dorothea Freebury, Librarian, and Mrs. Georgia Christensen, Assistant Librarian. Volunteer helpers are "Friends of the Library".

Those who have, through the years, assisted in 'the library are: Mary Stinson, Minnie McConnell, Dorothea Freebury, Melita Wall, Evelyn Richardson, Rosella Dodds.

# PALESTINE LODGE, NO. 46 A.F. AND A.M.

On the evening of July 21st, 1909, the Masons resident in Tofield held a meeting to discuss forming a Masonic Lodge. These men were:
Alfred Fugl, Brittania Lodge #23 of Saskatchewan;
Charles Spilsted, Wellington Lodge #341 of England;
Charles Cress, Norwood Lodge #223 Canada;
James Hammond, Palestine Lodge #357 of Detroit;
James Letourneau, Warren Lodge #150 of Minnesota;
Clarence Jamieson, Fidelity Lodge #428 of Canada;
James Mahaffy, Pawnee Lodge #17, Oklahoma;

Alfred Schultz, Enterprise #332, Iowa.

As a result of this meeting and after the necessary correspondence between the Grand Lodge of Alberta and the petitioners, a dispensation was granted on September 23, 1909, on the recommendation of Camrose Lodge #37.

On October 133, 1909 Palestine Lodge #46 U.D. was instituted and the following officers were installed and invested:

| | |
|---|---|
| Worshipful Master | A.F. Fugl |
| Senior Warden | C.H. Cress |
| Junior Warden | J.L. Hammond |
| Treasurer | J.A. Letourneau |
| Senior Deacon | A.E. Campion |
| Junior Deacon | A.F. Schultz |
| Inner Guard | J.F. Mahaffy |

Palestine Lodge #46 was named after Palestine Lodge #357 in Detroit which was Dr. J.L. Hammond's Mother Lodge.

At the time of Institution in 1909, Palestine Lodge in Detroit presented Palestine Lodge In Tofield with a lovely Lodge Bible.

As of 1968, Brother Hammond is the only surviving charter member. He now resides in California, but is still a member of Palestine Lodge. Brother Hammond has attended Lodge here on two occasions in the last eight years.

In the summer of 1910 fire destroyed the building in which the Lodge Hall was situated. Temporary quarters were used until the new Hall Block was completed.

On October 24, 1934, the 25th anniversary of Palestine Lodge was celebrated by a banquet at which over 130 guests were seated. The head table was decorated with yellow chrysanthemums sent by Palestine Lodge #3 of Detroit, Michigan. Sixteen Lodges were represented at the meeting which followed the banquet.

During the years of World War II, parcels were sent overseas, and financial support was given to the Victory Bond Campaigns, the Red Cross, and the I.O.D.E.

At present there are several second generation members of Palestine Lodge. These are Graham Allan, D. Dodds, Thomas Jacobs, Arnold

Swift, Douglas Murray, Malcolm Murray and Allan Maxwell.

In the Spring of 1955 the old United Church purchased by the Lodge and after some renovations the first meeting was held in the new quarters on the 21 of June 1955.

In 1958 an addition was built to the Lodge Hal. Kitchen facilities and a new heating plant were added.

The 50th anniversary of Palestine Lodge was held on March 15, 1960, with several Grand Lodge officers present. A service on Thanksgiving for a half century of Freemasonry in Tofield was conducted by Rev. Bro. Dr. E.J. Thompson, at that time Principal of St. Stephen's College.

Brother Penman of Edmonton presented Palestine lodge with three handmade, inlaid gavels which he had made from Oak from the old Hudson's Bay store in Edmonton.

In the course of fifty years' use, the Bible, which had been presented by Palestine Lodge #357 of Detroit, Michigan, had become rather shabby. So, Brother Bernie Brown, of Edmonton, had it recovered and it was presented anew by Brother D.W. Jacobs.

In the evening 175 guests were served a turkey Banquet by the ladies of Ionic Chapter of the O.E.S., thus bringing to a conclusion a most successful 50th anniversary celebration.

Over the course of years several of the members have been appointed officers of the Grand Lodge of Alberta. These were:

| | |
|---|---|
| A.J.H. McCauley | Grand Organist |
| T.P. Newbigging | District Deputy Grand Master |
| D.W. Jacobs | Grand Steward |
| T.W.A. Webb | District Deputy Grand Master |
| J.W. Chapman | District Deputy Grand Master |
| H.W. Lovell | District Deputy Grand Master |
| Rev. D.K. Allan | Grand Chaplain |
| W.A. Swift | District Deputy Grand Master |
| N. Phillips | Grand Steward |

In 1968, Palestine Lodge A.F. & A.M. #46 was host to 274 Masons from many points in Alberta and beyond on Tuesday, April 16, on the occasion of the visit of a Masonic Degree Team, arranged by Corporal

Roy Murray of Tofield, Worshipful Master of Palestine Lodge.

Preceding the meeting, which was held in the Tofield Community Centre, members of Ionic Chapter, O.E.S., served the guests a turkey banquet.

Seated at the head table and introduced by Bill Christensen, banquet chairman, were: Grand Master., Bernie Brown; Senior Grand Warden, Dr. P.J. Kendal; District Deputies, Cliff Jones, Edmonton, and Frank Rogers, Blindloss; Chairman of the Higher Education Bursary Fund Ken Crockett; Captain of the visiting Degree Team; Stan Harbin George Thiessen,Don Goss and K. Schroeder.

Following the banquet, the regular April meeting of Palestine Lodge was held, during which Harry Wilkie, John Wall and Floyd Irwin, all of Tofield, were received into Masonry.

Following a short business meeting, the chairs were turned over to the visiting degree team, who conducted the ceremony for Messrs. Wilkie, Wall and Irwin in a brilliant display which set a high standard for the work. Both visitors and members of Palestine Lodge were especially impressed with the crisp precision and perfection displayed by the highly-famed team, whose reputation had brought the large turnout in the first place.

The guests represented 64 Alberta lodges, including 21 Edmonton lodges, two lodges in Ontario, and one lodge in each of British Columbia, Quebec and Saskatchewan.

As well as those Grand Lodge Officers introduced at the head table, there were present six Past District Deputies, two Past Grand Registrars; two other Past Grand Officers, 76 Past Masters, and 15 sitting Master.

The register was signed by members from Calgary, Oyen, Mannville, Stettler, Cold Lake, Athabasca, Coronation, Westlock, Chauvin, Camrose, Vegreville, Tawatinaw, Edgerton, Sedgewick, Viking, Rimbey, Hughenden, Wetaskiwin, Wainwright, Whitecourt, Two Hills, Chinook, Castor, Alix, Blindloss, Lamont, Greisbach, Irma, Alliance, Forestburg, Holden, St. Paul and Edmonton, which sent 98 members.

# TOFIELD KNIGHTS OF PYTHIAS

When in 1955, the Masons moved from the room over the former McLeod's store to their new lodge room, an interesting document was found. Apparently the room had been shared by other lodges because this document is a report of the committee on selection of officers for the Knights of Pythias Lodge in Tofield. While the document is not dated, it must have been formulated prior to 1912, since one trustee's term of office expired then. The list of officers is as follows:

Chancellor, Arthur McMullen; ViceChancellor, Ernest W Rogers; Prelate, Rev. Allan M. McColl; Master of Work, Morris Mahaffay; Keeper of Records, John C. Kelley; Master of Exchequer, Roy S.Rudd; Master at Arms, Johnston Ferguson; Inner Guard, Dr. Norman Terwilliger; Outer Guard, David H.Mitchell; Past Chancellors, James A. Younie, Frederick McHeffey, Rev. Allan McColl, John C.Kelvey, Representatives to Grand Lodge; James Younie Morris E. Mahaffey. Trustees Ralph Davison to January 11, 1912; Norman Smith to January 1, 1913; Robert Mitchell to January 1, 1914.

The document continues:"In making these recommendations, your committee has borne in mind only what it considered to be the best interests of the lodge and its future success, and has endeavoured to select those who have manifested an interest in the lodge and its work. The remaining portion of the present term is very short and makes necessary a change of officers at the new year, so that practically all the new members will have ample opportunity to manifest the faith that is in them by practical service in official station."

In selecting those upon whom the honour of Past Chancellor shall be conferred, we have considered the matter only from the standpoint of equitable merit for the following reasons:

Had the lodge continued, Brother James A. Younie would have earned the honour of service. He had done much toward the reorganization of this lodge and we believe he deserves the honour.

Frederick McHeffey is one of the old-time members of the former lodge and one of the first to lend encouragement to the formation of the new lodge. His faithfulness and fidelity will be augmented and the

118

necessity of serving will be more than counterbalanced by the generous assistance he will gladly render the lodge as proof of his appreciation of the honor conferred.

The position of Prelate will be honoured and dignified by the services of Brother McColl in that station and the peculiar duties of the office should make it specially fitting that one of his profession should be placed therein. It follows, therefore, that so long as he remains a member of this lodge, he should remain in that position, thus precluding the possibility of his earning the honour by service in other capacities. Hence, we have suggested he be rewarded in advance for the duties we believe he will cheerfully and acceptably perform.

The position of Keeper of Records and Seal and Master of Finance is one of the most important in the lodge, about which revolves all the business procedure and without faithful and competent service therein, the lodge cannot hope for a full measure of success; when once the right member is found for that place, he is invariably retained there indefinitely, thus precluding the possibilities of his earning honours by service in other capacities and we believe, therefore, that the Keeper of Records and Seal should be given the honour of Past Chancellor, so he may devote his time and energies to the proper discharge of the duties devolving upon him, without feeling he is being deprived of honors that otherwise might come to him. In that spirit, and for that purpose we have named Brother Kelley as one of the Past Chancellors.

*Faithfully Submitted, M.W. Ferguson, C.E. Jamieson., Committee*

# THE WOMEN'S INSTITUTE

Enterprise...Initiative...Community Pride: These are the marks of the Women's Institute. And so it was with the Tofield Women's Institute. The first written record we can find is of meetings being held in 1915 with Mrs. Thomas Jacobs, Sr., as president. These meetings were held in the homes of various members.

It was the ambition of these ladies to have their own club rooms and so it came about they were able to rent the upstairs rooms of Mr. Taylor's Store. Here they had rest rooms and a club house till March, 1921 when they moved into a small building on Main Street, known to many old timers as the Institute Rooms.

With them, moved the Tofield Library which had come under their custody in May of 1920. Mrs.Innes Sr.was librarian.

The first Women's Institute Convention to be held in Tofield was March 15 and 16, 1921 in the Variety Theatre.

In May, 1921 a Child Welfare Clinic was held. Institute members urged all parents both town and country to bring their children.

The ladies worked hard for their money, sponsoring an annual banquet and play each year. One play held in March of 1921 was called: 'My Wife's Relations". Admission for adults was 50 cents, and for children it was 35 cents. A dance was held afterwards, with admission being a dollar per gentleman.

Many a whist drive was sponsored by the organization and we find that Mrs. Wm. Glover was awarded a nice pair of towels for regular attendance in 1922.

Apparently the ladies worked for charitable causes, for in 1922 a plant sale was held for the benefit of the Salvation Army. "If you cannot bake, bring fruit. If you cannot do anything else, bring a quarter," was their slogan.

In July of 1922, the Women's Institute donated the Lunch Booth erected on the Fair Grounds. They also sponsored the yearly cleanup program of the town and offered prizes for the nicest yard.

Perhaps for aggressiveness, enterprise and progress made, the Tofield Women's Institute ranks first among local organizations. From a small beginning they reached membership of nearly 50 by January, 1923. Their activities enterprise large numbers of people. (One of the best concerts, both in respect to attendance and talent, ever held in Tofield was presented by the Women's Institute at the Variety Theatre. With an attendance of 250 people. Mrs. Harold Hicks immensely pleased the audience with a Lancashire song and dance).

Tea was served every Saturday afternoon from 2 to 5 o'clock and many tired mothers found the Institute Rooms a haven after shopping.

The list of officers for the year 1925 was as follows: President Mrs. M. McHaffey. lst vice Mrs. Innes. 2nd vice Mrs. Parkers. Secretary Mrs.McKerrol. Assist. Sec. Mrs. Baptist. Treasurer Mrs. Doak. Press Agent Mrs. Wright. Boards Mrs. Hopgood. Librarian Mrs. Parker. Assist. Librarian Mrs. Allen. Directors Mrs. Ward, Mrs. North, Mrs. Dodds. Auditors Mrs. Baptist, and Mrs. Swift.

One especially enjoyable meeting in 1923 which provided a huge success,was held in the home of Mrs.J.B. Warner, but as the Warner children had the chicken pox it could not be held in the house, so all moved down to the banks of the creek for a very enjoyable afternoon.

The Women's Institute financial report of 1920 reads Total Receipts $1199.04 from which donations were made to 'Alton House for Girls','Pencil Sharpeners for the School', 'Fair Building', 'Children's Playgrounds' 'Social Service League', and 'The Xmas Box".

At 15 cents for tea and 25 cents for membership, this shows what an energetic club they were. However, membership dwindled in the 1930's till the officers of the day, Mrs. Ward (president), Mrs. Pincott (secretary) and Mrs. Peter Lerbekmo (treasurer), felt they could not accept another term and the Women's Institute sadly closed its doors.

*Mrs. John Thomson*

# PIONEER COMMUNITY PASTURE

The first Community Pasture in Central Alberta was formed by the Blackfoot Stock Association at North Cooking Lake in 1920.

The annual fall roundup begins toward the end of September. Then, the cattle are corralled, separated, counted and assigned to the rightful owners. It is an exciting time at the pasture headquarters. The pasture still occupies a tract of land nine miles long and six miles wide, twenty miles east of Edmonton and south of Highway 16. In the early days, the region was known as the "Beaver Hills."

The tract first was set aside by the Dominion Government for a forest reserve during the 1800's and was leased for a grazing reserve by the Blackfoot Stock Association in 1920. The next such community pastures on record in this area are the Twin River Grazing Reserves which were organized in 1935 and 1936. By the early 1940's there were eight experimental grazing reserves in Central Alberta.

Two roving forest rangers were appointed to look after the Beaver Hills forest reserve in 1895. Ranger Bill Stevens and his guide, Black Jack Sanderson, a Sioux Indian, had a shack at Blackfoot Springs on the old Beaver Hill Lake Trail which at that time was the main trail to Tofield from Edmonton.

A great deal of logging was carried on at the forest reserve before the turn of the century. Matt McCauley, who became the first mayor of Edmonton in 1892 operated one of the first sawmills in the district. In 1894 a great fire swept through the region. A year later on October 22, a prairie fire started south of Beaver Hill Lake, at township 52, range 23. It swept through the forest reserve and persisted in the ground over winter.

Much of the big timber was destroyed; logging was practically at an end. Nonetheless, a fine growth of grass followed on the burned over areas and a veritable haven for livestock resulted.

When the Blackfoot Stock Association was formed in 1920, 150 men signed up. The membership fee was one dollar each. Nearly all were farmers from Tofield, Lamont, Fort Saskatchewan and Clover Bar.

For one dollar the provincial government leased them 40,000 acres within the reserve for one year. In the same year, the association borrowed $12,000 from the Merchants' Bank in Tofield to finance fencing the pasture. A fence of four strands of barbed wire with solid cedar posts was completed the same season. The south side of the pasture fence was constructed and built by Jim Gray, the father of Jack Gray, the present rangerider and manager.

The association charged members $2.50 per head per season. It was very dry during the early twenties and horses were brought in from Camrose and as far south as Stettler and Big Valley. When the bank loan was due for repayment, there were no funds in reserve to meet it and many of the members dropped out. The remaining ones paid it, however, and it was $420.00 each.

Mr. Pincott, J.M. Verge and John Morrow each acted as secretarytreasurer for some years. The provincial government took charge for the subsequent eight years, after which the farmers again formed an organization known as the Blackfoot Grazing Association. This is a nonprofit organization working in conjunction with the department of lands and forests. Expenses are paid and remaining funds are used for improvements.

In 1947 Jack Gray took over the management of the reserve and the community pasture, using as his headquarters buildings erected in 1912 by the Dominion Government. The membership fee is now five dollars a year. Approximately 1100 head of stock are on the pasture each season at $6.00 per head. All stock must be vaccinated and, with the exception of purebreds, dehorned. For deciding the pasture's capacity, a cow and calf is taken as the equivalent of one and a half head and a yearling as threequarters.

Manager Jack Gray keeps one hired man and at least three good saddle horses, for there are many miles of fence to ride and repair. Jack says,"an elk will jump the fence but a moose goes right through it." He estimates there are around 100 head of deer,40 to 50 moose and perhaps 25 elk lie says that elk, unlike moose,"yard up" in the bush and are seldom seen. One of the most likely places to look for the elk or moose with their young is at the salt licks. They also graze in the swamps at twilight where the grass grows green around huge old tamarack stumps that measure up to three feet across. The wood therein is still hard and sound and they bear mute testimony of the logging operations that were carried on there over one hundred years ago. Salt has to be supplied regularly for the wildlife as well as the livestock. No hunting is allowed at any time. The beaver have made a wonderful comeback inside the fence, thus helping to ensure plentiful supplies of water in the pasture.

Cattle put in the pasture from the west gate are eartagged in the right ear and those admitted at the east gate are tagged in the left. A crossfence dividing the pasture prevents cattle entered from the west ranging on the east side and vice-versa, thereby simplifying the fall roundup.

One whole section inside the pasture has been enclosed with a fence. A gate to this fenced section opens into a stronglyfenced one acre corral called the "catch fence". The cattle are rounded up in groups. Each group is hazed into this oneacre catch fence, where they are counted. Then they are released into the fenced onesection corral. Further separating by brand can be carried on then and finally the animals are run into the corrals for their owner.

This year, Jack Gray's children, Caroline 15, and Ronnie, 13, who ride as though to "the saddle born" will be taking part in the fall roundup, hazing the cattle in golden September sunshine along the fence that their grandfather helped to build forty years ago.

This article is reprinted by permission of the author, Mrs. Irene Williams and by courtesy of the Winnipeg Free Press.

# THE TOFIELD F. W. U. A. #620

The first U.F.W.A. local in Tofield was formed October 24, 1925. At a well attended meeting, Mrs. W.D. McNaughton of the provincial organization, stated the advantages of belonging to a local branch. It was unanimously voted to form such a group. Officers elected were: President Mrs. Johnsone Ferguson; VicePresident, Mrs. J.B. Warner; Secretary-Treasurer, Mrs.Hingston; Directors: Mrs. W.M. Parker, Mrs. A.N. Booth, Mrs. J. L. Gray, Mrs. C. Baptist, and Mrs. F.O. Ball.

A feature of the afternoon was an address by the "Red Cross Lady", Mrs. Mary Conquest, who was impressed by the coincidence of the Red Cross speaker at a Farm Women's meeting, in a hall owned by the Women's Institute.

On March 10, 1949, at a meeting at Mrs. J. Appleby's home it was voted to change the name from the United Farm Women of Alberta, to Farm Women's Union of Alberta., in line with the change in the Provincial Organization. Mrs. A. Torrie made the motion which was seconded by Mrs. Jas. Dunki, President, and Mrs. McConnell as Secretary-Treasurer agreed to continue in office in the new local.

Junior locals in Alberta are the responsibility of the Women's groups, and in this area three such locals were formed: The Bardo Junior U.F.A. organized by Mrs. McNaughton in 1931; President, Ivan Foshaug; VicePresident, Margaret Moen; Sec. Treas., Mabel Jevening; Leaders, Mrs. Finseth and B. Anderson. The Tofield Junior also by Mrs. McNaughton in 1931; President, Harold Schultz; VicePres. Leda Baptist and Elgin Seale. The Ketchamoot Junior, in 1935 formed by Mrs. A. Torrie, was succeeded by Mrs. McNaughton as District Director; President, Stanley Sears; VicePres. Allen Harrison; Secretary, Margaret Mitchell.

These three locals were active for a relatively short time, and disbanded when interest waned.

In its forty-two years of life, the Tofield F.W.U.A has made a very great contribution to the community and to many humanitarian projects. Generous donations have been made yearly since 1925 to the Red Cross. Yearly support goes also to the C.N.I.B. the Unitarians, T.B. seals, the Salvation Army, and the Cancer Society, Prisoner of War fund, the Winnipeg Flood Relief Fund, and many, many others. Locally they have donated to curtains for the community hall, movie projector for the school, the Lions' skating rink, coffee pots for the Community league. They loaned 100 dollars to the Community League and later donated it outright.

During the war years the Red Cross was devotedly supported by the farm women, who knit sweaters, scarves, mittens, and socks in an endless stream and pieced and tied quilts in endless dozens, to be turned over to the Red Cross to be used as they saw fit. Woolen blankets, slippers and layettes were donated to the Tofield Hospital. For the last twelve years salvage drives were sponsored, which have turned in literally tons of used papers and clothes to the Red Cross and Salvation Amy.

Old timers will remember the annual whist drives put on by farmers, men and women, in the Old Variety Theatre, well supported by town and country alike. In 1931, there was the Art and Handicrafts exhibit, not for prizes, but to show the exceptional beauty and skill which went in to the making of so many wonderful articles. This display was written up for the Mercury by Mr. Worton, who gave great praise to all concerned in the exhibit.

And no member who attended them will forget the birthday parties, each October, which were something to marvel at, and to treasure in memory. The F.W.U.A. cook books deserve mention; these recipes collected from members throughout the province were compiled and printed first in 1928. At last count, over 65,000 were distributed, going to all parts of the world, where many are in daily use. The Tofield local has handled between five or six hundred and still the orders come in.

Membership through the past years has included the vast majority of farm women of the district; very few names do not appear somewhere along the line. Under the capable leadership of Mrs. Moos, president and Mrs Crispin, secretary-treasurer, Centennial year was entered with high hopes for continued good times and worthwhile endeavours in the future.

—*Mrs. John Thomson*

# THE TRENT RANCH

Mr. G.A. Trent bought, in 1910, what was known locally as the Logan Ranch which, lying on the west side of Beaverhill Lake, was comprised of approximately 19 quartersections of land. For a few years following his purchase of the Logan Ranch, Mr. Trent traded horses. People were able to pasture their horses on his land and he would then try and sell these horses to out of town buyers for the owner. He also ran about a thousand Merino sheep but found this breed not suitable for conditions in this area.

"On Dec. 30, 1927, Mr. Trent sold the entire ranch by contract to a group of Mennonites, consisting of seven families for $126,000. The deal was made by the Canadian Colonization Company, a subsidiary of the C. P.R. The seven families took possession on Jan. 1, 1928. Representing the Mennonites was W.A. Klassen, while the vendee was G.A. Trent," records the Tofield Mercury of Dec. 30, 1927.

Mr. Henry Schroeder, son of H.G. Schroeder, one of the original

Mennonite buyers, gives the following account of the early days on the former Trent Ranch.

"My father, H.G. Schroeder, came to the Trent Ranch with his family in the winter of 1927–28. We moved into a 'leanto' which had been an oat bin, a cattle shed and rumour had it a chicken house. The inside was lined with a very thick type of wallpaper which made ideal homes or nests for those little, flatbellied creatures that came for dinner in the middle of the night—bedbugs. These nocturnal invasions forced the family to spend nights in a granary while the house was being fumigated with burning sulphur to destroy the pests."

"At times we had two extra families overnight. Some slept on the table, some on coats and blankets under the table. It was quite a chore getting organized in the morning."

Mr. G.A. Trent had sold his ranch to seven families under one contract. Participants in the deal were: H.G. Schroeder, J.A. Heidebrecht, A. Froese, P. Goertzen, A. Peters, John Peters and Frank Peters. The ranch contained Sections 16, 17, 20, 21, S ½ of 28, SE ¼ of 30, S ½ of 34, SW ¼ of 30 and all the lake shore bordering this land was leased from the government.

The land was divided into seven parcels and numbered. Ownership of the land was decided by lot, the numbers of the parcels of land being drawn from a hat. Not everyone was satisfied with the results of the draw and the procedure had to be repeated until all were satisfied. Finally, when the smoke cleared, Mr. Goertzen settled on SE ¼ of 30., Mr. Froese on S ½ of 28, Mr. Heidebrecht and Mr. Schroeder on 20, A. Peters on NW ¼ of 17, Frank Peters on SW ¼ of 17, and John Peters on 16 close to the lake.

Land had to be fenced and buildings erected where none existed. The agreement was that the families moving into houses would help the others build the necessary dwellings. This arrangement was responsible for differences of opinion.

Wells had to be dug and water in sufficient quantities was not always found. J. Peters couldn't find enough water so every day he led his cattle out onto the lake where he watered them through a hole in the ice. By March the lake was frozen to a considerable depth as it was shallow. The distance to the water hole seemed even longer on a windy, cold day.

Goertzen from SE of 30 led his cattle to our place on NW of 20, for quite some time and we boys enjoyed watching the occasional bull fight when the cattle came together (by accident, of course!).

Much land had to be cleared and broken. Most of the breaking was done by hired machinery but the clearing was done by hand. I remember the long cables we tied to the bigger trees (there were some whoppers!). The team of horses strained at the end of the cables while the axes chewed away at the roots of these giants.

After breaking came rootpicking using the axe and grub hoe. One fall we picked roots far into December; there was no snow and very little frost to hamper the work.

One year, Heidebrechts and Schroeders cleared and broke 80 acres. This was sown to Marquis wheat the following spring and a splendid standard resulted. Then in early August, we had a tremendous storm which laid the field flat. Most of it stayed that way, and of course, cutting and stooking the grain was quite a chore. Our fathers tried to cut the lodged grain by using pickup arms on the binder and going just one way but the binders were unable to stand the strain and breakdowns were frequent. Horses had a difficult task as they had to step lively or the binder would jam.

Then came stooking, which involved tearing the sheaves apart. We boys had a taste of this hard work, too. Later the men on the threshing crew had their turn trying to make those horrible bundles behave. Although 48-50 bushels per acre were threshed, at least a quarter of the crop remained on the ground.

We went to MacKenzie School which was located on the N.W. corner of N.W. ¼ of 73, 52-18-W.4. We drove in a buggy or democrat in the summer and used a cutter in winter. Usually two or three families shared one outfit. We boys took turns at driving or, at least, at holding the reins. Many a runaway ensued. In later years, I have wondered what our mothers must have felt when they saw the horses come galloping full steam into the yard with the cutter on its side or with just the tongue and double trees dragging behind!

We raised our own horses and had plenty of excitement breaking them for riding and for driving. In the spring, we usually had four horses to a plow with one behind pulling a section of harrows. Hay was made with horsepower also, with the teams pulling the mower, the rake, the sweep, the buck and later, the overhead stacker. In wet years, mosquitos were a real plague, nearly devouring the horses.

Then came the dry thirties! One poor crop after another and no other income—nothing with which to make payments on the land. Mr. Trent was very patient with us and helped in many ways, but gradually the people gave up. Some went to the Debt Adjustment Board to get straightened away; one by one, they left the ranch. My father alone chose to stay rather than to move again.

However, it was very hard going until the middle of the forties. The crops were poor and the prices low; even cattle prices went to pieces. I remember father sending a cow to market just before Christmas one year and getting a cheque for sixty-six cents after trucking and expenses. Can you wonder at Santa Claus sort of sneaking by that year?

As the farmers involved in the original agreement of sale left the ranch, Mr. Trent took over again with the aid of hired help. These men moved in, bringing their families, and later rented the land they had helped to farm. Mr. W. Morowski moved to the farm on the S ½ of 28 which had been vacated by Mr. Froese. Here he worked for many years. The Dales moved onto the farm of John Peters on section 16 where they raised sheep for a few years. Mr. B. Pikula bought S.E. ¼ of 30. Other workers on the repossessed Trent land were:Peter Bassaraba, Frank Sharun, Peter Sharun, Harry Litwin, Mac Reed, Steve Kozak, Fred Schacker, Nick Holowychuck.

Later Mr. Trent's two sons moved onto the ranch. Mr. G.A. (Art) Trent, took over the north half of section 17 and Mr. H.M. (Monro) Trent the south half of the same section.

When Mr. Trent passed away in January 1954, the ranch was divided among his children. George Arthur and Henry Munro were already farming this inheritance; Bessie Delves inherited the S ½ of 28; Jacqueline (Mrs. Gregg) part of N ½ of 20 and SW ¼ of 21. Evelyn (Mrs. McIntosh) the S ½ of 20 and also shared SE ¼ of 21 with Mrs. Gregg.

My wife and I were working for Mr. Trent when he passed away and continued renting the Greggs farm till 1953 when we moved to the Secord farm.

Having spent 25 years on the Ranch, I have many fond memories. I recall with nostalgia the childhood excursions into the woods to destroy the nest of crows and magpies. We couldn't resist climbing to the horned owl's nest; the papa or mama objected violently, knocking off my friend's cap and clawing him considerably. That event cured us for a while.

In winter, we visited the same woods to shoot rabbits to use as bait on our weasel traps.

The cattle roundups were always looked forward to with great pleasure. We enjoyed watching the branding and vaccinating of the young range calves. Learning to rope was a challenge which required much patience and perseverance to master. Learning to stay on a good cutting horse and later, training one's own horse were real accomplishments.

The trips to the Blackfoot Forest Reserve for willow fence posts had their ups and downs. Upsetting a load of 125 posts and having to reload with the temperature far below zero was not a pleasant experience.We were glad to get home to a warm house at night yet no one wanted to miss the next day's trip.

Threshing time was a highlight of the year. Fondly remembered are the keen rivalry to put on the biggest load of bundles, the occasional tricks and stunts such as plugging the machine, tying bundles together in an impossibletolift mass, and wrestling with other crew members. One 17year old who knew all about threshing unloaded too long from the side and so tipped over with half of his load; he looked and probably felt very foolish. A full crew consisted of 6 bundle wagons and two field pitchers and the separator man.

So ends Mr. Schroeder's chronicle of the Trent Ranch.

# IONIC CHAPTER,
# ORDER OF THE EASTERN STAR

Ionic Chapter No.72, Order of the Eastern Star was instituted at Tofield, March 28, 1928. Thirty members were initiated at this meeting. Sister L. McLean was installed as Worthy Matron and Brother McClurg was Worthy Patron.

Mr. John Chapman became a member in 1931. He was one of the most interested and active members. The furnishings and regalia were much improved by him.

During the 1930's when work was scarce a number of residents of the district were in very poor circumstances. Many hampers of clothing and food were distributed to those in need. Much credit is due to the local mail carriers who so kindly delivered parcels to the country people.

During World War II quilts were made and sent to the Red Cross and many of the members did knitting and sewing for the Tofield Branch of the Red Cross of which Sister Hammond was convener. Approximately 170 parcels of fancy food, candy and gum were packed and sent to the boys overseas.

With the opening of the Tofield Hospital in 1947 a lot of sewing had to be done. Many of the Eastern Star members helped with this. Baby layettes have been donated to many needy mothers.

For years the Red Cross Drive and the Mobile Chest XRay were sponsored by Ionic Chapter.

Ionic Chapter contributed to the O.E.S. homes for senior members. These cottages are located in Lethbridge, Calgary, Edmonton and Grand Prairie. Donations are made to a number of charitable organizations in the province.

Eastern Star Membership in 1967 was 56 with 3 Charter Members still on the roll, Mrs. Blanche Hardy, Mrs. Leona Webb, and Mrs. Rose Dodds. The Worthy Matron is Mrs. Evelyn Nolan; the Worthy Patron, Mr. Neil Phillips.

The fortieth anniversary of Ionic Chapter was celebrated in 1968 with Mrs. Daisy Young as W.M.,and Neil Phillips as W.P.

# TOFIELD LEGION

On April 19th of 1968, The Tofield branch of the Royal Canadian Legion celebrated its 38th year of existence. Much can be said for this organization, which has suffered many reverses and yet stayed active. It has through the years done a great deal in making the town what it is, aiding and working with other organizations, sponsoring various events, etc. However, its main interest has been in keeping alive the memories fallen soldiers who lost their lives in battle.

Following is a brief history of the Legion, which will bring back many memories to old-timers, and will be of great interest to other readers.

On April 19, 1930, a group of men gathered in the old town hall and were addressed by Captain Hudson, provincial organizer of the Canadian Legion. As a result, comrades Bill Chapman and A.B. Clutterham were empowered to take the necessary steps to secure a charter. The charter was granted on April 28th, 1930, and Cde. Bill Chapman was elected president and Cde. Clutterham secretary. This was the beginning of the Tofield Legion with a membership of 35, holding meetings in the town hall, and social gatherings in the old curling rink waiting room where a piano was at hand.

The charter members of 15 included John.W. Morton,, A.P. Harrold., A.J.H. McCauley, A.B. Clutterham, A.E.F. Carey, R.F. Skitch, T. Cookson, H.W. Lovell, John W. Chapman, R.W. Pincott, E.W. Rogers, W.C. Morden, H.A. Kendall, C.J. Carr and J. (Doc) Simpson. They bought poppies which were sold for them by the Ladies of the I.O.D.E., they held church parades and generally carried on the functions of a Canadian Legion branch.

Then came the "Great Depression" in the"Hungry Thirties" when many of the most loyal members moved away. Some were forced to quit and the group became quite small. However, a few still carried on; Cde. Clutterham still ordered poppies and the I.O.D.E. ladies still sold them, and with the profits the secretary paid the "per capita tax" on the few loyal members remaining. With the balance they supplied comforts and extras to families of veterans on relief or in want.

Finally, the small group was forced to resign and return the charter. With $300 in the bank, which was earned in the G. W. V. A. days putting on dances and whist drives, and not wanting to send this money to Calgary, the group decided to build a cenotaph as a memorial to those in Tofield and district who had made the supreme sacrifice for Canada and the British Empire. Cde. Bill Chapman and John Letourneau drew up plans, similar to the Fort Scott Memorial. Cde. George Brace and H. Lovell (members of the town council) succeeded in getting a large donation from the town for this purpose. Deciding on the present location as best suited for the purpose, construction of the memorial took place using field stone collected from the farms in the Tofield district. The cairn was erected by Mr. Frank Hisey of Ross Creek, an old-time stonemason, and Fred Imler of the Gas Company donated pipe for the railing. The Boy Scouts cleaned out the bush in the trees at the back and were later given a lot just north of the legion where they erected the flagpole, making a place of beauty for a memorial cairn and park, with a 50-foot frontage, which has been very well kept up through the years, and certainly is a credit to Tofield.

Sunday, Nov. 12th, 1939, was destined to become the forerunner of many solemn gatherings at the new memorial which was unveiled that day by Major General W.A. Greisbach, who was the original C.O., of the 49th Edmonton Regiment.

Approximately five or six hundred citizens assembled to witness the ceremony which started off with a parade of Veterans of the Boer War and World War I, together with 20 members of the Canadian Active Army. The ceremony continued with an address by Gen. Greisbach, after which an invocation was given by Rev. D.K. Allan. A massed choir under the direction of L.A. Broughton, high school principal, led the singing, and wreaths were laid on behalf of the local community and Edmonton Branch of the Canadian Legion.

No doubt that day made a deep impression on the hearts and minds of all present.

During the war years that followed, the traditional duties were still kept alive by the fallen comrades in the mind of the community by ordering poppies which were sold by the faithful I. O. D. E. ladies. They kept up the parade and services at the cenotaph on Remembrance Day.

*Editor's note: We realize this account of the Tofield Branch of the Canadian Legion is far from complete but we were unable to obtain further information.. However, no account of the Legion should omit the name of Dick Mutlow whose contributions to the Legion and to Tofield were innumerable. The Legion has done much charitable work and has cooperated with other local organizations in civic projects.*

## JUNIOR FARM CLUBS

District Agriculturalist, Fred Newcombe from Vegreville, first organized junior farm clubs in the Tofield district in the early thirties. Grain, swine, and beef clubs were organized with the aim of improving the quality of grain and of breeding stock. The highlight of this era in junior farm club work was the achievement of Helmer Moen and Joe Kallal who, after winning a trip to the Royal Winter Fair, proceeded to win the beef-judging competition against competitors from all over Canada.

In 1943, under the leadership of Mr. Lars Olsen, a teacher at MacKenzie School, a beef club for the boys and girls of the MacKenzie and Tofield area was organized. In 1944, the two areas each formed its own club; and Melvin Walker and Happy Holmes were the leaders. Joint achievement days were held by these two clubs for the next three years. In 1947, Ryley and Kingman organized similar clubs and the MacKenzie and Tofield clubs merged into one. John Moore became leader of the Tofield Beef Club and in 1967 is still in that position.

The Kingman club dissolved after three years.

The Tofield Beef Club has some achievements to be proud of. In 1952, Reed Francis and Alan Warner won a trip to the Toronto Royal Winter Fair by placing first in the Alberta beef-judging competition. In the judging competitions at the Royal, they won third place.

In 1953, Jimmy Brown and Darrel Sutton won the Provincial beef-judging competition and went on to win the Canadian competition. In

1955, one of the winners in the provincial eliminations contest was Doris Ferguson of the Tofield Beef Club, who then went to the Royal. In 1962 Don Wood won the trip to the Royal by first winning the provincial eliminations contest. His interest in beef club work continued; in 1967 he is on the adult committee which guides the 4H club.

A grain club was organized in 1952 with Bert Kellicut, Alberta Wheat Pool Agent, as leader; it lasted several years before disbanding. A swine club organized under the leadership of Bob Wyllie and Earl Rose carried on for five years.

A girls' home economics club was active for a short period under the leadership of Mrs. Doug Murray.

In 1957, the Tofield 4H Beef Club organized the PeeWee section of the club. The new club was for children nine to eleven years. In 1967, the PeeWee club is ten years old and has seventeen members.

Other activities of the 4H clubs have been: public speaking, debating and conducting meetings. These activities are in addition to the main purpose of the clubs to learn to feed, judge, and care for livestock.

Achievement Day is held early in June. An auction is held; the services of an Edmonton auctioneer, Don Ball, for years were donated. Following the auction, a banquet is held at the Community Centre where awards are presented to winning members.

# TOFIELD COMMUNITY LEAGUE

The Tofield Community League in conjunction with the Women's Auxiliary, has been an extremely important organization in Tofield. It has an enviable record of supporting worthy causes, sponsoring cultural activities, and encouraging any project of value to either town or country.

A meeting was held in the Town Hall on January 20, 1944, for the purpose of forming an organization to take care of the further business in Tofield and district. After a lengthy discussion it was moved and seconded by A.B. Clutterham and Ray Coatta respectively, that the name of the organization be "The Tofield Community League."

Carried.

Mr. H. Chandler was elected chairman; Father Schmeltzer as vicepresident, Mr. G. McFadzean as secretary, Reed Burchard, A.B. Clutterham, F. Imler, Mr. McDonely and S. Sears as directors.

It was agreed that membership should be open to anyone who wanted to belong, provided they pay the membership fee of $1.00 for the year 1944.

Mr. A. Bigland was appointed to draw up a draft of constitution for the Tofield Community League. W. Bellamy, A. Bigland and G. Holmes were elected as membership committee.

On the motion of G. Allan and R. Coatta, the League was to sponsor a minstrel show.

At the end of this first meeting there were 85 paid up members.

The next meeting of the Tofield Community League was held on February 21, 1944 at the dining room of the Royal Alexandra Hotel. After the supper and a sing song led by A.B. Clutterham, an address on "The Future of Youth in Our Community" was given by Mr. Clutterham. On suggestion by Chairman Chandler, the secretary was instructed to write to the Students'Union of both High and Public Schools inviting each one to select a member who would represent them on the executive of the League.

A committee was appointed to investigate the possibility of ladies becoming members of the League, or asking if they would rather form an auxiliary to the League. The ladies preferred the latter. The League was soon in action, setting the pattern of the activities which were to follow over the years. From its inception, the T.C.L. has been anxious to serve the youth of our community. To this end, it for years paid half of the cost of running the skating rink each year with the Town of Tofield supplying the remaining cost.

At one of its early meetings, the League made provisions for a representative from the High School to be on its executive. Some of these representatives in early years were: Ralph Harrison, Bob Lovell and David Yakabuski.

The school Christmas concerts were held in the Memorial Hall as were the educational films held on alternate Fridays and attended by every pupil in school.

The Search for Talent Shows by the A.C.T. were sponsored here by the Community League. One outstanding winner, Alfred Myrhe "young old-timer fiddler", later went on to win second prize in a fiddlers' contest in Toronto. A welcome was extended to him by the League when he returned.

The Scouts were given the Memorial Hall rent-free, and also some necessary equipment paid for. PeeWee Hockey was also donated equipment from the League which had a committee to run the hockey.

In the realm of sponsoring sports, the League has been very active. The Memorial Hall was used for dancing, for badminton as well as the youth activities. The League paid expenses for Lloyd Rohloff and Muriel Bailey to take leadership courses in physical training at Red Deer. These two people then conducted classes in physical training in the Memorial Hall under the sponsorship of the League. After the Red Cross Society no longer sponsored the July lst Sports Day, the T.C.L. took it over.

The T.C.L. is interested in the problems of its farmer members too. Agricultural short courses have been sponsored on many occasions. Mechanics' schools and welders' schools have been assisted. The Calf Club Achievement Day has been assisted by the donation of a cup, by donations towards equipping the site of the calf auction, and by paying for the meals of the buyers.

When the Kallal and Wood families won the Master Farmer Award, banquets were tendered in their honour by the League.

In the cultural field, the Community League has sponsored an appearance in Tofield of the University mixed Chorus. The University players, have also presented evenings of drama under the League's sponsorship In 1949 and 1950, exhibitions of local handicrafts were held in the Memorial Hall with the League's cooperation. Each year, for many years, the League has arranged for a Christmas Carol Festival with all the local choirs participating. This is one of the highlights of the Christmas season.

The Tofield Library when revived in recent times, had its home in the Legion Hall. Since the Community Centre was finished in 1956, the meeting room has housed the library, rent-free.

The T.C.L. also made available, rent-free, the hall for band practice.

The T.C.L. has contributed to the social life of the town with the weekly movies, the fall carnivals and the card parties it has held.

One of the League's really big affairs was the welcome-home banquet for the veterans. It was held in the curling rink with the space for two sheets of ice planked in, and long, beautifully decorated tables set up.

To celebrate the Coronation of Queen Elizabeth II a suitable program was sponsored.

The League has given leadership to many vital community projects. Our hospital was sponsored by the League, which undertook the necessary publicity etc, since for some time after Dr. Law's departure in 1941 there had been no permanent resident doctor. The League on hearing of Dr. Freebury's intention of coming to Tofield finished a room for use as his temporary office. This was later the kitchen of the Memorial Hall.

Blood donor clinics were sponsored by the League and the Women's Auxiliary for years.

When the need for an ambulance became apparent it was the Community League which spearheaded the drive to obtain it, as well as donating $500.00 towards its purchase. Pasteurization of milk was also a League project as was the obtaining of a dentist for the community. The need for running water for the town was publicized by the League.

The League has also built two community halls in twenty-five years of its existence. Building even one community hall is an achievement for an organization but the Tofield Community League has built two of them, both ornaments to the town.

The first, The Memorial Hall, was the dream of the community League in its early days. The moving spirits on the executive were Herb Chandler and George McFadzean. A carnival held in the old Variety Theatre furnished the League with $800.00. If this amount seems a fantastic amount to be raised at one event, it should be remembered that road crews and seismograph crews were stationed in town. The League decided to go ahead building a hall on a lot on which the town gave the League a ninety-nine year lease for one dollar.

The building committee was composed of A.C. Dodds, Bill Davison and Joe Kallal. The day the foundations were poured, it was cold and raw. Bill Davison hauled water from Shonts for the cement George McFadzean accompanied him to help work the pump. When this supply ran out Fred Imler emptied the Gas. Co. wells to finish the job. Reed Burchard, Arnold Swift, and Hans Christensen were also on the cementpouring detail. Some of the workers recall that while nine men worked mightily, there were eighteen sidewalk supervisors whose comments were: "You'll never build it, boys." How wrong they were proved to be!

When the foundations were ready, the construction of the frame building began. A.C. Dodds was the head carpenter and in charge of securing crews for the necessary volunteer labour were Reed Burchard, Arnold Swift and Hans Christensen. The trusses for the roof were secured from a commercial firm but the rest of the building was to the credit of local volunteer labour.

Finally came the opening night. A variety show was presented. The M.C. was of course, to be Tofield's own Horace McHeffey. The show was billed as "the greatest show under one roof." Thomas Jacobs says the title stretched the truth a bit; the final roof was not yet on. The weather man took cognizance of this fact and the rain came pelting down on the unfinished roof. Enthusiasm, was not dampened; the new hall was full and the show was good. Everyone remembers the solos sung so beautifully by Margaret Dodds (now Mrs. Roy Brown) daughter of Mr. and Mrs. A.C. Dodds.

Later a second minstrel show was held (the first one had been in the Variety Theatre). Once again, Horace McHeffey took a leading part. People still remember his leading act and how it startled the children. Also remembered is Art Francis' neat trick of laughing so heartily that he doubled over with mirth—doubled over far enough to see his lines for the show which he had carefully placed on the floor. The show had a large cast and "brought the house down."

Original members of the T.C.L. remember that the Memorial Hall had the distinction of being built before the blue prints were made. A plan was all that was required to build the uncomplicated building, but to get a theatre license, blue prints had to be registered at the Provincial Architect's office. Due to the combined efforts of Blake Clutterham, Floyd Baker, MLA., Walter Bellamy and a willing draftsman, the blue prints made the deadline.

The T.C.L. preferred to go on a "pay-as-you-go" basis with the hall but when it became necessary to have the theatre seats installed, a larger sum of money and loans were solicited from members of the community. These were later retired by lot up to a given amount each year.

Finally the kitchen of the hall was furnished and equipped. The W.A.T.C.L. had, of course, been most active all these years but the kitchen was their special project. Another project was buying and making the beautiful wine coloured velvet curtains for the stage.

A cloakroom was furnished and the Legion finished the space over the furnace for their own use.

Theatre equipment was installed and movies were shown every Friday and Saturday. Among the operators of the projector were Art Elliott, George McFadzean, Jack Whyte and Hans Christensen.

The Memorial Hall served the community well for eight years but on the evening of March 20, 1955, disaster struck. The hall burned down. By the time the fire was discovered, the whole inside was aflame, and nothing was saved except the spirit that built it in the first place. Next day the radio reported the Community League president Bill Davison voicing the feeling of the League by saying, "We will build again."

The officers on whose shoulders fell the burden of what was to be an extremely active year were President Bill Davison; VicePresident, Conrad Patterson, Secretary, George McFadzean; Treasurer, Neil Wilkinson; Directors, Thomas Jacobs, George Arnett, Lorimer Hunter, A.C. Dodds; Theatre Committee, Jack Whyte, Art Elliott, George McFadzean, H.E. Christensen, A.C.Dodds. The day after the fire a meeting was held in the Curling Rink. It was a unanimous decision to rebuild the hall and a new building committee was formed to carry out the task. This was composed of: W. Davison, A.D. Dodds,

D.W. Jacobs, G. McFadzean, A. Swift.

The insurance from the hall was $38,800 so this time the task of building was a bit easier. Watson (Tofield) Ltd. were the contractors and by December 13 the hall was ready for the ceremonial opening. Well, almost ready. The women's league members were washing and waxing floors into the small hours of the night, while the men's league members assembled theatre seats which had been delayed in transit. The weather was bitter cold, many roads were blocked but on December 14 came the grand formal opening.

The following news item was read over the radio station on the morning of December 14,1955: "Premier E.C. Manning will officially open Tofield's new $70,000.00 community centre this afternoon. Construction of the new fireproof and steel reinforced structure was started in March, 1955, immediately after the fire which destroyed the previous centre. The frontage of the completed structure is 70 feet wide and is finished in imitation marble. The auditorium, including the stage is 50 feet by 100 feet and also incorporates a large meeting room. Other rooms include a kitchen, a cloak room and a lobby. There is in the auditorium seating capacity for more than three hundred persons. Its 35mm motion picture equipment is of the latest design and is capable of showing vistavision and large screen as well as regular pictures. The new hall will serve all branches of Tofield's activities and business, religious or charitable organizations."

The great day arrived, Premier E.C. Manning cut the ribbon to declare the centre officially open. On the stage were the President, Bill Davison, Premier E. C. Manning; Senator Stambaugh; Earl Hardy, M.L.A, Mr. H.A. Pike, Superintendent of Schools; Conrad Patterson, Mayor of Tofield; George McFadzean; Howard Watson, and representatives of the firms who had serviced the hall. Congratulatory speeches and telegrams were the order of the day. T.V. cameras photographed the tightly packed hall.

After introductory remarks by Mr. Pike, Superintendent of Holden School Division, Premier Manning presented Barbara Phillips with the Governor-General's medal awarded for the highest marks in the Grade IX examination the previous June. Other gifts were presented to Barbara by Mrs. Thomas Jacobs, president of the Women's League, Charles Sears, Holden School Division Trustee and Jack Lampitt, the Grade IX teacher.

The P.P. C.L.I. band was in attendance. In the evening they gave a concert which will long be remembered.

The following two evenings featured dancing and the annual Christmas Carol Festival and the new Community Centre was initiated into serving the community as the Memorial Hall had done.

The July 1st celebration of 1955 was held in conjunction with the Golden Jubilee Committee, this being the year of Alberta's Golden Jubilee. A parade, barbecue, museum and Old Timers' tent were the features of the day. Dr. W.H. Swift formerly of Tofield was the guest speaker. The dance at night was to be held in the Ryley Community Hall as the new Community Hall was under construction.

The Tofield Library was given the use of the meeting room in the Centre rent free. The proceeds from the sale of the booklet "A Concise History of Tofield and District", written by the Jubilee Committee, Rev. K. Iwaasa, Rev. V.P. Cole, Mrs. Grace Phillips and Mrs Aileen Elliott, were donated to buy a library table and chairs for the library.

The backdrop for the stage in the Tofield Community Centre is the work of Joe Chubaty and Dirk DeFrenne. Mr. Pete Kuc, with beautiful flower beds, has beautified the front of the Community Centre.

1959 was an important year for the League.

Mr. H.A. Pike was the guest speaker at the T.C.L. annual meeting in January stressing the need of good relationship between school and community. The 1959 executive were: Norman Glover, President, Bill Finn, Secretary; Horace Sellers, treasurer; Mrs. J. E. Stinson gave the library report, stating that the Tofield Library now qualified for a $200. grant from the Dept. of Extension.

During the year, a series of card parties was held to repair calf pens on the exhibition grounds at the request of the Calf Clubs. A visit of the University Mixed Chorus was sponsored; a Band Concert was given by the Tofield Band under the leadership of Rex Boyles to commemorate Jubilee Year; the annual community auction was held; Donkey Baseball was brought to town and with the help of the Tofield Golden Jubilee

Committee, this year, the Community League actively supported the yearlong celebration of the Golden Jubilee of the Town of Tofield. The "Tofield Mercury" recorded the following account of the final event of that year.

"Members of the Women's Auxiliary to the Community League arranged the supper to which all attending contributed. Head table guests included: Father Purcell, Mr. & Mrs. Harold Weatherill, Mrs. Edith Rogers, Rev. and Mrs. S. Bell.,Dr. and Mrs.W.H. Freebury, Mr. & Mrs. H.A. Pike, Mr. and Mrs. Norman Glover, Mr. and Mrs. A. Maxwell and Mark Ferguson.

Mrs. Edith Rogers, daughter of Dr. Tofield, after whom the town was named, cut the three-tiered Jubilee cake made by Mrs. Mabel Boyles and decorated by Mrs. Norman Stauffer. Rev. Bell, Chairman, introduced the people who had come that year to live in Tofield. Mr. Glover, president of the Community League, welcomed the newcomers. Mr. H.A. Pike, Superintendent of Schools for the County of Beaver, replied.

Mrs. Grace Phillips was presented with a bouquet of long-stemmed red roses by Dr. Freebury, as a token of appreciation for her work done as Press Secretary for the Jubilee Committee.

Selections by the Tofield Bank introduced the program. A pageant produced and narrated by Mrs. Phillips employed about fifty children and in different scenes showed Chief Ketchamoot (after whom Ketchamoot Creek and district are named) and his Indian tribe around the campfire; Indian war dancing; Robert Logan's trading post; square dancing to the Spilsted orchestra; choir practice at the home of George Cookson, Sr. pioneer sports enthusiasts returning after a successful day in Vegreville; Dr. and Mrs. Tofield at work; Tofield town moving to its three different town sites; Tofield's first election.

Charles Kallal's films of the events of Jubilee Year completed the evening's entertainment."

During the years, the Community League has sponsored both adult education courses and the Red Cross swimming lessons for the children.

As well as those mentioned previously, two men who gave greatly of their time and talents to the League during their terms as president were W.B.Worton, partner in the I.G.A. Store and John Baergen, manager of the Tofield Co-op Store.

In 1967, the League suffered the loss, through death of its president, Lionel Borton. The remainder of the term was filled out by J.C. Lampitt,with Peter Nickel as secretary and Hans Christensen as treasurer, a post he had filled efficiently for many years.The League cooperated with the Tofield Centennial Committee in every way to make the Centennial year a success.

The 1968 executive consisted of :. J. C. Lampitt, president; Ed. Watson, vicepresident; Father Scriven as secretary, and Rita Halverson as treasurer.

The debt on the Community Centre has been reduced to less than $10,000.

# WOMEN'S AUXILIARY TO THE TOFIELD COMMUNITY LEAGUE

The Women's Auxiliary to the Tofield Community League was organized in the Town Hall in October 27, 1946. Its first executive consisted of Mrs. Ed Kallall Jr., President; Mrs. H. Bowick, VicePresident; Mrs. C.Hallett., Secretary Treasurer.

The main objective of the W.A.T.C.L. was to assist the men's league, particularly in raising money.

Reading between the lines of the organization, one senses that this was an exceptionally energetic group of women. In the first two years of the auxiliary's existence it had supported a Superfluity Shop; held raffles; held Christmas Jamborees for the school children; in conjunction with the annual Christmas Concert donated impressive sums to the men's league; sponsored an amateur night, also the University Players; bought a piano for the hall; ran a popcorn stand at the carnival, equipped the Memorial Hall kitchen with dishes, cutlery and cupboards; sponsored Mrs. Stinson's annual music recital; organized the Cancer Fund drive and taken tickets at the show part of the time.

In 1940, the W.A.T.C.L. took over the refreshment booth at the Exhibition Grounds on July lst. This particular enterprise has expanded into the serving of meals at the Annual Sports Day.

Since Tofield at that time did not have running water, many entries in the minutes concerned the securing and storing of water for the various events catered for in the hall. This is one aspect of the "good old days" for which no one will have any nostalgia.

Soon the W.A.T.C.L. secured a popcorn machine. This was a real revenue-securing addition to the Hall. The women took (and still take) turns at popping the corn for the shows. A new booth was built on the Fair Grounds for the exclusive use of the W.A.T.C.L.

Over the years, Mrs. Irma Francis has been president for the largest number of terms. Mrs. Hazel Patterson holds the same record for the secretary's office.

Donations were made to the band, to the Coronation Committee and a $50.00 Scholarship was set aside to be awarded annually to the Grade IX student with the highest marks in the Departmental exams. This has been won by Lorraine Lee, Barbara Phillips, Vera Tiedemann, Glenda Patterson, Lorraine Allan, Elaine Sorrel, Tom Christensen and Ruth Dickson.

A sizeable donation was made to the Ambulance Fund. Lunch was served for the opening of the new Bank of Montreal. In fact, the history of the W.A.T.C.L. is one long series of lunches, banquets, receptions, dances catered for. It proved an effective way to raise money, for in addition to equipping the kitchen, and check room in the hall, the beautiful red velvet curtains were bought and made by the Auxiliary for the stage.

Just when the W.A.T.C.L. had begun to feel able to let up a bit in their efforts, the Memorial Hall burned down and the next few years read like a carbon copy of the first few years. Another piano, more curtains for the stage, more dishes, cutlery and tables for catering, more stoves and cupboards for the kitchen, another popcorn machine, and now stacking tables for banquets were among their projects. In 1959 Mrs. Mabel Boyles was president of the W.A.T.C.L.; Mrs. Ingrid Jacobs, vicepresident; Mrs. Hazel Patterson, secretary, and Mrs.

Mildred Watson, treasurer. At no time had the group been a large one, but it had certainly been an effective one, as its record of service shows.

Due to declining members this group disbanded in December, 1964.

## TOFIELD LIONS' CLUB

Tofield Lions' Club, a branch of Lions International was organized in Tofield in 1953, and held its Charter Night in May, 1955, at Lakeview Pavilion.

Clifford Patterson was the first President and Harry Wilkie first SecretaryTreasurer. Although many changes have taken place in the membership in the life of the Club, three Charter Members still belong and membership remains at the original level. Lion Henry Paege a former member of Tofield, was a member of the Chipman sponsoring Club. Tofield Lions' Club is justly proud of projects in Tofield, such as operating of the skating rink, the Museum which was a brainchild of Gordon Garford, the present Lions' Playground and equipment supplied therefore. The Club has also assisted Tofield Community League on July lst Sports Days, and given help to other organizations and individuals at various times.

## TOFIELD GUN CLUB

*The material for this article was made available by Alan Warner.*

The Tofield Gun Club was first formed in the year 1958. After the idea had been "kicked around" for a month or so the club was formed with the following executive elected: President, John Hutchison; Vice President, Gordon Garford; and Secretary Treasurer Alan Warner.

John Hutchison., who was the Calgary Power assistant in Tofield at that time was the prime mover in the organization of the club, which was known at that time as "The Tofield Rifle Club". Some of the first members were: Bill Friesen, Earl Brown, Arny Klassen, Allan

McAllister, George Thiessen, Dave Morris, Peter Swizinski and Bob Nahrebeski.

The club began as strictly a smallbore target shooting club, using the facilities of the CIL Dominion Marksmen awards program for sporting rifles. The first range was a bend of the creek, directly north of the house on the A. Warner farm. The range was small, about 25 yards long and 10 yards wide, and was fenced with snowfencing to keep cattle out. A wooden shooting platform was built at the firing line, but the members soon found this was unsatisfactory due to the builtin wobble from the movements of the shooters.

The first junior club was formed that year, also, with an enrollment of about 25 youngsters. Larry Murray was the first winner of the Northwestern Utilities Trophy for the best shot in the Junior Club.

A Ladies' Nite Shoot was held that first summer, with Frances Garford winning the honours as the best shot amongst the fair sex. Another social gathering was held in late summer when the members and their wives gathered to say goodbye to the Hutchisons at a wiener roast. At this wiener roast the club honoured their first president by making him an Honorary Lifetime member, in recognition of his efforts in organizing the club.

## 1959

One of the more notable events of 1959 was the evening that some adventurous member brought his shotgun out to the range and when the light became too dim for rifle shooting, a few lumps of dirt and the odd "cow chip" provided some primitive aerial targets. Sparked by this experiment, a Western Practice trap was secured from the Bardo community where it had been used many years before. Since the club no longer was confined to rifle shooting, the name was changed to the present "Tofield Gun Club".

The first organized trapshoot was held that fall and the scores were even worse than might have been expected, as the loaders had a mania for what the shooters came to know as grasscutters, thrown at a 45Th angle and at an altitude of 6 inches.

# 1960

The year 1960 opened with the news that the club would be forced to move its range because of the noise factor. A search of the district disclosed a ravine about one-half mile from town that seemed usable. After securing the blessing of C. F. Kallal, the owner, the members went to work with a will; brushing, levelling and building a trap house of railroad ties.

Most of the summer was spent working, but there were a few shoots, notably some interclub visits with Viking. These trips to Viking were enjoyed by all who attended, and at one of the first held in Tofield, Jack McArthur of Viking shot the first 25 straight at trap on Tofield grounds.

The club secured a building formerly used as a school, from the County of Beaver, and at the same time acquired "squatters' rights" on the lot on 7th Ave. East, where it was located at that time. This building became a clubhouse and indoor range. A hole was cut in the back wall and a range tunnel was constructed of railroad ties. A pile of dirt backed the end wall to stop stray shots. The bullet trap used was constructed by Bill Friesen and N. E. Stauffer using heavy gasoline casing as a basis. This proved to be a very effective and adequate bullet trap.

The acquisition of the building and the new range seemed to be the cohesive force necessary to really start the club on its way. Since 1960, it has become much more stable and effective in its operation.

# 1961

The executive for this year consisted of Bob Nahrebeski as President, J. B. Warner, Vice President; Dick Whyte, SecretaryTreasurer, and Range Officer, Alan Warner.

A social evening featuring slides and movies was held in April, this type of evening being one of the most favoured type of socialto be held since that time. Club crests were designed and made of leather by Larry Willson for the members.

## 1962

In this year the club became incorporated under the Societies Act of Alberta. This was also the first year that permits were issued to club members to carry pistols to the club range, and CIL pistol competitions were entered.

Executive for this year was: President, A. Klassen; 1st Vice President., A. Warner; 2nd Vice President, G. Thiessen; SecretaryTreasurer, E.L. Willson; Directors R. Nahrebeski, G. Garford, and W. Friesen.

Dues were raised to $3.00, and range fee for non members set at 50 cents per day. Then at the Annual Meeting in November of that year the dues were again raised to $5.00 per year and family memberships set at $5.50.

The first game supper was held in the club building with each member bringing one guest. It proved very successful. A turkey shoot was held as a means of raising operating funds.

## 1963

In this year the old Western practice trap was retired and a regulation trap purchased from the Edmonton Gun Club.

A wall was built in the building to separate the club room from the firing line in an attempt to reduce the noise problem. Jackets were secured from CeeJay Mfg. in Edmonton.

A letter of protest was sent to several organizations in regard to roadside brush spraying, as it was felt that this was detrimental to game bird chick populations.

# 1962

The "Digger" type Australian Army hat was adopted as official club regalia, and the first shipment was received.

Mr. and Mrs. George Kidd were guests at the Game Supper, to which the ladies were also invited for the first time. In preparation for this the walls and ceiling of the clubroom received their first coat of calsomine in many years.

The executive for this year was unchanged from 1962

# 1964

The executive for this year was: President ,Norman Stauffer; lst Vice President, A. Warner; 2nd Vice President, Ray Henriksen; Secretary, E. L. Willson; Directors, Friesen, Garford and Holtsbaum.

This spring again saw the club searching for an outdoor range. A location three miles north of the Creamery was chosen and brushed off, courtesy of A. Klassen and the Northwestern Utilities Caterpillar. The trap house was moved and rebuilt of concrete blocks, and both 100 yd. and 20 yd. ranges were set up.

The club also participated in the Gun Show held by the ASCCA in Edmonton.

The club also took an active part in lobbying against proposed federal legislation restricting the ownership of guns.

The First Annual Black powder Shoot was held July 5th and was moderately successful.

Two small .22 rifles were purchased for use by Junior members.

# 1965

The following executive was elected: President, W.Friesen; lst Vice President, G. Garford; 2nd Vice President, Glen Reil; Range Officer, A. Klassen; Secretary L. Willson; Directors, Harry Huser, N. E.

Stauffer and A. Warner.

A very successful black powder shoot was held at which the NUL trophy for stakecutting teams was presented for the first time.

The club members began to show up as winners in black powder shoots throughout the province and interest in shooting and old guns increased considerably in this year.

The Tofield club was featured in a U. S. magazine in June of this year as an example of what with limited funds can do, with full support of members.

# 1966

The 1966 executive consisted of Glen Reil, President; Ray Hendriksen, 1st VicePresident; A. Warner, 2nd VicePresident; L. Willson, SecretaryTreasurer; Roy Murray, Range Officer; and G. Garford, A. Klassen, and Jack Haise as Directors.

This year the club was on the move again, only this time it was the building. A foundation was poured directly east of the skating rink on the fair grounds and the members managed to skid the club house onto it by means of the county graders. All labour was volunteer, and the club managed the difficult job in a minimum of time, under the capable direction of Gordon Garford and Bill Friesen. The inner dividing wall was removed and a concrete or wooden tunnel is to be built on the rear of the building as an indoor range.

A ten-year lease on the outdoor range was secured from the owner, Stanley Schacker. A bench rest was added to the outdoor facilities, as well as a primitive running deer target holder.

The club was complimented at the annual Blcack Powder Shoot by Mr. Jimmy Allen of Hargwynne, Alta. He stated that in all his years of competition in this field, Tofield ran the best shoot, and thanked the club for the invitation on behalf of all the visiting shooters. As Mr. Allen has been shooting these old guns for the past sixty years, the club was very grateful for his words.

Plans were laid in late fall for the 1967 Black powder Shoot to become a Centennial shoot with expanded prize lists and a change in competitions, in hopes of making it a memorable occasion, to celebrate Canada's birthday.

The Warner-Thiessen Memorial Trophy for club competition was purchased. It was awarded to Gordon Garford as the best allaround shot in the club., with Arny Klassen being a very close runnerup.

In the eliminations for this trophy, George Thiessen became the first Tofield member to break 25 straight at trap.

# THE TOFIELD HISTORICAL SOCIETY

The Tofield Historical Society was formed on April 8, 1961, on a motion of Mrs. Jack Appleby and J. R. Francis at a meeting of interested persons held in the Tofield Town Hall. The first slate of officers was comprised of: Harold Schultz, president; Conrad Patterson, vicepresident; Mrs. Grace Phillips, secretary; Mrs. Edna Bowick, treasurer. The directors were Mrs. Mary Tiedemann, Mr. George Arnett, Mr. James Francis, and Stanley Dunham.

The newly formed society was registered according to the provisions of the Society Act after a constitution had been prepared and adopted.

In October, the Amisk Creek building located on the Tofield School grounds had been donated to the Historical Society by the County of Beaver for use as a museum. The chairs used by the original council of the Town of Tofield were donated to the Society by the Tofield community League in whose care they had been.

Display counters were donated by Graham Allan, Jack Whyte, and Watson's Ltd.

Artifacts of pioneer life were contributed by many local residents; display cases for pictures made by Jim Francis; arrangements made of various classifications of articles and improvements made to the museum by Harold Schults, W. McHeffey and W. Lancaster.

During the years since its inception, the Historical Society has taken an active part in the annual Dominion Day celebration sponsored by the Tofield Community League by acting as hosts to old-timers, presenting them with identifying ribbons and serving them coffee. In addition to this service, the Historical Society has always had an entry in the parade and has had an exhibition of pictures and artifacts of pioneer days on display. This exhibition has been much displayed and has been very much enjoyed. Mrs. Mary Tiedemann has donated some beautiful handmade quilts to the Society; these have been raffled to the financial gain of the Society.

A guest book in the museum has been signed by visitors from near and far as well as by many groups of school children who have visited the museum as part of their school programs.

The officers for the Society remained the same until 1966, with the addition of Dave Heidebrecht and Wm. Lancaster as directors. In 1966, J.R. Francis replaced Grace Phillips as secretary while S.J. Sears and C. Appleby became directors. In 1967, E. Wood became a director. Mrs. Bowick moved away; the treasurer's duties were taken over by the secretary.

In 1967, the Society decided to publish a book containing a written and pictorial history of Tofield. It was felt that this would be a valuable project, since it would form a permanent record of our town and district.

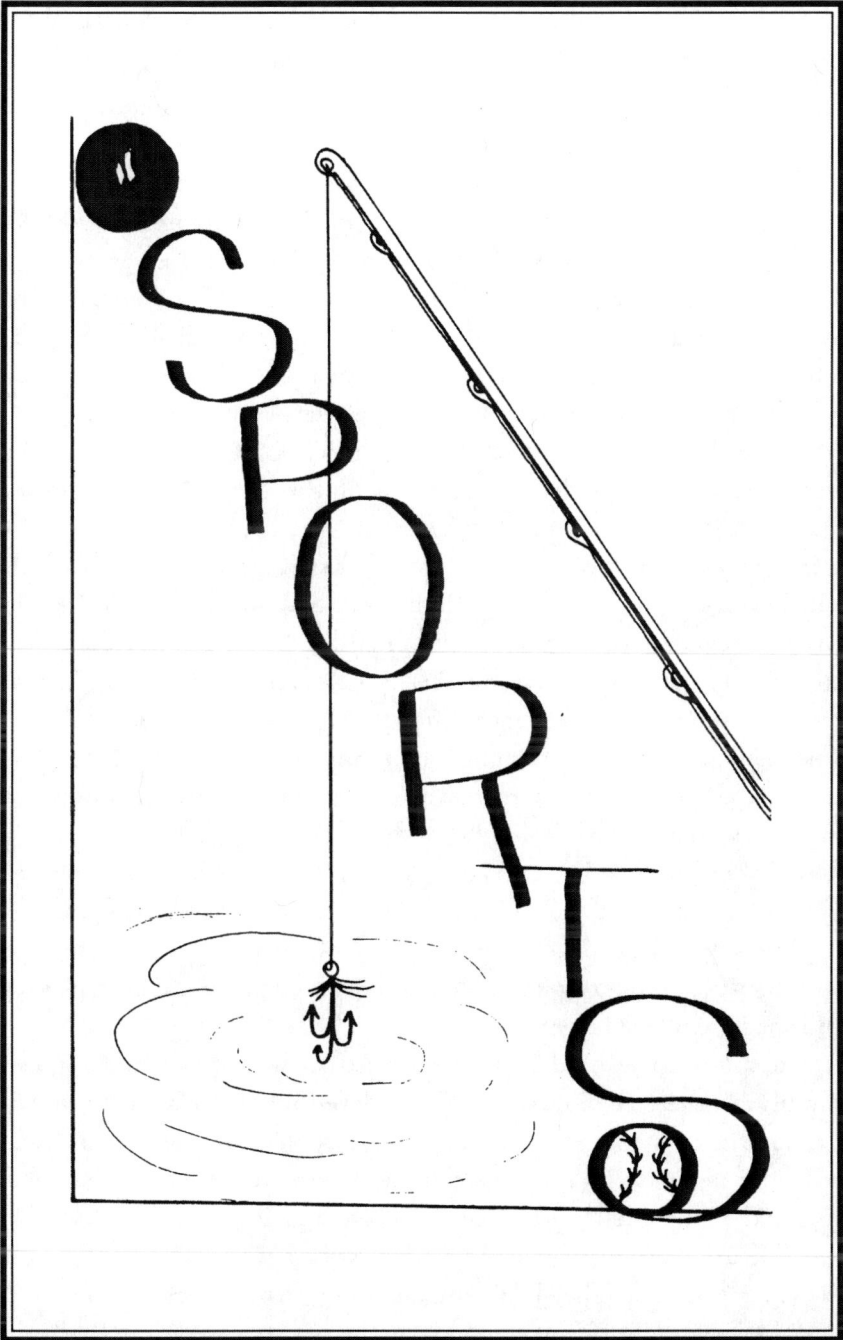

# FABULOUS HOCKEY TEAM OF YEARS GONE BY

Our pioneers took their recreation seriously. It was a community affair and thoroughly enjoyed by every one.

Hockey was a very popular game. We have a picture of the first organized hockey team who were E. A. H. L. champions of 1909. In the picture [not available] are to be seen: P. Wimbles, G. Haines, Dr. Tofield, W. Spilstead, H. K. Adams, N. C. Legge (bank manager here then), Don Cameron, Stewart Hall, A. D. Ferguson, H. E. Diamond. This team was apparently highly successful and led to the formation of Tofield's most famous hockey team, the Silver Seven in 1910.

Three local men, Harvey Adams, "Shorty" Carter and Jim Hannan were responsible for the organization of the Silver Seven. Gordon Haines was imported from Chipman and Stanley George brought in from the farm. Both were assured jobs that they might play for Tofield. Mr. Stanley George said that Herb Diamond was the fastest skater he had ever seen and lent great power to the Silver Seven. The other members of the team in 1910 were: Oliver Letourneau, Gordon Haines, Herb Diamond, Stanley George, Jim Charlesworth, and George Bisset. The manager was Harry Rogers. Jim Hannan was a sponsor of the team and was kindness itself to the players. He owned the Royal Alexandra Hotel which still stands in the original place of its building. Here Stanley George and Gordon Haines stayed. Mr. and Mrs. Hannan were like parents to the boys. Their small son, Bud, was the team's mascot.

Hockey in those days was a seven man 60 minute affair. There were no substitutes and no replacements. It was tough going and both players and spectators loved it.

In spite of the hard playing required to win games under these conditions, there were no fights ("We played for the sake of the game, not for the money") and few accidents. Stanley George got his nose broken in a game with the University of Alberta team but Dr. Hamond soon fixed it up and no permanent damage was done.

The uniforms were green and white with a white T for Tofield on the green sweaters. They had pennants in the same colors.

No one seems to remember who the referees were but the little silver handbell they used in controlling the game is in the possession of Mr. Rufus Wilson. When up, the silver bell was idle and the Silver Seven were no more.

Of the 1910 team, four members are still alive. Oliver Letourneau, Gordon Haines and Stanley George are gone. The first two died in accidents. Letourneau died when his car left the road at Lindbrook; Haines, according to reports, was found in the Saskatchewan River at St. Paul with his hands and feet wired together. Ward Somers, who is a druggist at Devon, and Stanley George who later played hockey with the Victoria Cougars in 1918 19 with Lester and Frank Patrick and who lived for many years on his Ministik farm, were the sources of information for this article.

# THE MILLIONAIRES HOCKEY TEAM

The history of "The Tofield Millionaires," another well known hockey team of the early 1920's, was given to the Mercury by Grace Phillips, secretary of the Historical Society. It is taken from a record of Tofield's hockey activities kept by Roy Lee.

When the Silver Seven hockey team was at the height of its fame, Roy Lee was a sportsminded youngster who haunted the old covered hockey rink. Here, Roy Lee watched admiringly as his special heroes,Gordon Haines and Herb Diamond, as well as his cousins Herb and Bob Lee, won the plaudits of Tofield hockey fans as they demonstrated one scintillating play after another. In these days, Roy says, the rink would be packed to the rafters; excitement and betting both ran high. Unfortunately, the excitement subsided as the team disbanded when three of its star players, Gordon Haines, Jack and Herb Lee enlisted in the Canadian army.

In 1918, George Bissett, Herb and Bob Lee came back to Tofield, and a new hockey team was formed, with Jim Hannan as manager. This team was known as the "Tofield Millionaires." This intriguing title was a reference to the amount of money it took to feed the members of the hockey team while enroute to games on the train. They were young, healthy and hungry, and the diner service on the CNR profited accordingly.

George Bissett, who had been one of the younger members of the Silver Seven, now played defense with Roy Lee for the Millionaires for two or three years. Roy says Bissett also blocked as many shots on goal as the goalie. Games with the Bashaw team boasted two former members of the Silver Seven, Jim Charlesworth and Smokey McDonald.

The Millionaires were members of the Gas Line League which was comprised of teams from Wainwright, Viking, Holden, Ryley and Tofield. The "Dawson Cup" was put up for competition but, though the Millionaires won it several times, it never came into their permanent possession. Several games were played against Camrose, and Roy Lee reports that the Rose City had a never-ending source of players in the persons of the Hanson brothers.

The Millionaires disbanded in 1924. Roy Lee then played on the Camrose team for some exhibition games in 1924 and in 1925 was offered a job in Camrose which carried the stipulation that he play hockey for Camrose. The Camrose team, he says, was a hired team, sponsored by the town, and to whose support Mr. H. Boggs, a Hereford breeder and Roy's employer, contributed heavily. At the end of the year, Mr. Boggs was $800 in the red. However, the team won the Killam cup, so presumably Mr. Boggs felt well repaid.

Roy Lee later returned to Tofield and played defense with the Millionaires, who were reorganized under the management of Mr. W. Worton, late editor of the Tofield Mercury.

Mr. Lee has recalled and listed the hockey players of the Tofield area from the famous Silver Seven era until 1940.

## SILVER SEVEN TEAM: 1909-10

H. K. Adams (manager), Wm. Spilsted, D. R. Cameron, G. M. Haines, H. E. Diamond, N. Sutherland, J. Lee Jr., D. Ferguson, C. Jamieson.

# SILVER SEVEN: 1910-11

J. D. Hannan (manager), J. Charlesworth, Stanley George, G. M. Haines, H. E. Diamond, G. M. Bissett, J. O. Letourneau, Herb Lee.

# SILVER SEVEN: 1911-12

H. E. Rogers (manager), J. A. Charlesworth,, J. W. Saners, G. M. Haines, G. B. Bissett, Herb Lee, Bob Lee, J. H. McDonald.

Mr. Lee comments that the seventh man was very important; he was known as "point." He played any position and was in most plays. All players were 60-minute men.

# TOFIELD MILLIONAIRES 1919-1924

Jim Hannan (manager); Norman Smith, George Bissett, (goal); Dr. Bain, Stan Livingston, Roy Lee, (defense); Bert McIntosh, Archie Pruden, Harold Weatherill, Bob Lee, Bud Hannan, Scotty Lee (wings); Laurie Scott, John Letourneau (centre). "Point" was dropped from this team., but an extra line of forwards was carried. The caretaker during this period was "Shorty" Carter; referees were George Agnew and A. B. Clutterham. Laurie Scott turned professional and played with the Saskatoon Quakers in the "Old Pro" League.

Roy Lee recalls some of the highlights of hockey in the early '20' s.

In 1920, the team journeyed to Camrose for a game. Billy Webb drove one of the cars, a sporty Model T Ford complete with side curtains. These were not too adequate protection against the temperature, which registered fifty below zero. The frost in the air reduced the visibility to the point that the players, let alone the few fans present, could scarcely see the goals. Players and fans alike had frozen toes and heels as mementos of the game.

All these discomforts were not enough apparently. Coming home, the driver missed the corner at Kingman cemetery, where they should have turned, and they drove around the long way, by the site of the present Grand Forks Community Centre. At least the Model T kept on chugging away till Tofield was reached!

## THE THIRD TEAM 1925-1939

Mr. W. Worton (manager); Dan Craig, Norman Glover, Jack Whyte (wing); Les Glover, Herb Martin (defence); Sid Worton, "Crow" Worton, Lee Burnett, Jack Bowick (forward). Referee, Bob Whyte; caretaker, Bearisto.

## THE TOFIELD CURLING CLUB

The history of the Tofield Curling Club really begins in Vegreville. In fact, it could even be credited to the Liberal party, and this is the reason:

While Tofield was still very young, several prominent citizens., among them Mayor J. Letourneau, Mr.Cress Mr. Emery, and Mr. McCauley, journeyed to Vegreville for a Liberal Convention.

Their Vegreville hosts, wishing to entertain them, and no doubt impress them, took them to see the "roarin' game" as played in Vegreville.

The Tofielders' reactions were immediate and emphatic. Whatever Vegreville could do, Tofield could do as least as well! They were determined that Tofield should have a curling rink. And that is how it all began.

A Curling Club was formed in 1909 with Dr. McQueen as its president and A.J.H. McCauley as secretary. Mr. Ben Barkwell had built a covered skating rink on the northwest corner of the Fair Grounds. This was the first covered skating rink on this railway line and to give it further distinction, a sheet of curling ice was now added in the form of a lean-to on the north side. Later another sheet of ice was added and curling was off to a flying start. Mr. Barkwell then sold the rink to the town for the sum of $500.

Some of the men who began the curling traditions of Tofield were: Charlie Cress, the first station agent here; A.J.H. McCauley, secretary of the town; Clarence Jamieson, druggist; J. 0. Letourneau, first mayor of the town; Mark Ferguson, council member; Jack Bowick, George McLaughlin; W.D. Swift whose son, Arnold, and grandson, Donald, carry on the family tradition; John Warner, who was such an enthusiast that he often walked in from his farm to curl when the roads were too bad to drive; M. Emery; Lem Abbott, pioneer barber; Cap Lee of baseball fame; Roland Murray, who was prominent in Tofield's sports; J.G. Jobb, proprietor of the iron foundry; Chris Hammond, tinsmith; Dr. Morrison and Dr. McQueen, veterinarians; John Morton, who for years was a one-man draw committee; E.W. Rogers, pioneer merchant; J.W. Carter, auctioneer; Rev. Alex Stewart, Presbyterian minister; John Lee; Wm. Lee; Ward Somers, druggist, and no doubt others of whom we have no tangible record.

The first caretaker of the rink was Bill Bowick. In addition to the usual duties of a caretaker and ice maker, he had some extras. Light for the rink was supplied by gasoline lights which were fed by pipes running the length of the rink. It was no small task to keep these lights burning brightly. At times the lights, according to one veteran curler, would grow so dim that the curlers could not see the skip's broom.

At bonspiel time, the two sheets of ice proved inadequate for the 20 to 25 rinks entered. So two extra sheets were laid out on the adjacent covered skating rink.

In 1926, curling entered a new era in Tofield. Here the name of J.W. Chapman must be honored, for it was largely due to his enthusiasm and efforts that a four-sheet covered curling rink was built a block east of the Royal Alexandra Hotel. He had promoted the idea for several years and through donations, social events auctions, and volunteer labor, the rink was finally erected. In fact, as one of Mr. Chapman's contemporaries said, "Anything short of theft or murder, John Chapman would do to raise a dollar for the rink."

The first bonspiel was held in 1920 with the Women's Institute serving lunch to the curlers. By 1923, there were 22 participating rinks from Edmonton., Viking, Wetaskiwin, Wainwright, Camrose and

161

Fort Saskatchewan. The Grand Challenge was won by Schofield of Edmonton, but rinks skipped by Chris Hammond and A. A. Beirnes took second and third while Slavik of Viking took fourth.

During this period, the Dawson Cup, the McCauley Cup, the Pincott Cup were played for up and down the line with Camrose and Fort Saskatchewan also participating. Tofield won its share of honors.

Over the years many Tofield curlers have acquitted themselves admirably, but probably none has won so many trophies as George McLaughlin. He has won the Grand Challenge and the Grand Aggregate in Edmonton five times between 1932 and 1951, the Grand Aggregate in Calgary in 1926, the Grand Challenge in Wetaskiwin, Wainwright, Camrose and of course, in Tofield. He was also president of the Alberta Curling Association.

When curling became more highly organized, and zone playdowns came into vogue, the Club began to dream of matched rocks. The expense involved was considerable, but fortunately Tofield possessed two curling clubs. The Ladies' Curling Club also wanted matched rocks and worked hard to make the dream a reality. With new facilities for serving and with water now coming from taps the ladies increased their activities. Coffee and lunches were served during the regular curling schedule, as well as meals during bonspiels. The Ladies were able to contribute a sizeable amount towards the purchase of matched rocks. The remainder of the cost was financed by loans from members and from current funds. The matched rocks were purchased in 1955. In 1958 the Zone 12 playdowns were held in Tofield with Dobry of Viking emerging victorious.

In 1959 the High School Curling Zone finals were held here with New Sarepta being the winner. Through the years, the Tofield Curling Club has encouraged High School curling. Every Saturday morning was set aside for them, and High School rinks have participated in the regular schedule. From this has come such present curlers as David Yakabuski, Tubby McCallister, Warren Watson, and, of course, Jack Whyte, who started curling while in High School in 1934 and has curled here for 34 years, with the exception of two winters while he was away working.

During the years, there has been fun and fellowship in the club. Friendly games are played with other towns and from one of these has come a recurrent story of the early times which may be of interest. It has been told by many people and so there are many different versions. It seems that one of Tofield's rinks, while participating in an out-of-town bonspiel became slightly inebriated. One member was, to put it bluntly, "out cold." His teammates conceived the brilliant idea of taking him to the local undertaking establishment; he was placed in the morgue. When he awoke in strange surroundings with a lily in his hand, he recovered his sobriety very quickly. The story doesn't say whether he ever went curling with the same rink again.

In 1959, in recognition of Tofield's Golden Jubilee the Tofield Curling Club held a banquet. With Dr. W.H. Freebury, president, at the head table, were pioneer curlers: Jack Bowick, John Warner, J.L. Hay of Ryley, George McLaughlin of Edmonton, Cliff Lee, Edmonton; Dr. F.F. Law, Edmonton; John Slavik, Viking; Mark Ferguson, "Shorty" Carter, Edmonton; W. Somers, Devon. Other head table guests included Bill Worton, Bill Christensen, George McFadzean, Neil Phillips, J. Yakabuski, Father Leshinski, Conrad Patterson, Art Francis, John Widynowski, Dirk De Frenne, Olaf Haugen and Bill Davison.

Since 1959, the Tofield Curling Club became incorporated. A new four-sheet, artificial-ice rink has been built on the Tofield Exhibition Grounds.

In the year 1960 the farmers in the area surrounding Tofield formed an afternoon Curling Club and rented the ice for one afternoon each week. With sixteen rinks they were able to fill the four sheets of ice twice weekly. This has proven very successful as it has carried on for several years. Each year they have had the same number of rinks. Each year the play has been very closely contested as trophies go to the winners. With four sheets of artificial ice everyone has been able to have lots of curling. For several years the enthusiasm ran very high with the men's and ladies' clubs both. very active. In November of 1965, the Ladies' Club decided to disband; mixed curling was then organized. This proved to be very successful, so one game a week was scheduled. This has been carried on for several years. With several men curling in the mixed draw, the number of curlers in the men's draw was cut down. This meant that on certain evenings, sheets of ice could be rented to rinks who wanted an occasional game.

1967, our Centennial Year, added an extra bonspiel and turkey shoots! The curlers were shooting curling rocks instead of guns. This proved very entertaining and added a little money to the club funds. In the spring of 1967, curling ended with the Centennial Bonspiel. Forty local rinks took part, many wearing their Centennial costumes.

The following High School students have participated in the zone playoffs over the past number of years: Wayne Moore, Don McKernan, Clayton Everitt, Bruce McFadzean, Dwight Sears, Dave Allan, Ray Pittet, Ted Whyte, Jack Nolan, Duane Sears, Robert Wall, Greg Whyte, Kevin Pike, Brian McFadzean, Allen Everitt, Dale Christensen, Doug Everitt, Pat Nolan, Dave Lampitt, Reg Regehr and Bill Sears.

High School curling occurs two afternoons a week during the season. Mr. Lloyd Cribb has been the supervisor from the High School staff.

# TOFIELD LEGIONAIRES

Tofield Legionaires Junior Baseball Team was organized in 1954 with Graham Allan as manager, Doug McKernan as coach and E.O. Pederson as assistant coach. The lineup consisted of Denzil Solberg, Eddie Williams, David Yakabuski, Leo Rurka, Bill Creig, Allen Bjork, Marshall Slewka, Eddie Slewka, Lawrence (Red) Williams, Bob Nahrebeski, Mike Badum, Wayne Lawson, Dale Barrow, Leonard Lawson, and Arnold Bailey. David Allen was bat boy and Lois Solberg was scorekeeper.

In 1954, the Legionaires eliminated Camrose and Wetaskiwin to go to Taber to play in the Provincial Junior Baseball finals. The games at Taber were split as were the two following games in Tofield. The fifth and deciding game was played in Tofield and resulted in the Legionaires winning the Junior Baseball Championship.

In 1955, Red Deer was eliminated by Tofield who then played, and defeated, Lethbridge in the Provincial Finals by winning 3 out of 5 games.

So for two consecutive years, Tofield held the Provincial Junior Baseball Championship.

# GOLF

Early in the 1920's a golf course was laid out on the site of the present Tofield Mennonite Church. Interested golfers were Harry and Edith Rogers, Ernie and Clara Rogers, bank manager Doak and his wife, J.A. Constantine and his wife.

The course was maintained for several years but finally enthusiasm waned and there was no golf in Tofield until 1964 when the present golf club was formed.

The course was laid out on land owned by Charles Kallal just south of the highway. This land is now owned by W.R. Davison.

The Tofield Town and Country Golf Club, as such, was officially organized in 1966. Shares were purchased by those interested and the equipment was taken over from Charles Kallal.

In June 1967, a successful tournament was held. The paid-up membership for 1967 was 27 individuals and one family. 156 names were registered in the Fee Book as indications of $1.00 per day participants. Those under 16 years of age enjoyed golfing at no cost.

The future of this Golf Club appears uncertain at the beginning of 1968. However, the members are hopeful of being able to keep the course in operation. They feel the opportunity for this type of outdoor recreation serves a useful function in the Tofield district.

# TROPHY WINNING DOGS

The last decade has brought recognition to Tofield as the home of champion dogs. Both the Chesapeake Bay breed and Black Labradors have won championship trophies.

Charles Nolan raised Chesapeake Bay Retrievers for many years before his passing in 1967. In 1960, he registered his "Tofalta Kennel" through the Canadian Kennel Club.

Although he had raised show dogs Mr. Nolan was more interested in field trial dogs and during his years in field trial work, he was an active and willing worker in the Canadian Chesapeake Club, spending much time helping to organize field trials to the betterment of the Club.

He won several field trial trophies with his favorite "Lucky" and also with his promising young prospect, Creachainn Nick."

Also engaged in field trial work is Leo Rurka, with his Black Labrador Retrievers. A member of the Edmonton Sporting Dog Club, Mr. Rurka has, in his ten years of competition, placed in many trials with puppies, juniors, qualifying dogs, and open all-age dogs. One of his dogs, Bandit of Carmoney has amassed sufficient points to become a field trial champion. To Bandit's credit, as a sire, are five dogs that have been sold in the United States as well as many more which have been bought throughout Canada.

Mr. and Mrs. Rurka, both members of the Tofield School Staff, live just north of Tofield and here they have their kennels.

# Pictures

1. Doctor Tofield
2. John Peter Pruden
3. George Cookson Sr.

4. Mr. Weslake and his ox team

5. and 6. Transportation of 1910

7. A meeting in Tofield of the Vermilion Presbytery.

8. Standing: Doctor Morrison, Don Ball, Frank Ball, R. Murrey.
Kneeling: John Lee, George Agnew, Marvin Pruden. Seated: Glen Woods,
A. Dodds.

9. Odd Fellows Parade in front of the old town hall.

10. Lem Abbott and his Boys' Band. Back row, left to right: Klask, Art Smith, Gordon Jobb, Allen Lewis, Barney Kendall. Second row: Ted Paradis, Cole "Twin," Cliff Lee, Mr. Abbott, Cole "Twin," Oscar Brooks, Hingley.

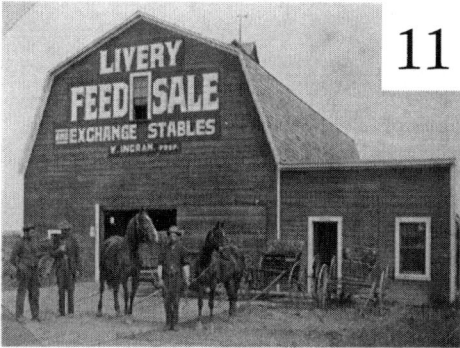

11

11. W. Ingram Livery Stable
12. Art Elliott, Len Phillips,
Jack Grover, Allen Bjork, Bob
Nahrebeski, Bill Enns, Arno
Binder, Leonard Lawson,
Claude May, Raymond
McGinitie. Front row: Don
Niemetz, Wayne Lawson, Rod
Sutton, Ed Williams, Lorne
Phillips, Alfred Driediger,
Ed Maziuk, Stick Boy-Cliff
Oslund.
13. An engine used at the
Tofield coal company

12

13

Old Tofield, March 1st '07

14. Main Street in Tofield No 1, 1.5 miles east of present site
15. Main Street in Tofield No 2, one block west of present school
16. Homesteaders loghouse

THE LAKEs IN CREE

BEAVER HILLS LAKE A-MISK-WA-CHI

COOKING LAKE O-PI-MI-NOW-WA-SIOO

HASTINGS LAKE A-KA-KA-KWA-TIKH

THE LAKE THAT DOES NOT FREEZE

BEAVER CREEK A-MISK-WA-CHI

BEAVER HILLS A-MISK-WA-CHI

17

18

19

17. *Taken from a survey account. By Pallister.*
18. *Tofield Silver Seven, 1910-1911. Standing left to right: Herb Lee, George Bisset, Oliver Letourneau. Seated: Gordon Haynes, JD Hannan, Coach Jim Charlesworth, Stanley George.*
19. *Basketball Team. Standing left to right: Mrs. Nora Olson, Mrs. John Blackburn, Mrs. Earl Moore (Mary Francis), Ida Assmo. Seated: Unknown, Mrs. Adams (Alma Erickson), Agnes Bruha, Mrs. H. McGinitie.*
20. *Tofield Town Hall*
21. *An ox team coming through Tofield, 1907, fall.*

22. A Sunday School Class. Left
to right: Alban Harriman, John
Letourneau, Cecil Letourneau,
teacher Gertie Francis, Rose
Francis, Alex and Pat Gladue.
23. Tofield second school
building. Built on the southeast
corner of the northeast half of
section 36 TP50, R-19, the place
where John Rempel lives now.
George Cookson Sr. homstead,
Harold Martin, teacher.
24. Guy Walker's hounds with a
tired coyote.

25. Odd Fellows and Rebekah gathering
26. Stripping at the Tofield coalmine. Standing on the step, left to right: Jack McCusker, Al Innis, Rufus Wilson
27. Queen's Hotel in Tofield No. 2

28. School picnic 1909
29. Breaking with steam engine. Steated: Pete Ingram. On tank: Jim Ingram Sr.
30. A lineup of Fords that G. McLaughlin sold in 1916.

31. *Left to right: Bayard Carlisle, Jean Whillans, Mary Klask, Alymer Harriman, Harold McMullen, Neville Kirk. Second row: Bertha Neal, Marjorie MaHaffey, Ina McMullen, Ila Murray, Bernice Griswold, Harold Weatherill. Third row: Kathleen Secord, Jean Secord, Ruffy Leffer, Julia Klask, Keitha Lee, Wilma Kirk, Mildred Griswold, Nola Hannan. Seated: Jessie Hopgood, Alice Rude, Mr. Nidrie, Edith Herndon, Cynthia Price. Seated on floor: Allen Lewis, Bill Swift, Robert Lane, Frank Carter*

32. *The William Thompson home with Mrs. C. Blake, Mrs. Earl Moore, John Thompson*

33. *The Pioneer Young Ladies. Standing: Fanny and Lilly Rickner, Amanda Henderson, Mary Francis. Seated: Gertie Francis, Oma Rickner, Lina Whillans*

34

35

36

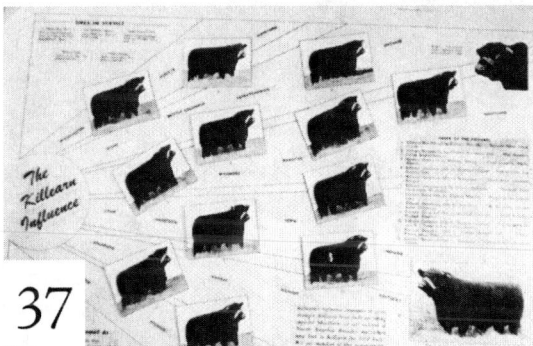

37

34. The Tofield
Millionaires. Back row:
Roy Lee, George Agnew,
Jim Hannon, Dr. Bain.
Middle row: Pat Gladue,
David McIntosh, Archie
Pruden. Third row:
Harold Weatherill,
Norman Smith, Lepensee
35. Dr. Tofield and his
grandson, Max Rogers
36. Quilting Bee. Standing:
Mrs. Letourneau, Mrs.
Gertie Chapman, Mrs
Bensen, Mrs. NS Smith,
Mrs Lem Abbott, Mrs.
Harvey Adams. Seated:
Mrs Jim MaHaffey, Mrs
Maxwell, Mrs Harper,
Mrs WM Lee, Mrs
Emery
37. Where Killearn bulls
were sold

38. *Tofield's first brick school, 1910 or 1911.*
39. *Alberta Jr Champions, 1954. Standing: G Allan, manager, Bob Nahrebeski, Denzil Solberg, Eddy Williams, Dave Yakabuski, Dale Barrow, Arnold Bailey, Eddy Slewka, Coach Doug McKernan. Front row: Leo Rurka, Mike Batum, Bill Crieg, Lois Solberg, Allen Bjork, Marshall Slewka, Lawrence Williams*
40. *Laying of the railroad steel 1909.*

41. Lakeshore school. Mr. Muro, teacher. Back row: Olive Pruden, Ned Pruden, Flo Pruden (Mrs. Kortzman), Anne Pruden, Sophia Norn, Harriet Pruden, John Pruden, Bill Pruden. Front row: Mary Pruden, Carrie Pruden, Lilly Norn (Mrs H Tiedemann), Ellen Rowland, Walter Pruden, Jack Phillips, Charlie Pruden, Marvin Pruden, Jim Rowland

42. Henry Woods steam outfit. On plows left to right: Billy Wood, Henry Wood, Jim Gray, Marion Hays with wide-brimmed hat

43. The outfit that the Coombes family came with to the country from Oregon. Another family bought it and returned over the same trail.

*44. Tofield fall fair. Picture taken about where the steel bleachers are now.*

*45. Tofield school 1905. Back row: Alice Gladue, Amy Morton, Venah Rickner, Betsy Gladue, Amanda Henderson, Fanny Rickner, Lilly Henderson, Oma Rickner, Harold Martin. Teachers-front row: Cecil Letourneau, Pat Gladue, John Letourneau, Wardy Whillans, Jim Francis, Jason Henderson, Rose Francis, Clara Gladue, Mabel Francis.*

*46. Jack Cookson's home about 1912. George Cookson Sr, and Mrs G Cookson.*

47. *The Logan boat on Beaverhill Lake*

48. *Bardo Brass Band about 1912. Back row: Chester Ronning, Pete Johnson, Palmer Andersen, Ole Bartness, Hilmar Johnson, Olaf Anderson, Torfin Brocke, Lyman Roram, Albin Anderson, Doug Black, Harold Johnson, Ingwold Haugseth, Pete Haugen, Ben Anderson*

49. *Farming on a big scale: Warners.*

50

51

50. *Tofield's first fire engine, 1910.*
51. *Hiram Phillips and his oxen*
52. *Kallal brothers in a duck shoot*

52

53. *Railroading with horses*

54. *Main Street looking south from in front of Swift's Garage*

55. *Ox team back of Queen's Hotel, town no. 2*

56. Baseball, January 5, 1914. Left to right standing: AA Story, Guy Owens, Unknown, Roland Murray, Ralph Davison, Shorty Carter, Joseph Rogers, Mike McCusker, Unknown, Unknown, Jim Hannan, Unknown, Unknown, Unknown, Scott

57. East side of Main Street. Corner of third avenue and Main, looking south
58. Speaks for itself.

59. Main Street looking south, Queen's Hotel, right side 1910
60. More large scale horse farming at Warner's.
61. Tofield Skating Rink, built in 1910

62. Curling team.
Standing left to right: John
Lee, George McLaughlin,
Walter Rogers, Wardie
Somers
63. Fish caught in
Beaverhill Lake, June 13,
1913.
64. Orange Lodge Parade
65. A goose shoot.
RE Emery, Davidson
Manners, Josh Noland

66. Tofield's first gas light.
Standing left ot right: JO
Letourneau, RE Emery,
Arthur McMullen, Unknown
in front of Swift's Garage
67. An early ranch (note the
sod, or straw-covered roofs)
68. Tofield station 1967
during demolition
69. All ready for an evening
duck shoot
70. Baling hay with horse
power. Left to right: Art
Hosler, AF Schultz, OA
Schultz, Marvin Rickner, a
passing trapper. 1907.

68

69

70

71. Wayne Lawson, Mrs. Jim Ingram, Annis Ingram, Leonard Lawson, Mrs. J. Lancaster (Edith Davidson). Seated: John Sears, Mrs. S. Sears, Ida Coombes, Mrs. H. Schultz, Mrs. Foshaug Sr., Mrs Wilford, Mrs J Ingram Sr., Mrs Sears Sr., Mrs Bill Mitchell, Bill Mitchell, Mrs Charlie Whillans. Front row: Sam Stirret, John McGinitie, Chester Coombes, Tom Roram, Charlie Whillans, Henry McGinitie, Jason Henderson, Leslie McGinitie

72. Nailing on a 60-year plaque on the old Bank of Montreal building. Left to right: Horace Seller, present bank manager, Dr. Freebury, mayor, Mark Ferguson, the first depositor in 1907, Bert Everitt, Ed Watson, Arnold Swift, Conrad Patterson, Graham Allan, Harold Weatherill

73. Our Centennial Queen, Mrs Petra Stauffer, 1967.

74. Our Mayor, Dr. WH Freebury, 1967.

75

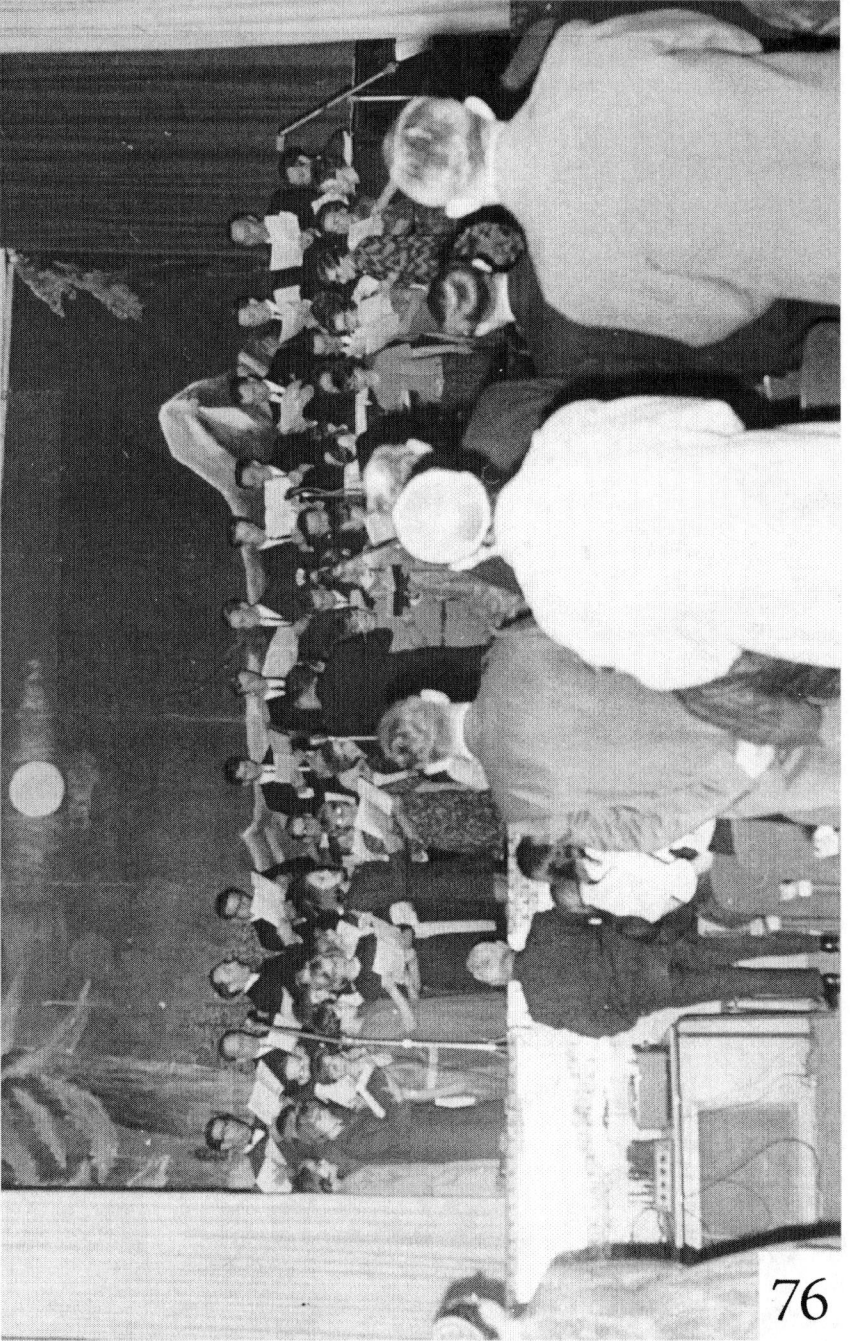

76

75. *Tofield Community Centre Festival of Christmas Carols, 1967.*
76. *Mass Choir at the Festival of Christmas Carols, 1967.*
77. *1967 Girls' Basketball Team. Standing left to right: Margaret Hallett, Gwen Sears, Karen Davison, Mr Eastlick, coach, Cherle Astley, Gwen Klassen, Victoria Wall. Kneeling: Marjorie Moore, Frances Schultz, Terry Moore, Linda Ozubko, Beth Ingram.*

78. *1967 Boys' Basketball Team. Back row: Art Korbie, manager, Bruce Bowick, Ron Foshaug, Jim Allan, Don Maurer, Jim Hart, Ken Dodds, Brian Schultz, Mr. Eastlick, coach. Front row: Allan Everitt, Robert Foshaug, Darryll Reil, Duane Stauffer.*

79. *Queen Petra at the Bethany home, Camrose, Mrs Kindley, Mrs Fosshaug Sr, Mrs NB Ness, Evelyne Stauffer, Mary Erickson*
80. *Mr and Mrs Claude Gallinger in Centennial Dress.*

81. *Tofield 1967 council. Standing, left to right: Bert Everitt, Allan Herndon, George Boese, Conrad Patterson, Gabe Pittett. Seated: Mrs Rita Halverson, secretary-treasurer, Dr. WH Freebury, mayor, Arnold Swift.*

82. *Centennial co-ordinating committee. Standing left to right: Gabe Pittett, David Halverson, Mabel Boyles, Larry Wilson, Marie Worton, Father Scriven, Jim Francis, Thomas Jacobs. Seated: Grace Phillips, Mrs Petra Stauffer, Dr. Freebury, chariman, Miss Chimko, Bill Christianson*

83. This home has a little more history attached to it than most log buildings. Built in 1896 by Martin Finseth family, from 1902 to 1905, it was the home of the Finseth store and from 1903 to 1915 the Bardo post office occupied one corner of it. In 1921, the lean-to was taken down. Three generations of Finseths have lived in it. 1959, LeRoy and Mary had it raised and had a full-sized basement put under it. It is believed to be the oldest log building in the Tofield district still in use.

84. St. James Anglican Church situated on the northeast corner of the southeast quarter of section 31-51-18. The wedding of Andeline Norn to Roy Ross, Lily Tidemann is the small girl in front.

85. The orginal home of PB Anderson. Seated is Mrs PB Anderson,
Emma (Mrs R Eide). Standing: Magda Anderson, Mrs George
Henderson, Camrose. Picture taken in 1915.
86. The Reverend Bersvend Anderson and his travelling outfit. PB
Anderson's second home, with the original house behind the sleigh

*87. Bardo Log School building, No 434 NWT, taken about 1908. 1) Adelia Rorem, 2) Inga Horte, 3) Palmer Anderson, 4) Chester Ronning, 5) Netrus Ronning, 6) Talbert Ronning, 7) Harold Ronning, 8) Hazel Ronning, 9) Magda Anderson, 10) Olaf Anderson, 11) Martha Anderson, 12) Ruby Rorem, 13) Nora Rorem, 14) Lyman Rorem, 15) Alma Ronning. Teacher: Mr. JW Bower.*
*88. Taken the day of Reverend BA Anderson funeral, June 1917, showing Bardo Church.*

89. *Breaking with steam engine, Bill Bowick riding back plow, John Lee next standing, unknown, Charlie Bowan sitting on engine seat, Charlie Ingram sitting on right wheel, Pete Ingram with white collar, other unknown*
90. *Bathgate post office. Also home of Messers Morrison and Walker. Note the old gramophone and telescope. Right to left, seated: WH Gold, JW Mullen, and Mr Morrison*

91. *Logan tombstone, picture taken April 1968, at St. James Anglican Cemetery*
92. *These two big ones did not get away.*

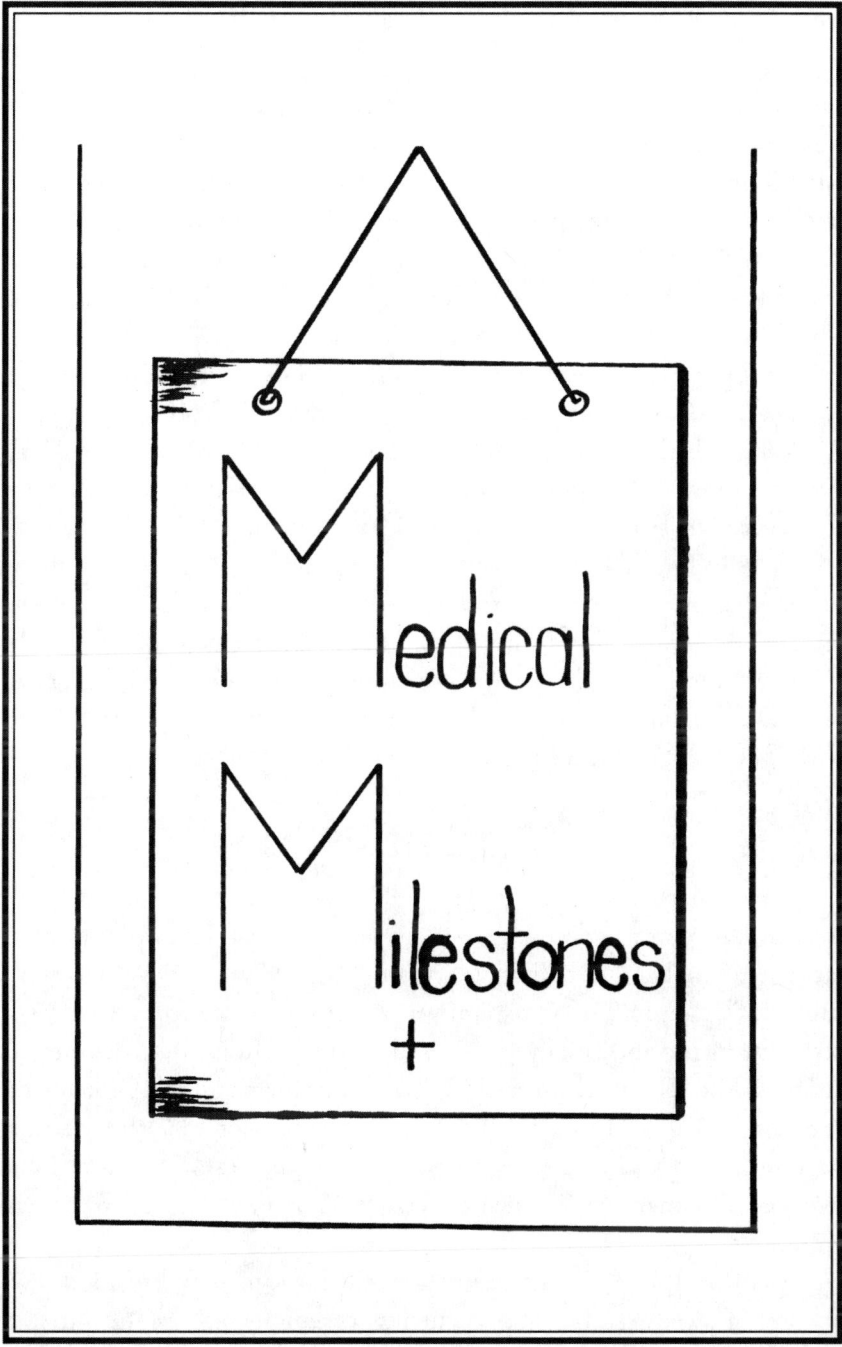

# Medical Milestones +

# MEDICAL SERVICES IN TOFIELD

Dr. J.H. Tofield, whose biography appears elsewhere in this book, was Tofield's pioneer doctor serving the area from 1892 to 1918. Dr. MacKennon, Dr.J.L.Hammond, Dr. Kirk and Dr. McDonald were also in the town for varying periods between 1906 and 1918.

In 1918, Dr. N.L. Terwilliger cane to Tofield, serving until 1921 at which time he moved to Edmonton. From 1921 to 1926, Dr. Bain was the Tofield doctor. Dr. Paul was here in 1923.

Dr. Frank F. Law, whose former office still stands on Main Street though now used as the C. Ferguson residence was in Tofield from 1926 to 1941 at which time he joined the Allan Clinic in Edmonton. Dr. A.E. Caldwell now of Viking, was in Tofield from 1941-1943. For the next three years, Tofield was without a resident physician.

In 1946 Dr. W.H. Freebury opened a practice in Tofield in a room in the Memorial Hall made available to him by the Tofield Community League. At various times since then, Dr. Freebury has been assisted by Dr. Chai, Dr. Louis, Dr. Clarke. For several years, Dr. G.M. Price has been Dr. Freebury's associate. Recently Dr. Singh has been associated with Drs. Freebury and Price.

# TOFIELD HOSPITAL

Tofield had never had an active treatment hospital The only hospital facilities had been Dr. Tofield's home and Mrs. Gray's Maternity Home. The absence of a hospital was a serious hindrance to keeping a resident doctor and finally in 1944, due to the efforts of civic-minded citizens, the Tofield Hospital District was formed. In 1945, under the supervision of Hon. W. W. Cross, Minister of Health, the first hospital board was elected. George McFadzean, Stan Sears and John Warner were members of the first hospital board, with J.E. Stinson as secretary.

In Nov. 19, 1947, the 20-bed Tofield Municipal Hospital was opened. Preceding the ribbon-cutting ceremony at the hospital, a program was held in the Memorial Hall. Rev. H.B. Ricker, Mayor A.B. Clutterham, F. R. Murray, E.E. Maxwell, Floyd Baker, M.L.A., Miss M. Dodds Dr. J.L. McPherson of Ryley, Dr. M.R. Bow, Deputy Minister of Health and George McFadzean all participated in the program. At the hospital door, unlocked by Matron Miss M. Smith, prayers were offered by Rev. Orme of the Holy Trinity Anglican Church, Fr. Gorman of St. Francis of Assissi Roman Catholic Church and Rev. H. B. Ricker of Tofield United Church.

The first staff consisted of Miss Mattie Smith, matron, Miss Kay Rutherford, Miss Marie Slavik.

Mrs. H. Ewert, was the first patient, as well as the first maternity patient; she named her baby William Howard Ewert in honour of Dr. W.H. Freebury, the attending physician.

Miss Kay Kozak became matron in 1948 and continued till 1963 when she was succeeded by the present matron Miss Ruth Kraus.

In 1956, a 10-bed addition was constructed, giving the hospital room for 31 beds and 9 bassinettes.

## STATISTICAL REPORT 1968

| | |
|---|---|
| Total Inpatients admitted, adults and children | 1230 |
| Total new borns | 60 |
| Total outpatients admitted | 1605 |
| Percentage of occupancy 1968 | 71% |
| Total Patient days | 8,027 days |

## HOSPITAL PERSONNEL, 1968

Medical Staff
    Dr. W.H. Freebury
    Dr. G.M. Price
    Dr. K. Singh
Administrator
    Mr. J. Ramsbottom

Accountant
  Mr. D. Roth
Office Staff
  Mrs. A. Fisher
Nurses
  Miss R. Kraus
    Director of Nursing
  Mrs.M. Worton
  Mrs.J. Mitchell
  Mrs.M. Dickson
  Mrs.E. Koziol
  Mrs.K. Walker
  Miss R. Ancheta
  Miss M. John
Nursing Aide
  Miss E. Galenza
  Miss G. Tkaczyk
  Mrs. A. Oliver
  Miss S. Yaranon
  Miss A. Olaveja
Ward Aides
  Mrs. M. LaRocque
  Mrs. J. Ozubko,
  Mrs. A. Nachtigal
  Mrs. J. Mazur
Technician
  Miss S. Wenstob
Kitchen Staff
  Miss E. Wideman
  Mrs. J. Othen
  Miss H. Tiedemann
  Mrs. E. Ferguson
  Mrs. A. Snortheim
  Mrs. S. Melezko

Laundry Staff
  Mrs. F. Mierou
  Mrs. M. Roberge
Housekeeping Staff
  Mrs. R. Ross
  Mrs. M. Gunther
  Mrs. V. Lehman
Maintenance
  Mr. Wm. Backschaat

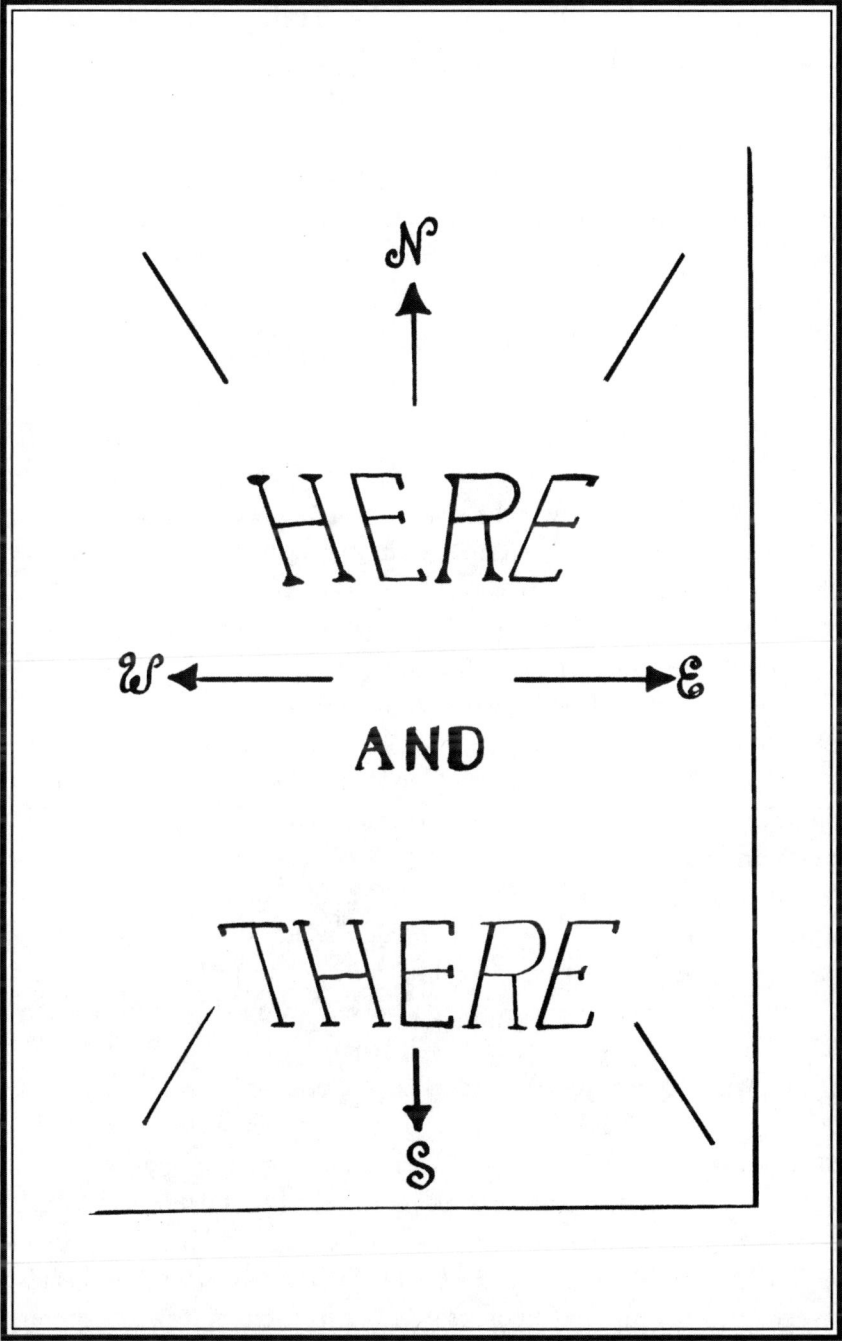

N

HERE

W ← → E

AND

THERE

S

# HISTORIES OF SURROUNDING DISTRICTS

Histories of the Deville, Cooking Lake, Amisk Creek, Lindbrook and Spilstead areas have been made available to the Tofield Historical Society. Since the pioneers of these districts were an integral part of the development of the area the Tofield Historical Society is pleased to include these histories of these contiguous areas in its book.

## SOUTH COOKING LAKE

Cooking Lake as a stopping place goes back to the days of the old Carlton trail, the overland route from Winnipeg to Edmonton in the 1880's. Around the turn of the century, the first homesteaders coming to this district used this trail named by the Indians. Cooking Lake in Cree means "place where we cook."

Sheriff Robertson is one of the first names well known around Cooking Lake. He came with his family to that district in 1892. His mother was the first white woman to ever set foot on Kony Island, an island in Cooking Lake. He built a substantial lodge of native logs in 1898 on section 24, at South Cooking Lake. The lodge withstood the ravages of time and weather for more than 60 years and is still a landmark on the shore.

At that time, John MacFadden was camped on the shore of a small lake to the west which bears his name, "MacFadden Lake." He had driven a horse herd up from Montana earlier that spring.

Next came Daniel Grummett who settled on the South shore in 1893, and has many descendants in the surrounding districts. The Grummett family kept the post office in Cooking Lake. On Saturdays the settlers came from far and near on foot and on horseback to collect their weekly mail. Settlers from North Cooking Lake came across the lake to this post office. Distance meant little to Dan Grummett. He has been known to start to Edmonton on foot across country at five p.m. and be back by daylight with the box of shells he went for. He was also an excellent violinist and all of his family, three sons and two daughters, inherited his gift. A jack of all trades, he was also the carpenter when the Anglican Church was built in 1908, and built a fireplace of fieldstone for Sheriff Robertson.

From 1893 to 1906 Cooking Lake district filled up rapidly. One of the earlier settlers was Sid Edwards, 1901, who hauled freight from Edmonton to Cooking Lake and later with a team of oxen broke the first sod on many homesteads.

Mr. Keen, who had a greenhouse on the south shore, sold bedding plants in Edmonton, hauled via team and democrat over the Old Cooking Lake Trail. Eddie Keen, whose byline is familiar to readers of the "Edmonton Journal" is a grandson.

Mr. Walton's four daughters and three sons made their home a popular one. It was a gathering place for the young people and 20 guests was a conservative number for Sunday supper.

Billy Murphy's homestead is now part of the Alberta Game Farm.

Will Bufton's homestead was west of the present Lakeview in 1902. Bert and Fred Williams and their mother were family friends in Chicago and they arrived in 1904.

The country south of Cooking Lake was rolling and heavily timbered. Mr. Chadwick had a sawmill where the village now stands. Settlers hauled their own logs to the mill where they were sawn into rough lumber at $4.00 per 1,000 ft. B.M. Many of the homesteaders were from the old countries and had been apprenticed to different trades. Working at their trade part of each year in Edmonton helped many over the first rough year. Everyone lived off the land as much as possible. Rabbits and partridge, an occasional deer and even bear meat during the winter, were items of homesteaders' menu.

The lakes were full of pike and mullet (jackfish) and suckers to the homesteaders) which made a welcome change in springtime. Wild ducks and berries of all kinds were plentiful all summer.

Trapping muskrats in the spring was also a source of revenue. Later on came the beef, cream cheques and small crops on every homestead.

Franklin School was built in 1908. Mrs. Portas, Mr. Walton and Brockett Moneypenny were the first trustees. Miss Gertie Stinson was the first teacher.

A few of the names who arrived before 1908 were Chambers on whose homestead Lakeview Pavilion now stands; Uprights who had the first B.A. service station in the village; Hepharts, Browns, Bradshaws, Portas, Bob Bell, Moneypennys, Morehouse, Haleys, Bairds, Chadwicks, Edgar Hayman, George Weslake (originally at Cooking Lake) Oswald Defieux and many more.

In the Cooking Lake district there were many homesteads filed on by single young men. So every male living alone on a homestead, whether he was 18 or 80, was called an "old bachelor."

During the late winter of 1907 these bachelors held a meeting, appointed a secretary (Brockett Moneypenny) and each one donated one dollar to provide refreshment at what was to become an annual affair, "The Bachelor Ball". It was the windup in the spring of the settlers' social season. Formal invitations were sent out to more than 50 families, children and grandparents included within a 20-mile radius. Sheriff Robertson loaned his lodge for the occasion. The music was furnished by Dan Grummett with violin and Art Quilley with a flute. The cooking was done by Mrs. Trudgeon (a daughter of Mr. Grummett) who was later to become Mrs. Murdock of Ministik. She was assisted by Ada Chambers. At twelve midnight sandwiches, cakes, even lemon pies, tea and coffee were served followed by an hour of impromptu concert, in which everyone participated.

Then the dance was resumed, lasting sometimes until daylight if the roads were bad. The labour, music, etc. were all donated free and the memory of these "get-togethers" lingers long in the memory of the old-timers.

Farther east on the south shore of Cooking Lake lies the Ministik Lake district. In 1910-11 there was quite a summer resort at White Sand Beach. There were several cottages built there.

There was a large boat (The Daisy Girl) owned by Mr. Firth and Mr. Hull, editor of the Edmonton Bulletin for many years. This boat met passengers from the daily C. N. R. train at North Cooking Lake and delivered them to White Sands on the south shore.

The first Postmaster in Ministik was Pete Anderson, and, later, his parents. They lived in a small house directly opposite the present consolidated school. They were a quaint old couple who spoke such broad Gaelic that a newcomer found it difficult to understand. The mail was brought out to Cooking Lake via team and buggy and then taken by horseback to the postoffice. In wet seasons the horse would often bog down on the way.

Ministik School was built in 1909. There was a debenture taken out for $88. The lumber was bought from W. C. Swift of Tofield and hauled to the school site by Andrew and Archie Ferguson. Bob Mair, secretary, Peter McKerral and David Swabey were members of the first school board. The first teacher was a Mr. McCauley, who boarded at the Robert George home, who were the first owners in 1908 of the homestead where the present school and Ministik Community Hall are now located. Church services were also held at this home. The first written record of the old school is in 1910, when fourteen pupils were enrolled from May until December inclusive. The teacher was Mrs. Irene Verge. The old school, still in good repair is used and owned by the United Church for weekly services. The original desks and the copper handbell which was used to keep order down through the years are still there.

The lakes were used for travel in winter; the ice was smooth travelling and often cut off many miles "as the crow flies".

In 1912, Ed Donnelly took out a contract to build the main road right through to Tofield. He hired a crew of eight men with teams to use plows, scrapers, and fresnos, which were the only road machinery available. He moved his tent camp every few miles as the work progressed. Ernie Haley was one of the local men who worked on the road and his wife cooked for the men; their seven-year-old daughter attended school from the road camp. The school was open all summer and closed January and February the first years. Deep snow and cold made it difficult for young children to attend. Maintenance of the road provided a source of revenue in the district later.

Bert Williams filled the sloughs on the side road leading to his homestead with the stones he picked off his first fields, and covered the stones with dirt scraped from the hills to enable him to drive out to the main road.

Fred Butler, fresh from Agricultural College in Toronto, came to Ministik in 1909. He and Bert Williams and Myra George formed a debating society in 1910, which provided a social outlet for all.

Stanley George played on the Tofield Hockey team several years. Mr. Eva and family lived on the homestead north of Bert Williams in 1907. They were, previous to that, missionaries in India.

Bill Stewart ran a sawmill with a huge old steam engine for many years near the Ministik Lake.

Jack McNish, foreman of a lumber camp near Edson spent his summers on his homestead.

The first man on Atkinson's place pushed his belongings from Edmonton with a wheelbarrow, but did not stay long.

The Camerons had the place where the present BA Service Station and Coffee Shop is now.

Frank Doherty owned the quarter where the Catholic Church now stands, south of the hall.

Following are a few names of the first settlers: Wingroves, Bacheldor, Barnes, Olivers, Bosses, Ralph Ablett, Heitmans, Bert Robbins, Steele Murdoch, Dick Allen, Jack Blair, Quigleys, McBain, George Huff, Dick Wilson.

There was a quaint character on the west end of the lake who drove one horse and one steer for a team. He claimed that the dim trail leading past his place was made by rustlers driving stolen cattle to southern Alberta.

Ministik Lake itself and 10,000 acres of virgin territory is a Federal Sanctuary. By an order of the Minister of the Interior, in 1911, all vacant lands adjoining the lake and the smaller lakes beyond were set aside for sanctuary, to provide protection for the birds which migrate from one country to another. An agreement was signed in 1916 by His Majesty's Ambassador Sir Cecil SpringRice, G. V. C. O., and Mr. Robert Lansing, Secretary of State, U. S. A.

There are good houses and good cars and prosperity in Ministik and Cooking Lake districts, due in large part to the beef and cream cheques down through the years.

Irene Williams

# SPILSTED DISTRICT

*The information for this article was obtained from Mrs. John Warner, nee Alice Spilsted.*

This district was named after Charles Spilsted who after hearing of the wonderful free land in Alberta, left his English farm home in July 1903 with his wife, their six sons and one daughter for Canada. The family spent one year in Cranbrook, B.C., and another in Kimberly, B. C.

Mr. Spilsted spent two months driving with horses to many places around Edmonton before sending for his family to join him in October, 1905. He rented a house in Strathcona and here he left his wife, daughter, oldest son, and youngest son (to complete his education) while the others completed a log house and barn on the homestead which was ten miles west and two miles south of Tofield. In June, 1906, the family was reunited on the homestead. The trip to the homestead took two days with two teams and wagons over primitive trails, including corduroy roads, uncut brush and plentiful mudholes which could only occasionally be avoided. When the mudholes could not be driven around, both teams had to be hitched to one wagon. It made, says Mrs. Warner, an interesting trip for greenhorns!

Many people looking for homesteads were welcomed at the Spilsted home. The home became a stopping place, the guests sleeping on the floor, as was the custom.

Other early settlers in the district included the Chillman family, the Mickleboroughs, John Druce, Doanes, Mr. and Mrs. George Everitt, Harry Saul and Miles Barrow, Dawson Manners, George Perkine as well as others who were in residence for only a short time. Guy Owens who lived in the Ketchamoot district, had previously proved up a quarter section used entirely for slough hay which was later bought by the Spilsteds.

As the settlers increased in numbers the need for a Post Office arose. It was applied for under the name "Happyland" but the grant came in the name of "Spilsted." When, later, the school was built, somehow the "Spilsted" was misspelled "Spilstead" and to the disapproval of the family, the latter spelling was retained. When the rural mail routes were established, the Spilsted office was closed but, until that time, Walter Mickleborough carried the mail once a week, in summer by democrat and in winter by jumper (sleigh).

Will and Carmen Spilsted were often called on to supply music for dancing and parties. Violin, guitar, organ and the occasional piano were the means of entertainment by Will and Carmen for the pioneers of the Tofield area. Will and Carmen Spilsted lived in the town of Tofield during their retirement as did Bert and Polly Spilsted. The only living member of the Spilsted family in 1967 is the daughter, Alice, who married John Warner and lived in the Lakeshore district. Mrs. Warner now lives in Tofield. John Jr. the eldest son farms in the Lakeshore district. Herbert the middle boy lives with his wife Carol and sons Kevin and Christopher in Edmonton; John Jr. married Irene Bailey. They have one son Bruce (who married Isla Hielter) and one grandson, Brian; Allan married Joan Murray. Their children are: Michael, Lynn and James.

The Mickleborough family of the Spilsted area came from London. The family consisted of the father, three sons and two daughters, one of whom married Fred Doane a neighbour and moved away. On the Mickleborough farm, there was a fairsized lake called Gamblen Lake but mostly known by the family name. All the neighbours were welcome to use Mickleborough's homebuilt boat to go to the island in the lake where they could pick the wild raspberries, gooseberries, cranberries, and black currants which grew in great profusion. For several years, a pair of vultures proved a great attraction on the island as they nested and raised their young.

The John Druce family were also English. The son, George, and daughter, Mary, (Mrs. Gus Schmidt) and Dorothy (Mrs. Ivan Broen) still live in the district. Miles Barrow married and his family grew up in the district; he has retired and lives with his daughter.

Percy Mason returned to England after several years and now lives near Canterbury by himself, still riding a bicycle at 82 years of age.

Dawson Manners left and opened a store in Jarrow. He married a Tofield School teacher.

# DEVILLE

On a cool October day in 1906, a group of five—four Irishmen – Sam and Jim Adams, John Coleman, John Morrow and an American from North Freedom, Wisconsin, Jack Dickie, wended their way east from Edmonton by the old base line trail for eighteen miles, then as best they could for another fifteen miles through brush, swamp and muskeg. They had pooled their resources to buy a team of horses, a wagon, and supplies for the coming winter. They reached the northeast shore of Cooking Lake by nightfall—unhitched their weary horses, built a campfire, had a lunch, pitched their tent and bedded down for the night. Tomorrow each would be out scouting for a quarter section of land on which he would squat and establish a home. This land was part of the Cooking Lake Forest Reserve and although it was all burnt over and not yet surveyed or open for homesteading, its choice lay in the fact that it was good rich sandy loam. It lay in a sloping valley between Wannison Lake and Hastings Lake, with Cooking Lake on the west and Islet Lake on the east.

At one time this area had evidently been an Indian hunting ground. Many a time the writer plowed up what was reported to be large balls of pemmican which was sundried buffalo meat, pulverized and mixed with melted fat and wild berries such as cranberries, saskatoons, and bakeapple. It was in balls as large as a football, and had been buried in the earth by the Indians for emergencies. It was tough as rubber but not decayed. Many Indian relics such as arrowheads, flint spear heads, stone battle axes, pemmican pounders and tanning scrapers were also turned up.

The main idea of squatting in this district was the rumor that the railway from Winnipeg to Edmonton might come through this location, and the settlers guessed it would be on the north side of Cooking Lake.

They decided to squat on a quarter section each, and by the end of November each had built a log shack of a kind in order to establish a claim. On Jack Dichie's quarter, a large two-storey house was built and the five boys batched together for the winter. "We made our headquarters there, and built a log barn. Everything possible was homemadeour beds were made from poles, mattresses were gunny sacks stuffed with hay; pillows were made from duck feathers, tables were native poplar; apple boxes nailed to the walls served as shelves; we cooked on iron stoves. Throughout it all, we were warm, comfortable and healthy.

The winter of 1906-07 is remembered as the winter of the deep snows and low temperatures— sometimes as low as 60 degrees below. We ate the odd partridge, but the writer hereby acknowledges his indebtedness to the lowly bush rabbit. Rabbits were eaten every day— stewed fried, and baked. We also had lots of pork and beef, as we could buy a dressed hog or a quarter of beef for five cents a pound from the occasional settler who would pass through with a load on his way to Edmonton. The Cooking Lake trail and the old Beaver Lake trail were the two highways travelled by the early settlers from Tofield and Beaver Lake districts. Such familiar names as Francis, Cookson, Ingram, Woods and Shupe come to mind.

All the creeks and lakes had fish, and creeks flowed all winter. There were deer, elk, lynx, fox, mink and muskrats, and these meant ready cash for their fur and hides.

The only settlers near this part of the country when the squatters came were Peter Donald and his family. The Donalds whose grandfather homesteaded on a quarter section which is now Bonnie Doon in Edmonton, lived on the creek outlet of Cooking Lake. The Jonas Ward family lived on the creek on Hastings Lake at the northwest end. Another family was the Augustus Gladue family, who had a well established ranch at the outlet of Hastings Lake. He had moved from Beaver Lake years before to take advantage of the luscious pastures and hay meadows along Hastings Creek. Many a weary traveller between Beaver Lake country and Edmonton was glad to make camp at the Gladue ranch, and share the hospitality of the Gladue home. This ranch was the outstanding land mark in the district during the early days. Jack Saunderson lived on the west end of Cooking Lake. He was a Sioux guide with General Middleton during the Riel uprising. He came to Edmonton from Fort Pitt and was land guide for many parties around Edmonton. He ended up as a guide for Charlie Bremner, valuator and appraisor for the C. P. R. Charlie set him up on a quarter section of land on Cooking Lake, where he eked out a living trapping. Jack was quite a story teller, and was welcome wherever he went.

The settlers had guessed right about the railway for in the summer of 1907 the Grand Trunk Pacific surveyors came along, and construction gangs followed in 1908. By this time we had left the big house we shared during the winter, and had all moved into our own log shacks and improved them considerably. With the coming of the railway, other squatters began to come into the district, most of them squatting on the south end of the Forest Reserve. Among these earliest settlers were: Alex Morrow, Hugh Adams, John Adams, Robert Adams, Bert Dunn, Jim Morrow, Hedley Bryenton, Charles Magee, William Doxee, John Watherston, J. M. Verge, Jim Scott, Fred Pennock, Peter Donald, Henry Donald, Roy and Guy Dunn, Jim McCaskill, R. Banford, William Ross, Teddy Owen, Bob McHarry, Walter Langton, Matthew Ferguson Sr., Andy and Archie Ferguson, Henry White, Julia Rowland, Pete Huston, Tom Scott, William Druiard, Jim Gray, Charlie Gray, Alex Love, Bob Donald, and Peter McKerral. I am mentioning these settlers as there are residents in the district today who will recognize many of these names.

With the coming of the railway, jobs were available working with the surveyors, cutting right-of-way, ditching, and building the grade for the railway. During the winter, earth was shovelled into miniature cars which were hauled by horses out to the grade on narrow gauge rails. I might mention that quite a few of the settlers were able to buy a team of horses or a yoke of oxen, and those who were fortunate enough took subcontracts building grade with a borrowed slip, and if they could double up with someone, they could get a fresno. This was slow hard work, but it paid $2.00 a day, and I honestly believe few of the settlers could have stuck it but for this ready cash. Many felt indebted to the late Mr. Jackson who contracted from Folley, Welsh and Stewart. He would give anyone a chance if they were willing to work.

When the grade was built and the steel laid, there were other jobs such as fencing and keeping the track level. There was no gravel, and the usual procedure when the track sank in the mud was to go into the bush and cut poplar poles, and haul them out, cut them into suitable lengths, jack up the steel and slip the poles under the ties. This was only good for a few days, at which time the operation had to be repeated.

By 1909 the railway was completed, and on August 13th, 1909, the writer rode from Tofield to Edmonton on the first passenger train from Winnipeg. By the time the Grand Trunk was through, most of the settlers had a few cows, and cream cheques were the life savers from then on. As land was cleared, grain was grown, and hogs and beef cattle increased, and the settlers were beginning to feel well established.

Now that the district was well settled, requests were made to Ottawa to have the district thrown open for homesteading, and giving the squatters the right to file on their land. After much negotiating, and with the help of the Honorable Frank Oliver, Minister of the Interior at that time, the land was eventually surveyed, and the old squatters got their claims, paving the way for new homesteaders.

It is of interest to know how our district was named. Various names were suggested for the new settlement, such as Dickieville, for the senior of the first squatters. New Ireland and Erin were other names suggested. However, when the railway built their station, they bolted up a big twelvefoot sign on the front of it"DEVILLE", in honor of the Surveyor General of Canada at that time, C. E. Deville.

In time, most of the bachelors married, and as the community grew and families increased, there came the need for a school. The local school had its beginning at a public meeting held in Mr. Ross' house in January 1912. Trustees were J. M. Verge, Mr. Kidney and Mr. Fowler. Money was raised by selling debentures to the Alberta School Supply Company. Interest paid was 6 ½ %. The site for the school was donated by the late John Coleman, who lost his life in the first World War. The school was built for $740.00 by Mr. Harrison.

The second annual meeting had four ratepayers present. At that time, the writer was elected president, and was connected with the board for the following 45 years when he retired and left the district. Early trustees were: Mrs. Mcmenomy, Mr. Fowler, Alex Love, Mrs. Bert Dunn, J. M. Verge, Mr. McCarty, Mrs. Owen Mrs. Bryenton, Alex Morrow and the writer J. Morrow.

Besides her active role as a trustee Mrs. Bert Dunn played a major role in helping the children. She gave much of her time in coming to the school to teach the children handicrafts, such as knitting, sewing, and woodwork which were exhibited in the Annual School Fair. Many of those children who now have families of their own, remember her helping hand with gratitude.

The school ran very successfully from its start in 1912, and had many pupils of which it is justly proud. In 1937, permission was granted to add another room to the school, to enable the students to take up to grade eleven. This was built for $415.00. Now two teachers were hired— a Junior High and a High School teacher.

The local school is no longer used, as pupils are now taken by bus to larger centers, under the Provincial Government's new scheme. It is now used as a community center, so still serves a useful purpose in the community.

In the winter of 1912-1913 the first store was built in Deville by Mr. Jim Caskill and a partner who was a fur buyer. This store served the community for a short time, as it burned. In 1914 Mr. McIntosh built a store and in 1916 sold it to Jack Curlett Sr. About 1924, Mr. Curlett's son Jack Jr. and his wife Laura took over. Around the same time that Jack Curlett Jr. was operating his store, Alex Morrow kept a store on his homestead farm, a short distance north of Deville then built a new store south of the railway station. The two stores served the community until Curlett's burned in 1930. It was never rebuilt. Morrow's store has continued to serve the district.

The first mail in the district was brought by saddle horse from South Cooking Lake district to Mr. Watherson's homestead. Later the Verges had it in their log home. When the railway was completed in 1909 the post office was moved to McCaskill's store, then to McIntosh's and Curlett's store. When Curlett's store burned, the post office was moved to Alex Morrow's store on February 24th, 1931, where it is at the present time.

In June 1956 Mr. Alex Morrow received a long time service badge for having given satisfactory service to the Post Office Department and to the people of Canada.

Several churches have served the district over the years; the first is believed to have been the Anglican Church from Tofield. Services were held in December 1912, presumably in the school. A Catholic Church was built shortly after this date. The United Church held services in the school for many years, sending student ministers out from St. Stephen's College in Edmonton. The Lutheran Church and the Mennonite Church have also served the religious needs of the community.

While Deville has become a prosperous district the struggling railway, no longer an asset to the district is slowly shrinking into oblivion. The stockyards, the elevators, the section gangs, water tank, and siding are all gone. Good roads, good trucks and good service have been a welcome substitute and nobody gives a second thought to the disappearing railway.

The early settlers are pretty well scattered today, and many have reached the end of the trail. Many of their families have enjoyed large holdings, and are enjoying the prosperity that well developed farms, good buildings, gravelled roads, electricity and gas brings. No longer are people dependent on trapping this has been replaced by dairy herds, beef stock, hog and sheep raising.

The district is fortunate in having the Blackfoot Stock Association pasture adjoining it. This is a 40,000 acre community pasture which started in 1922, and runs about two thousand head of cattle per season from May 15th to October 15th,and is under the capable management of Mr. Jack Gray.

Texaco Exploration has done some drilling, and has struck a strong gas flow. Drilling is continuing from time to time.

When the district was transferred from the Beaver Municipal District to the County of Strathcona, a new era of road development started high grades, and gravelling of all main roads something the district had hoped for after many years of only "good weather" roads. Councillor Andy Adamson played a large part in bringing these services to our district; later it was taken over by Rodger Parker.

The latest acquisition to the district is the new Provincial public picnic park set up in 1926. This is a quarter section of land on the north shore of Hastings Lake, owned by the Provincial Department of

Lands and Mines. It has half a mile of sandy beach, and good fishing with jackfish and perch. Many beautiful islands of spruce and birch are dotted throughout the lake, making it a popular spot for boating, fishing and duck hunting. Our local Member of Parliament, Mr. Floyd Baker, played an active part in developing this project, and "Baker Beach" is fast becoming one of Alberta's most beautiful public camp sites.

This is the story of Deville as the writer saw it. Looking back over those 58 years, I can sum it up in one phrase, "Those were the good old days".

—*John Morrow*
*March 1964*


## THE AMISK CREEK SETTLEMENT

*Mrs. Conrad Patterson, a former resident of the Amisk Creek district, wrote the following article.*

The rich land along the banks of the Amisk or Beaver Creek together with the stream, teeming with fish, seemed an ideal location for a settlement to the Flaatens, Bergs and A. Erickson who arrived there in 1894. But these Norsemen soon found they had English neighbors. Mr. and Mrs. Brown and their son had located about a mile and a half south of the present Picnic Shelter. Then they dug a home in the bank, shored it up with boards, covered the roof with sod and were ready for winter.

Mr. Erickson filed on the quarter north of them and Rudolph Berg and his son Robert settled on the land just south of Donald Yoder's farm.

No doubt they all hurried to the Dominion Land Office at Beaver Lake, N.W.T. to file on their homesteads but only Asa Erickson's document is available. It is dated June 16, 1894, number 268.

In October the P.C. Moen family arrived and Flaatens made room for them until they could dig a shelter in the bank about half a mile to the northwest. There were no boards for walls and floor but it was home and the happy family moved in in November, taking Mr. Erickson as a boarder.

"It was crowded with Pa and Ma Erickson, Einar, (a baby) and I, but oh it was fun!" said Mrs. Annie Patterson, at ninety-one.

The men were often away cutting logs but the women were too busy to be lonely. There were socks and mitts to knit, candles to make from tallow and made in a mould bought in Winnipeg. Mrs. Moen had a sewing machine and had been warned of the highprices of materials in Canada, up to thirty cents a yard, so she had a good supply of calicoes to make up at five cents a yard

The news that Annie was working age soon spread and before she left for a position at Dr. Tofield's, Mrs. Flaaten came over one evening and they made basques and skirts for themselves. They splurged that night and used two candles.

Annie's dress was a cream flannel with brown dots and cost ten cents per yard. She did love that dress.

Mrs. Moen's prowess as a midwife also spread and she helped bring many babies into the world. When she couldn't go in the early days, Annie had to. She went to Brown's and then to Major Fane's, east of the lake She was to care for an invalid daughter but she had scarcely finished the supper dishes when Major Fane placed young Frank in her arms. He evidently was in a hurry to get on with the business of his country and caught them unprepared.

Annie held the baby before the fire and kept him warm until the midwife arrived. It was a cold, stormy night and the lady lived about five miles away around the lake; Annie kept boasting about the fine baby until the poor mother was frantic with worry. She was sure something was wrong with him, but her fears were groundless; he was perfect. He's now a Conservative M.P. for VegrevilleBruce. (Editor's note: Major Fane resigned his seat in Parliament early in 1968.)

During the summer of 1895 the log houses were completed and the families moved in. Mr. Erickson was joined by his wife and daughter Alma. They brought some fine furniture and were the envy of the neighborhood.

Church services were sorely missed and when Presbyterian or Methodist preachers rode in, all the settlers gathered for worship and fellowship. There were no denominational divisions; they all used the same Bible and all believed in the same God; each took his turn hosting his neighbours, serving as he was able. Sometimes the refreshments were pretty meagre but that didn't count.

Occasionally the ministers served in other capacities. Rev. R.E. Findlay arrived at Erickson's and found that gentleman suffering untold agonies with an aching tooth. The minister reached in his saddle bag for forceps, pulled the tooth and won a lifelong friendship. No doubt he was invited in, to dry out after fording the creek, and given good Norwegian coffee.

The women longed for Ladies' Aid and walked to Bardo whenever they could, carrying their precious shoes. Sometimes they knit as they walked, the yarn fastened with a device hooked in their belts.

Mrs. Moen was the Bardo Ladies' Aid first Treasurer and Mrs. Flaaten and Mrs. Erickson were also Charter Members. They joined in on quilting, knitting, sewing, and talking, but all working toward a goal – a church.

However, in 1902, the ladies found it too far to go to Bardo; new settlers had arrived in their own community and they needed a church of their own.

Consequently, an Aid was formed. Mrs. P.C. Moen was elected President and Mrs. P.O. Flaaten, Sec.Treas. Other members were Mesdames A. Erickson., P.O. Moline, Oleana Lillo, and the Misses Annie Moline and Annie Moen. These two young members became Mrs. Roy Carter and Mrs. Alfred Patterson.

The first dinner and sale was held at Moens in the spring of 1903. A $100.00 organ was purchased with the proceeds and church was held in the school. But the women wanted a church, so when their savings reached $400.00 the men were asked to pitch in. The congregation was canvassed, other donors gave generously, Alfred Patterson donated land for the church and cemetery, and with a capital of $1075, the Pederson Bros. of Round Hill were contracted to build the church.

The church was incorporated on Dec. 31, 1914, under the name of

The Norwegian Lutheran Church of Amisk Creek. Charter members were: Mr. and Mrs. R.O. Berg, Mr. and Mrs. A. Patterson, Mr. and Mrs. P.O. Flaaten, Mr. and Mrs. Peder C. Moen, Mr. and Mrs. E. A. Moen, and Peter J. Aas.

Rev. Jothen, Pastor of the sixpoint Ryley charge conducted services bimonthly.

The minutes of the congregational meetings were written in Norwegian until 1930 although English was used for most church services after 1920.

A basement was built in 1928 and a kitchen in 1938. For a period of four months the church was used as a school after that building burned.

Some of the remarks overheard at the Lutefisk dinners served in the basement were most amusing. One young girl was passed a plate of lefse. She took a piece and placed it beside her place. Her companion asked her, "Aren't you going to eat it?" 'Is that what you do with it!" was her reply. Spread with butter and sugar, it would have made a sticky napkin.

Mrs. Gray liked flatbread but not that skin bread and one man knew what lye did to his sink so he wasn't taking any chances on eating lutefisk.

Membership was never large in the Amisk Creek church but we did have fiftyfive children and adults receive baptism; thirty were confirmed, but only seven at Amisk Creek and eight couples were married there. The women kept abreast of changes in their organization, raised hundreds of dollars for charitable purposes, added improvements to the church and even installed the power after the congregation had given its consent providing we would pay the bills.

Let us turn back again to about 1900. With the arrival of new families it became apparent that a school must be built. Lawrence Anderson bought Berg's quarter for $500.00, a magnificent sum, Gallaghers settled south of them, Sr. and Jr. P.O. Moline bought out the Browns, the William Lennie family and Hugh Black, settled east of them, L. Bolton, Andrew Patterson and his nephew Alfred, John L. Gray, Peter Aas, the Lillo family and others made the settlement positively crowded.

A meeting was called, early in 1903, consisting of L. Anderson, Chairman, L. Bolton, Sec. and John. L. Gray was elected as treasurer.

H. Black, a bachelor, donated land in tho southeast corner of Section 22 and the Amisk Creek School District, No. 799, N.W.T., was formed. A seal bearing this insignia was still in use in the minute book of 1937.

It was decided to build a 20' by 26' building. L. Bolton was asked to see M. McCauley about getting out 4000 ft. of lumber, debentures were issued for $410.00 and contracts were let as follows: W. Schultz for hauling lumber @ $5.00 per thousand, hauling lumber, nails, etc. from Wetaskiwin to Mr. Solberg for $42.00, delivering 2 cords of rock – A. Erickson, $12.50, laying foundations 1 ½' x 1 ½' – J. Adams – $10.00, building school – A. A. Story – $89.00 and seats for $15.00, hauling and piling lumber – C. Adams – $4.00, digging 2 holes, 3' x 4' x 5' – H. Gallagher, $1.50 and building 2 little houses – P. Aas – $9.00. The contract to rebuild in 1937 was let to A. Moen, and J. Ness for $2696.

The first pupils were Annie, Oscar, Nettie and Elmer Anderson, Alma Erickson., Einar Moen, Albert and Ingvald Lillo, Alex Lennie and Chanley Gallagher. They were greeted by John D. Gilchrist, a good teacher I am told . He must have been shrewd and a man of means as well, because in 1904 the board borrowed $197.00 from him at 8% to meet current expenses even though taxes had been raised from 3 1/8 cents per acre to 4 ¼.

The settlers worked hard but there was time for play too. Visitors were so welcome and when language proved a barrier, sign language was used. Mrs. Brown and Mrs. Flaaten had a great visit this way. Mrs. Erickson called on the Lennies, a fine Metis family. Mrs. Lennie dug some meat out of the ground, cooked it, spread a cloth on the grass and they sat down to enjoy the dinner. It was good even though it was skunk. Annie Moen went to her first picnic at Rowlands and found the only refreshment was a barrel of lake water. She didn't stay long. It was a long way home for supper.

I don't know what the men did for amusement except play outlandish pranks on each other. I suspect they watched the girls because one by one the bachelors married or moved on. I know there were house parties, ice-cream socials, Christmas concerts, quilting bees, and I feel sure the men were there, too.

Some of the girls formed a basketball team. Mabel Vaughn, Inger

Brocks, Mary Francis, Lena Anderson, Agnes and Emma Bruha had a lot of fun. Emma remembers playing Bardo and those Jensen girls!

Later football became the craze. A Young People's Society was formed and young and old alike took part in the programs. Again all denominations became one. Of course this was in the late 20's and communication and travel were no problem and I doubt we felt we were having as much fun as our forefathers had enjoyed under far more stringent circumstances.

The creek still meanders through the community but its channel has been diverted, bridged and dammed. Roads are gravelled and no longer is it necessary to skirt sloughs and then follow the creek's twists and turns to reach school as Alma Adams did. Progress has set in; progress has taken its toll.

The trend toward larger farms, the migration of young people to larger centres to seek employment and old folk retiring for a well-deserved rest has left many homes vacant. The school was moved to Tofield and now serves as the Historical Society Museum. The children are bussed to Ryley, and Ryley has become the centre for Luther League and 4H activities. More families have moved away.

Finally the church faced the insurmountable task of functioning with five families and a bachelor. The task was too great. But, before closing its doors, a glorious Fiftieth Anniversary celebration was held in August, 1964.

The church was filled with former members and friends out: two charter members, Mrs. Patterson and Mrs. Moen were duly honoured, there was great rejoicing but sadness too. Then in December, the doors were closed.

The little cemetery is kept by the young Patterson boys, Gary, John, David and Dennis and given a good trimming once a year by the sons and daughters of loved ones lying there. The church still stands as a symbol of fellowship enjoyed.

Although the community has dwindled, its spirit lingers; legends of its early days persist and many are the stories still being told.

# LINDBROOK

Lindbrook School District was formed early in 1910. The first trustees were: Mr. Lindberg, Mr. Sherbrook, and Mr. Asa Rogers. Mr. C. Blake was the secretarytreasurer. While the school was being built, classes were in a log building on the homestead of Mr. A. Anderson from May to December. The new school was built by Asa Rogers, assisted by Mr. Sherbrook and Steve Sullivan. After December 1, 1910, classes commenced in the new school with the new teacher, Mrs. Fielding, who had just come out from England. Other teachers at Lindbrook in the early years were Miss Metherikk and Mr. McCall. Later, Mr. McCall was to be principal at Alberta College.

The little log building which had been used for a school was used as a granary when a few years later Mr. Anderson sold his farm to Mr. W. Hooper and Pete Holland. Mr. Anderson moved to Miquelon district south of Lindbrook; a son, Helmer, still lives there.

Lindbrook acquired its name from a combination of parts of the names of the two trustees, Lindberg and Sherbrook.

The C.N.R. completed its main line through Lindbrook in 1909. The first passenger service occured early in 1910. In 1914, the Lindbrook station was erected. It stood until just recently when it was sold. A. Parish and Heinbecker elevator was built near the station in 1933, but it was torn down in 1951.

The road to Edmonton in the early years was just a winding trail. Though it was improved somewhat during the years, it was not gravelled until 1930.

Lindbrook Store was built in 1919 by Percy Swain. However, he did not complete the job as he fell from his wagon while hauling supplies from the store. He broke his leg, gangrene set in, and he died. His brother-inlaw took over and ran the store for a number of years.

Mr. Jack Leahy was well known throughout the district. Those who were fortunate enough to have a telephone could order groceries and have them delivered by Mr. Leahy.The children would all be waiting to see his old touring car come in sight for they would be certain to find a bag of candy or packet of gum tucked away in the grocery bag.

Mr. Leahy sold the store to Clark and Hicks who in turn sold it to Mr. Silversides. The store later belonged to J. Bracegirdle, Brown and Timelus. F. Garford, J. Hooper and to its present owner, Charles MacLeod.

Other old timers in the Lindbrook area included the families of Stine, Glenn, Steve Sullivan, Otto Lindgren, John Wozencroft, Andrew Scott, Tam Porter, Ed Cookson, Tam Cookson, John Bailey, Frank Kortzman, A. Gill, G. Braaten, Mrs. A. Smith, A. McHeffey, George MacKenzie, Jack Appleby, J. Brown, 0. Jensen, Robert Logan, W.Lancaster, A. Frary, R. Hammersley, John Wilson, Paul and Jesse McMullen.

# LEGEND OF MONARCH OF BEAVER HILLS

*by Irene Williams courtesy Winnipeg Free Press*

R.D. (Bob) Harris of Canadian Wildlife Service and Keith Williams, project manager and field man for Ducks Unlimited, stood admiring magnificent elk antlers mounted high on the wall of the Williams' home near Ministik Lake.

"By Jove, Keith." exclaimed Harris as he measured the antlers for a second time, "will you look at this? They are a royal head; a real trophy! How did you get them?"

"Well, it's a long tale, Bob," said his companion as he strolled off, "but strange as it may seem, that rack that you have just measured may be the proof of an almost legendary tale that has been told for many years through the range of Beaver Hills."

In this part of the Canadian West the country is rolling and well timbered, also dotting with innumerable lakes. It is an ideal game country and as late as 1900 one could travel by canoe, without portage, from Miquelon Lake, close to Camrose, right through the Beaver Hills via Oliver, Ministik, Cooking and Hastings Lakes to Beaverhill Lake between Tofield and Mundare.This route lies south and east of Elk Island Park situated on Highway 16 west of Mundare.

When Elk Island Park was being formed the moose and deer were very plentiful in that area but the elk were noticeably fewer in number.

Around solitary camp fires, however, the story oft repeated was of a giant bull elk who sank through the ice on Ministik Lake into twelve feet of water. The place was marked by hearsay as being one half mile west of the creek mouth which ran from Ministik to Cooking Lake.

The idea for Elk Island Park began in 1904 at which time 16 square miles were set aside as a game preserve and by 1908 the fencing of the original park area was completed. In 1913 the area was changed from its game preserve status to a National Park. It was not until 1922 that 36 sections (the southern part) were added to the park, with the addition of a few other small parcels of land from time to time.

There were many animals already within the fenced portion but the local residents, who originally requested that area be so preserved, were promised at that time that there would be at least 24 elk and 35 deer within the fenced area.

There seems to be no official record of the establishment of the fence or of the animals that were subsequently introduced, but there is a story handed down from one of the early settlers north of Cooking Lake who is now deceased.

Louie Daniel was his name. He was a Metis, well versed in the ways of the wild and a leader among men; slight build, weight around 135 pounds, wiry, with great stamina, about 5 feet 7 inches in height with jet black hair; an excellent horseman and a crack shot. He was known far and wide as a matchless guide and a man to depend upon.

He was given the contract of rounding up a nunber of the wapiti and getting them inside the newly fenced area of Elk Island Park.

He chose 12 young men whom he knew he could depend on to do the right things at the right time in the woods. They were all well mounted and they travelled far to the south and east and established their camp on the Hudson's Bay lands in the southern part of Beaver Hills They scouted the surrounding country for many miles during the next few days and, in so doing, they got the lie of the land and ascertained that game was plentiful enough for the drive.

Early one morning they broke camp and rode quietly many miles more, still to the southeast. In the chilly predawn they separated, each one several hundred yards from the other, and started working their way slowly northward toward the park. There was no excitement just a quiet, orderly, slow trek forward with an occasional glimpse of an elk drifting ahead of them.

It was a slow, difficult drive as elk cannot be driven like cattle. They have to move forward more or less of their own accord without being panicked or hurried and in some places it took over two hours to move them 100 yards. The riders spread into a half circle behind and on each side with the game forming a sort of island in the centre., moving slowly but surely ever forward.

There was one gigantic bull elk with a set of antlers that made him outstanding that they had sighted early the first morning of the drive, and when the word was passed along to tighten up the half circle it was also to watch for this prize specimen. But as the days passed with never another glimpse of him Louie Daniels began to fear that the wily elk had eluded them, and he silently resolved to return and stay in the Beaver Hills until he got at least another look at him.

There was quite a section of fence laid flat and men spread far out on either side waiting as the last day waned and the drive neared the end. The animals were herded quickly and successfully into the park without ever guessing that they were to spend the rest of their lives within the enclosure.

Everyone was well satisfied with the drive except the man who planned it and he wanted that big elk.

Later he quietly prepared for a lengthy stay and went back into the hills. He was an experienced hunter, but for once he seemed to have met his match.

He got only one long shot at the fleeing form of the old monarch. Although he followed the tracks for two days he didn't sight him again and had just about concluded that he must have missed when in the heart of the thicket he found where the old warrior had stopped to rest. When he went on there were uneven tracks as if the elk walked with a limp.

It was growing late in the day, so he hurried on, following the tracks, hoping to sight his quarry before dark. The elk was headed for the lake where the islands were close to shore. Although it was late in November the ice was not too safe.

"Surely," thought Louie, "he will not risk crossing that springfed lake to an island."

But the elk was wounded, weary and hungry and that was just what he intended to do. If he could get across and hidden securely in the little hay meadow that was invariably in the heart of the impenetrable thicket that formed each island his instinct must have told him he would be safe until his painful wound healed.

He was about half way across, in the centre of the channel where there was twelve feet of water, when Louie emerged from the bush and caught sight of him.

In the fading light it was hard to see but he took a chance on another long shot and the elk fell heavily. The ice cracked ominously and as the elk struggled to rise it sank beneath him.

As the early darkness settled like veiling smoke over the lake, a coyote howled eerily, and the waters closed silently over his head. So ended the last chapter in the life of the old monarch of the hills.

On a bright sunny day in June, many years later, with the waters of the lake a full 10 feet lower, around the same island appeared a green Peterborough boat with a redhaired girl of 16 years and a small blond boy rowing. They detoured a few feet in their course to avoid what appeared to be a snag protruding from the water.

Suddenly the boy said, "Wasn't it along here some place that elk was supposed to be? Let's go back!!"

So with the curiosity of youth they backed water a few feet and discovered that it was horns they had seen.

The water was shallow and after a struggle in which they were in great danger of overturning their boat in the bottomless black mud which formed the boggy north shore, they succeeded in retrieving a magnificent set of antlers which belonged to the huge elk of the long ago.

Perfectly kept by the alkaline water, they are now polished and preserved for posterity. Mounted high above a doorway facing the rising sun, the ancient monarch keeps silent vigil over the Beaver Hills where he ruled so long ago.

"It's a strange world isn't it?" said Bob Harris looking speculatively at the rack. "You were the small boy, eh? You and your sister found the last resting place of the old elk.

"I can see why you grew up to be a naturalist, but it is a coincidence that you are with Ducks Unlimited working on the same old lake."

# ORGANIZATION OF DISTRICTS THAT NOW MAKE UP THE COUNTY OF BEAVER NO. 9

## MUNICIPAL DISTRICT OF CORNHILL

In 1903 when the Local Improvement Ordinance was passed to provide for the organization of selfgoverning Local Improvement Districts this area consisted of four townships. The secretary for this setup was the late Mr. Thomson. This organization existed until 1912 when the Rural Municipality Act was passed allowing nine townships to an area with six councillors. The area not being classed as an organized area became the Rural Municipality of Cornhill No. 487 and held its first meeting January 6th 1913 with five Councillors. The first Reeve was T. J. Glenn and T.J. Rogness the first Secretary. The name of the municipality was chosen at the first meeting. Quite a number of names were submitted of which Cornhill was one. The name is of historic interest also, it dating back to the 12th century in the City of London, England. A road running between Poultry and Leadenhall streets bearing the name of Cornhill for 700 or more years. It was suggested that the site was an ancient corn (grain) market, though of this there is no actual record. It is now a busy street. The name Cornhill had a pleasant sound and there were visions of plenty of food – hence the name was chosen.

1914 saw six Councillors elected. T.J. Rogness was secretary until January 1915, when other business obligations forced him to resign.

John Weatherill, father of Harold Weatherill, later a councillor for this area, then became secretary and held the office until his death in March 1928. Routine business was carried on until this small district became a part of the enlarged District in 1943.

## MUNICIPAL DISTRICT OF BEAVER LAKE NO. 486

The history of the Ryley District is very much the same as that of Viking and Tofield. Being situated between the two the same trails were used and the living conditions of the pioneers were alike. A Post Office was set up for this area on the east side of Beaver Lake and one to the south.

The Ryley District is also a mixed farming area. The district had a large creamery and cheese factory which was destroyed by fire caused by a lightning strike in the late 1940's. It now has a $100,000 milk drying plant. Coal of very good quality is also available from mines at the south end of the district.

Very few records of this District are available but according to one of the old timers first Councillors for the Local Improvement District were Mr.Golden., Mr. Albertson., P.P. Kjosness and John H. Hill. This area also began with four townships. It was still an L.I.D. in 1915 but had been enlarged to nine townships.

## MUNICIPAL DISTRICT OF PATRICIA NO. 485

This District began as District 25-J4 consisting of four townships and Councillors Eli Latham,Peter Nelson and J.W. Suddaby and met June 17,1905. Eli Latham was elected Chairman and one member took the minutes. July 15, 1905 a secretary was appointed. December 1905 an election was held and one more Councillor was added, namely Mr. Hennessy. This added up to one Councillor for each township. The district remained as such until 1912 when five more townships were added, making a total of nine. Six Councillors were elected and the district was made into six divisions. The district being an Organized

Local Improvement District operated under the Local Improvement Act of 1907. The number assigned to it was 485. First meeting of this nine township area was held February 8, 1913.

## MUNICIPAL DISTRICT OF IRON CREEK NO. 455

This District began as District 24-J4 consisting of four townships and Councillors George Loades, J.E. Kringen and Mr. Havener. It met May 28, 1906.The next meeting held August 4, 1906 saw C. Barber present a fourth Councillor. This district remained as such until 1912 when it became an organized Local Improvement District No. 455 and five more townships added. First meeting of this area was held February 1, 1913.

The Provincial Government had Organized Local Improvement Districts operating under the Local Ordinance Act of 1907 and Rural Municipalities operating under the Rural Municipality Act of 1912. The Organized Local Improvement Districts were remaining as such and preferred the "waitandsee policy."

In 1918 the Provincial Goverment passed the Municipal Districts Act. Under this Act the Organized Local Improvement Districts and Rural Municipalities became Municipal Districts.

Local Improvement District No. 485 became the Municipal District of Patricia No. 485 and the first Reeve was M. McDiarmid.

Local Improvement District No. 455 became the Municipal District of Iron Creek No. 455. The first Reeve was Henry Ovens.

Local Improvement District No. 486 became the Municipal District of Beaver Lake No. 486, first Reeve was B. Lillemoe.

From the records it would appear that the Municipal District of Cornhill No. 487 had been a Rural Municipality in 1913. First Reeve of the Municipal District of Cornhill No. 487 was William Thomson.

1943 saw many nine township districts become a new enlarged district of which this area was one. The District included Municipal District of Cornhill No.487, Municipal District of Beaver Lake No. 486, Municipal District of Patricia No. 485 and Municipal District of

Iron Creek No. 455, a total of thirtyfive townships. The number and name assigned to the district was Municipal District of Ryley No. 480. The first Reeve was Henry Ovens and the SecretaryTreasurer was J. W. McMullen, former SecretaryTreasurer of the Municipal District of Beaver Lake No. 486. The name given the District was for organization purposes only. At the meeting of Council March 13, 1943 the name was changed to Municipal District of Beaver No. 480. On April 1, 1945 the Department of Municipal Affairs assigned new numbers to many districts. This one then became Municipal District of Beaver No. 73.

As time went on it was considered necessary to change the boundaries so that the Municipal District and the School District covered the same territory. This meant that for School bus transportation boundaries had to be changed to suit natural barriers.

Effective January 1, 1955 some territory was added at the east end of the district., some on the south and a small portion to the north. Some was taken away on the west and the south west corner. This coterminous area covers approximately 1400 square miles.

First Reeve of the revised area was John P.Rozmahel and SecretaryTreasurer J.W. Letourneau.

In November 1957 the Municipal Council applied for County status and effective January 1, 1958 the Municipal District of Beaver No. 73 became the County of Beaver No. 9. The first Reeve being John P.Rozmahel, and SecretaryTreasurer Olof Monsson, Superintendent of Schools was H.A. Pike.

In December 1967 an addition was started to the County office located at Ryley. This was completed in late spring of 1968.

January 1, 1969 Reeve of the County is J.H. Roddick; SecretaryTreasurer, A. Robert Cross and Superintendent of Schools, Marvin S. Bruce who, while on leave of absence, is replaced by W. Bock.

# Early Families of Tofield

# BIOGRAPHIES OF PIONEER FAMILIES

The committee responsible for the compilation of this book felt that for practical reasons the accounts of pioneer families should be limited to those families who were in this area by 1910. After this date, a large influx of immigrants entered the Tofield district; the pioneer era was over.

Members of the pioneer families were asked to submit their family histories. If direct contact was impossible friends of the family were consulted.

Since the excellent history of the Bardo district, "Pioneers of Bardo, Alberta" by Ragna Steen and Magda Hendriksen contains biographies of the families in that district, no attempt has been made to duplicate this material. We are well aware, however, of the invaluable contribution made to Tofield area by the Bardo pioneers.

Those submitting biographies were encouraged to record family legends and experiences as well as the relevant statistics and dates. While this anecdotal approach has enlarged the book, thereby increasing its cost, we feel that the spirit of the pioneer era has been accurately presented for future generations.

# THE ABBOTTS

The Abbotts were a pioneer family of Tofield. Lem Abbott was barbering in Ed Kallal's pool room in 1908 and living near the Maxwells with whom he and his wife Emmeline shared many happy social hours.

Lem was musically inclined and generously donated his talents to the town band and to the Tuxis Boys band, which he directed.

The Abbotts took an active part in the town activities. Mrs. Abbott was a charter member of Ionic Chapter O.E.S. and an avid bridge player.

Two years after Mrs. Abbott's passing in 1957, Mr. Abbott went to live with his daughter, Mrs. Clara Brady, her husband and family, in Edberg.

# H. K. ADAMS

One of the real old timers of Tofield was Harvey K. Adams, Mr. Adams was one of the general merchants in the original hamlet of Tofield, on the present John Rempel farm.

Mr. Adams was born in 1878 in a log shack on a farm in Newton County, Mo. When he was fifteen, he went with his family to the newly-opened Cherokee Strip in Oklahoma. They filed on a townsite lot where the city of Pawnee eventually arose. His father founded a meat and food business which young Harvey took over when his father died.

He got many Texas longhorns to butcher as the Texas cattlemen used to trail them up to Oklahoma to feed them out on corn for a year and most of them would be big brutes five or six years old when they reached the Adams' slaughterhouse.

On January 1, 1898, he journeyed 150 miles to Wichita, Kansas to marry a young farm girl he had met in Oklahoma.

In a letter written from Laguna Beach, California, in April, 1959 Mrs. Adams said their two children, Arthur and Audrey, were both born in Tofield.

In 1903, the Adams' came north to Butte City, Montana and worked in the butcher business there. A young man from Butte went to Edmonton to investigate business conditions and on his return reported them as being good. This was J. W. Morton, who, with Harvey Adams, formed a partnership to establish one of Edmonton's first butcher shops known as Morton and Adams.

Later Morton and Adams moved to Tofield, ahead of the coming of the Grand Trunk Railway. Mr. Adams took a contract from Pat Burns to supply construction crews with meat. After the construction crews passed Edmonton, he went to work with Burns, who had meat contracts for construction camps as far west as Jasper.

In Mr. Adams' time the price of cattle was somewhat lower than it is now. He remembered trailing 1,400 lb. steers to Edmonton and selling them for 3 ¼ cents a pound, the price for the times.

Even at that price, cattle raisers made money because there was no grain feeding, thus making for lower production costs.

After working for Burns, Harvey Adams became a drover, working part time out of Edmonton and part time out of Tofield.

In 1919, he came to Calgary as manager of a branch of livestock commission firm of Wood, Weiller and McCarthy. Two years later, he and his bookkeeper, Roy Ferguson, bought out the Calgary branch of this firm and carried on as Adams, Wood and Weiller. Later this firm was managed by Art Adams, son of Harvey. Art's son, Pete, is following in the family footsteps in the business. Neil Morrison, son of Mr. and Mrs. Adams' daughter Audrey, is also in the firm.

Harvey Adams was always too busy to engage actively in service clubs, but, for a period he was associate director of the Calgary Stampede. The organization to which he later devoted time is the Southern Alberta Old Timers' Association.

## SAM BETHEL

On a site overlooking Beaver Lake, five miles north of Tofield, between Highways 14 and 16, is the Bethel place, a weatherbeaten, two-storey frame house rising above the surrounding fields. This house was built in 1910, replacing the small tarpapered original shack. In about the some period the rail fences had been discarded and replaced with wire. The old log barn, although shaky, still stands but many other buildings also built of log, have disappeared.

Mr. Samuel Bethel filed on this property before the turn of the century. As the dense growth of trees had to be cleared before buildings could be erected, the family did not come to the homestead for a few years. During this time they resided in Wetaskiwin where Mr. Bethel managed a Burns' Butcher Shop.

In 1905, travelling by team and wagon, he brought his wife and three small daughters, Mary, Mildred and Alma, to their new home. Mrs. Bethel was no novice to frontier life as she, in 1876, had moved with her parents, the Joseph Stohrs from Illinois to Kansas. As this was only a few years after Kansas had been admitted as the thirty-fourth state to the Union, Indian scares were still commonplace. In later years Mrs. Bethel entertained her children with tales of these early adventures. The Stohr family later settled in Nebraska and here Rosa met and married Samuel Bethel, a young Irish immigrant.

The year following the move to the homestead, Melvin and Myrtle (twins) were born and Hubert arrived two years after. For the new arrivals Dr. Tofield, and Mrs. Than Noland (a close neighbour) were in attendance. It is interesting to note that the birthplace of the twins is listed as Logan. They were possibly two of the first children registered in this area.

In those early years the Bethels' neighbours were the Pruden families, the Norris', Phillips', the Than and Jos Noland families and Henry Wood family, (with whom Sam had shared the terrifying experience of a train wreck on an earlier trip to the territory). This community is now known as Lakeshore. To the north (the McKenzie district) lived the Chris Moos, the Logan, Trent, Roberge, Norn and, of course, the McKenzie families. In time several families from Quebec, including Seales, Fergusons and Booths came to the neighborhood. The Jack Monroes acquired the quarter just south of the Bethel property and became good neighbors In many cases the former homesteaders sold to the new arrivals.

During this time of change other people came and left. Some became discouraged with the demanding pioneer life and soon departed. But many fond memories remain of one colorful couple the C.D. Cays, who once lived on the farm now owned by Rod Rudzcki. C.D. was a retired British sea captain and his wife, Elsie, a New York heiress. It is difficult to imagine them in a pioneer community. They were frequent visitors at the Bethels' and along with their three Airedale dogs Currie, Haig and Tig, were a source of awe, wonder and amusement to the children. Mrs. Cay smoked (very gracefully too) and she also wore a blonde wig! This was fascinating. In 1914 Captain Cay was recalled to his ship for active duty and Mrs. Cay stayed on the farm, caring for their livestock. Following the war, they sold the farm and left for Hollywood. The movie making industry was in its infancy, and it is reported that D.C. became an actor. This story is quite credible as he was a handsome and debonair gentleman.

True western hospitality prevailed in the Bethel household. Dances, card games and skating parties were frequently held. Sam was generous with his belongings and his time. Horses were shod and equipment repaired in his primitive blacksmith shop. He was willing at all times to attend and care for sick animals in the community. His interest centered in livestock, primarily SuffolkPunch horses, Shorthorn cattle and Berkshire hogs. He was an organizer and director of the early Tofield fairs and was always an enthusiastic exhibitor. He was a member of the Stock and Swine Breeders' Association.

Mrs. Bethel was endowed with a wealth of good common sense and also possessed a keen sense of humor. These characteristics gave her the strength to brave the hardships, privations and sacrifices of a pioneer wife and mother. She could produce a proverb for almost any situation. ("Spare the rod and spoil the child" was the one most often quoted). She too was a kind friend and neighbour and her youthful outlook and lively interest continued throughout her long life.

In 1926, Mr. Bethel became ill and suffered the loss of a leg. He died four years later. His widow remained on the farm until her death in September, 1954 at the age of 86.

Mary is the only member of the family remaining in the Tofield area. She and her husband, John Wood, live on a farm near the original Henry Wood's homestead. They have four daughters and one son. Mildred (Mrs. Mildred Seale; deceased) left two daughters. Alma (Mrs. Bob Bradley) lives in Nelson, B.C., Myrtle (Mrs. J. McDonald) of Okotoks has two sons. Melvin(deceased) left two sons and two daughters. Hubert and his wife Annie also have two sons and two daughters. These two families live in Vancouver, B.C.

# BIG BILL BLOSS, COLORFUL OLD TIMER, DEAD

This article was written by Margaret (McCauley) Wood in 1938, following the death of Bill Bloss. It was printed in the Tofield Mercury and is reprinted here because of its historical significance.

"Tragically ending his life by hanging, at the advanced age of 89 (he would have been 90 the following day) Bill Bloss, a colorful figure of the West, passed away Sunday night. His wife predeceased him in 1913. There were no children.

Big Bill Bloss is dead Let not the manner of his death overshadow the true character of the old man. Those who knew him best well know his courage, independence and indomitable will. As a young man his life was filled with romance, excitement and adventure, such as few of us can ever hope to experience. A pioneer of the pioneers is gone. To quote his own words spoken during a serious illness six years ago, "Aye, a lot I've seen in my time, more than most, perhaps. Life has been kind to me. So many I've seen come and go in the making of this country of ours. But looking back over my life it seem to have been a lot of fun more than anything else. Aye, a great adventure. I have no desire to live longer and be a burden to anyone. I hope I may soon be in the happy hunting grounds."

He was born in Indiana, October 3rd, 1849. In 1869 he left home and went to Minnesota, and in April, with a team of oxen and wagon, began freighting from St. Cloud to Dakota, carrying supplies for the soldiers in the first Riel Rebellion. There were eighty wagons in the outfit and more than once they were attacked by the Sioux Indians. These trips took all summer and the winters he spent at Detroit Lakes, Minnesota, fishing and hunting.

The Spring of '72 found him the head of a small party freighting from Braynard Minn. to Ft. Lincoln on the Missouri River, just across from where Bismark now stands. In the spring of '73 he went west with a government engineering party under General Stanley. It was a big outfit, 29 companies of soldiers and over 300 mule teams. They were surveying a route for the Northern Pacific Railway.

In the spring of '76 he was waiting at Ft. Buford to join the troops which were being sent up the river. A post settler asked him to go to Bismark to bring back men and oxen, promising they would be back before arrival of the troops. However, they were away much longer than they intended, and on their return they heard the news of the Custer Massacre; thus quite by accident Bloss missed the fate of Custer and his men. He joined the troops at this time serving General Miles. He carried despatches for General Crook from Ft. Buford up the Yellowstone to General Terry's boats. Here he delivered them to the famous Buffalo Bill who carried them the rest of the way.

In June of '77 Bloss and another made a trip from Miles City to Seattle on horseback, took the boat to San Francisco and train to Los Angeles. There they fitted out with saddle horses and packs and went east, skirting the Mojave desert, near the borders of Mexico to Fort Tuna on the Colorado River; across the river 125 miles north, then east 200 miles to Iron Springs and 30 miles again to the Colorado crossing just below Grand Canyon; north again 100 miles to St. George. From St. George down the valley towards Salt Lake City 300 miles; then to Ogden, Utah; north to Franklin, Idaho; still further north to Lemki, the Indian agency at the top of the mountains; east to Virginia City, Montana, to Bozeman, then down the Yellowstone to Miles City. That was May of '78. The trip had taken eleven months.

The years '79, '80 and '81 were spent hunting big game in the Big Horn Mountains; part of the time for himself and each fall acting as scout and guide for Old County gentry. There were many big names among them and it was then that he met the uncle and father of our present Alberta Lord Rodney.

In the spring of '84 he was freighting in the Rocky Mountains as far west as Golden, B.C. The C.P.R. was being built through that year.

In the spring of '85 came the war. Bill Bloss served under General Strange and pursued Big Bear as far as Fort Pitt. In July of '85 he came back to Calgary and the next spring went freighting again between Calgary and Edmonton.

In the spring of '87 Bloss went to Lacombe and had a cattle ranch there for four years. In the spring of '91 he came to Beaver Lake. Since that time he has been ranching and farming in the Tofield district until six years ago when he retired from active life.

—*Margaret (McCauley) Wood*

# THE JACK BOWICK FAMILY

Jack Bowick was born in Fettercairn, Kincardineshire, Scotland, in 1881. In 1892 he came to the United States and then to Edmonton. In 1905 he and his wife came to Tofield, in the company of James and Omar Mahaffey.

Among his remembrances of his early days in Alberta was the driving of the golden spike which symbolized the completion of the Canadian Northern Railway.

He also remembered the discomforts of a trip to the Pembina valley when a snowstorm was raging. He was wearing, of all things, a derby hat; a handkerchief tied over the hat and around his ears gave some protection against the bitter weather but still, he was forced to turn back.

On his arrival in Tofield, Mr. Bowick filed on a homestead which consisted of four quarters of land and was situated one-half mile north of Henry Woods' home. The Bowicks travelled to their homestead in a lumber wagon over roads that were far from good. The sloughs, swollen by the wet spring, had covered much of the road so a new trail had to be made, following the higher ground.

The Bowick homestead was proved up in 1912. In the meantime, Mr. Bowick worked for the Tofield Coal Company. The first shaft for their mine was sunk in 1907. Mr. Bowick managed the mine for Crafts, Lee and Gallinger from 1907 to 1910. Later, this became a strip mine, reaching a production of 145,000 tons per year and being shipped as far as Winnipeg.

By 1913, Mr. Bowick was working for the town of Tofield, finishing up the gas well near the present Baptist Church. When the drill went too deep, salty water flooded the well one thousand feet in six minutes.

In 1915, Mr. Bowick bought a steamer that pulled three 24-inch plows. These weighed 1575 pounds each. He and his brother Bill, together with Cap Lee owned this outfit which was used to break up virgin land at the rate of seven or eight acres a day. This was an unheardof speed in breaking the land which had been covered by solid forests of poplar at the coming of the pioneers.

The Bowick family often saw Chief Meechum and his band travelling by wagon and horseback to and from their permanent camp at Blackfoot Lake. Chief Meecham's favorite article of attire was a derby hat.

Mr. Bowick was instrumental in moving the buildings from the original site of Tofield to the Crafts, Lee and Gallinger townsite. When Tofield was again moved in 1908, he again assisted the process both with horse outfits and with his steamer. He moved the present Masonic Hall with six teams of horses. It had to be jacked up to be raised onto a high foundation. To do this, 64foot timbers were used.

Mr. Bowick returned to the mine later. Here, as master mechanic with steam engineer's papers, he worked until 1923.

He also moved the present Graham Allan house and the present Coffee Shop which was once the L. C. Hay Store and was situated on the site of the present Walter Kendal house.

In 1940, the Bowicks moved to Barrhead, returning to Edmonton in 1947. In 1951, they went to Kelowna and in 1955 returned to Tofield to retire.

Mr. Bowick was an active curler. Some of his fellowcurlers were John Lee and George McLaughlin, with whom he curled in 1913.

He recalled playing baseball in shirt sleeves on January 5th in 1914.

Mr. and Mrs. Bowick retired in Tofield where they lived for several years prior to their deaths.

In Tofield they were close to their grandchildren, Bonnie, Bruce and Colin, children of their deceased son Harry and his wife Edna (Shaw) Bowick. Nearby in Edmonton are Mattie and Connie, Keith in Barrhead, Bob in Kingman, and another son, Jack, in Kelowna, B.C.

# DOLPHUS CAMPION

Mr. Campion was born in 1884 in the Duhamel district. His mother, widowed when Dolphus was a year old, carried on the freighting business begun by her husband. With horsedrawn cart two trips were made each summer to Calgary hauling supplies for the Hudson's Bay Company. Sixteen carts with two riders in charge composed the train of carts which Dolphus remembers. He recalls the loss of one canvas-wrapped load off the ferry over the Red Deer river at the site of the present city of Red Deer. The load, he remembers, was recovered and reloaded before the train resumed its journey.

Dolphus has another amusing memory concerning a ferry, this time on the North Saskatchewan River at Edmonton. The ferryman, thinking his load of horse drawn vehicles complete, pulled away from the shore leaving one horse and buggy to wait the next trip. The horse felt differently about being left; as the ferry began to move he made a plunge, landing with all four feet on the ferry. The lady driver had but little choice; she had to hang on, sit well in the center of the seat to balance the floating buggy and hope for a safe landing on the other shore.

In 1907, Dolphus Campion married Esther Dumong of New Norway and settled in the Hay Lakes district. Here he took up freighting trips which frequently took eight days and were not without their difficulties. Once, when a horse balked halfway up a hill refusing to go further, another teamster came to Dolphus' assistance by the strange device of putting sand in the balky horse's mouth, he succeeded in distracting its attention and, forgetting its balkiness, the horse proceeded up the hill.

Moving to Tofield district in 1910, the Campions homesteaded the northeast quarter of section 4, township 51, range 19, W 4th. Seven children were born to the marriage, four sons and three daughters. All four boys served in World War II, one being killed in action.

Mrs. Campion died in 1924, Mr. Campion remained in the Hasting Lake district taking an active part in community life, serving on the school board and in other organizations. In addition to farming, Mr. Campion kept a small herd of cattle; he also trapped and fished.

Retiring from farming, he bought a half-acre of land in the southwest corner of W. Fontaine's land on which he built a small house in a poplar grove. Travellers on Highway 14 would often see Mr. Campion enjoying either the sunshine or shade according to the weather. Here he remained for 12 years before moving to a small house near Lindbrook Store in 1964. Until recently Mr. Campion regarded a walk from Lindbrook to Tofield as just a bit of exercise! In his life span of 83 years, Mr. Campion had seen, and been a part of, the development of the West.

# THE COOKSON FAMILY

George Cookson was born in Lancashire, England, August 17, 1837. He married Louisa Lloyd and to this union were born seven children; five sons, John, George, Thomas, Herbert, Edmund, two daughters, Annie and Ida. Herbert died in infancy.

It was in 1890 that John who was the eldest in the family decided to come to Canada. His first stop was in Manitoba, where he spent a year before coming to Alberta. The first railway tracks were being constructed between Calgary and Edmonton and he obtained employment with the C.P.R. A year later his brother George also decided to come to Canada and he arrived in Calgary on his 23rd birthday. For awhile the brothers worked in Calgary for the James B. Little brickyard. Shortly thereafter, this company moved to Edmonton and the Cooksons worked for them here also. Early in 1893, Thomas Cookson informed his parents that he wished to join his brothers in Alberta. It was then that the family all decided to emigrate to Canada. Jessie Porter who was engaged to John Cookson came with them. Prior to the family's arrival; John and George had filed on their homesteads and erected a log house in readiness. The family arrived in Edmonton in December, 1893; on December 12, 1893, John and Jessie were married in the old McDougall Church which is still standing. It was bitterly cold at this time of the year and John was unable to obtain a marriage license in Edmonton. He walked to Fort Saskatchewan to get one, a distance of some 17 miles. The Cookson family made the trip to Tofield shortly after their arrival in Edmonton. The weather was intensely cold: the first night they found shelter in an old abandoned trapper's cabin. The mud had fallen from the chinks between the logs so the travellers hung blankets around. There was an old stove in the shack, and they cut enough firewood to keep themselves warm the temperature that night was 62 degrees below.

John stayed in Tofield to assist his family to establish themselves and to prove up their homesteads.

George Jr. remained at his job in Edmonton. His wages were needed to assist the whole family. He stayed on in Edmonton working until 1898 and it was during these years he worked for the Edmonton Cartage Co. which was owned by Matthew McCauley. It was in 1900 that Annie Cookson was married to Matthew McCauley, who was the first Mayor of the town of Edmonton.

After his marriage to Annie Cookson, Matthew McCauley lived a few years on the shore of Beaverhill Lake on what is now part of Dan Dodds' farm which later sold to Henry Wood. He became warden at Fort Saskatchewan jail. After his retirement there, he moved to Sexsmith. Two sons, George and John, were born to this second marriage. Annie McCauley, widow of Matthew passed away in 1947, following a brief illness. For the last fifteen years of her life, she lived in a world of silence, for she had become stone deaf.

In the early years, the home of George Cookson, Sr. became the centre of religious activities in the Tofield area. The Cooksons had obtained an organ from the first Anglican Mission in Edmonton and this was a welcome addition to the church services. Mr. Cookson was an accomplished organist and many happy hours were spent gathered around the old organ for a get-together and a sing-song.

George Cookson Sr., was the first postmaster and the post office was located in his home, one mile east of the town's present location. When it came to naming the town he was approached and was asked if he would allow them to name the town Cookson. However, being a modest man, he felt that he didn't deserve this and suggested that the town be named after Dr. Tofield. This was a good choice, for here was a very dedicated gentleman, loved and respected by all who knew him.

On May 17, 1909, the Cookson family were sorrowed with the death of their beloved mother, Louisa Cookson. Following the death of his wife, George Sr. went to live with his son and daughter-in-law, John and Jessie. He passed away in 1924 at the age of 87 years.

George Cookson, Jr. was married on June 27, 1905, to Winnifred

Whillans who had come west with her family from Ottawa. Her father, Rev. Robert Whillans performed the ceremony at Tofield. George and Winnifred had four children, John, Arthur, Edna and Helen. Edna who was the eldest in the family tragically passed away from spinal meningitis at the age of 8 years. Helen married Art Lampitt and is now living in Sherwood Park. John joined the Edmonton city Police force and today has attained the rank of DetectiveSergeant. Arthur joined the R.C.M.P. and is now the Chief of Police for the city of Regina.

George Cookson passed away November 13, 1952, and his wife Winnifred on December 5, 1960.

Ada Cookson went to Victoria where she received her training in the school of nursing. She served overseas during the first World War; then went to San Francisco where she remained until her death in 1944.

Edmund Cookson married Olive Ingram on March 4, 1917. Their homestead was in the Lindbrook district. Edmund passed away on February 14, 1925 from acute appendicitis. He was only 42 years of age at his death, and he left three small children, Lloyd, Margaret and Nola.

Thomas Cookson also had a homestead in the Lindbrook area directly across the road from his brother Edmund. Tom served overseas with the Canadian Army during the first world war. It was while he was in England that he met and married Mabel Taylor on February 2, 1919. He brought his bride here until 1934, but due to illness and war injuries, they sold the farm and moved to Victoria where Tom passed away in 1945. His widow Mabel, now lives in Sudbury, Ontario where her son Cecil Cookson and daughter Mrs. Eileen Spiers reside.

The Cookson family were always active in activities of the United Church; both John and George served on the church board and were elders for some time. They were both members of the choir. Mrs. Jessie Cookson taught a Sunday School class for over forty years and was also president of the Ladies' Aid for many years During the early days, their home was open for the student ministers of all denominations. John and Jessie lived on their farm southeast of Tofield until 1953, when they took up residence in Tofield.

In 1943 John and Jessie celebrated their golden anniversary. A program and reception were held in their honor in the United Church. John Cookson passed away February 9, 1956 at the age of 89 years. His widow Jessie passed away, August 16, of the same year at the age of 93 years.

# THE COOMBES FAMILY

*Editor's note: The material for this article was obtained in an interview with Mr. and Mrs. Coombes in 1964.*

Mr. and Mrs. Chester Coombes pioneered in the Ketchamoot district. Mr. Coombes came to Tofield as a two-year old in 1894. He had come with his family by covered wagon from Colusa County, California, where he was born, so his earliest memories are of that long trek.

His parents, Mr. and Mrs. William Coombes, left their California home in 1893 for land in the state of Washington. They spent the winter in the town of Fairfield, near Spokane. During this interval they heard of the wonderful homestead county in the Beaverhill Lake area. When spring came the family set off by covered wagon for Beaverhill Lake. Over the mountains they went, and Mrs. Coombes had many moments of terror when the high mountain bridges had to be crossed. She refused to ride across, preferring to trust her own feet rather than those of the horses.

One of Chester Coombes' first memories is of himself, as a two year old boy, "helping" his father drive the team across tricky places while his mother shepherded his sisters, Mabel, Ethel and Amy along on foot.

Soon the mountains gave way to the rolling prairie, and parkland. When the little party reached Lacombe they were taken in tow by a land guide, E. Thompson, who was paid by the Dominion Government for guiding families to homesteads. On the trip to the Beaverhill Lake Country, Mr. Thompson's services were shared by three other families, the Charlie King, Gene King and Hugh Gallagher families. They arrived at their destination in September, 1894. Already here, Mr.

Coombes remembers, were the John Johnson, Lerbekmo, Haugen, Anderson, Erickson, and Flaaten families. Very shortly many other families were added to the community.

Just after the Coombes family had got settled, the Joe Dutton family who had lived here in a dugout for a short time, decided to return to Oregon. They purchased the canvas and the framework which had supported it on the Coombes covered wagon to make their own covered wagon more comfortable for the return journey. On their safe arrival at Corvallis, Oregon, they had a photograph of themselves and equipage taken, and sent a print of it to the Coombes family.

The Coombes had arrived in September and in October, another little sister made her appearance; she was the first white child born in the Ketchamoot and Bardo areas. She was named Eva. In due course, Margaret, Leslie and Myrtle arrived, to complete a family of eight children. Of these, Ethel (Mrs. Violet) and Chester are deceased, but the others survive. Mrs. Brown (Ethel) lives near Bawlf, as does Mrs. Jensen (Amy) while Mrs. Garvia (Eva) and Mrs. Johnson (Margaret) are in Orbelle, California. Leslie lives at Vulcan, Alberta.

The Coombes family were fortunate in finding land with a residence in fact two residences already built. Before they moved to the Amisk Creek area, the Hugh Gallagher family occupied one of the log houses on the farm on the S.E. ¼ of 165019W4th and Coombes family lived in the other. The good fortune of finding a ready shelter was the result of someone else's ill fortune. The gentleman who had constructed these log houses with sod roofs, also had another occupation. According to legend, he was a horserustler in traditional western style. Mr. Harry Neal, being the rustler's victim, did not accept his loss calmly. The rustler was convicted, and automatically lost his homestead rights. One cannot "prove up" a homestead while incarcerated.

As well as provisions for human habitation, the Coombes farm boasted a good log barn. A well, the source of which was a spring, was a most valuable asset of the farm. There was no school near the Coombes residence. The older girls stayed in town (the first Tofield) with the family of J.O. Letourneau, and attended school north of town. Later when Anderson school was built, the Coombes children attended there.

252

Mr.Harry Erwin and Mr. Jas. Younie are the two first teachers of the Anderson school, and Mr. Coombes remembers them, as well as the twice-a-day five-mile walk in quest of an education.

Mr. Coombes remembers clearly the early farming days of Tofield. He remembers starting farming with a team of oxen. With these powerful, if slow, beasts,he recalls breaking the prairie sod on his present farm. He borrowed a seed drill to sow his crops, though he remembers seeing as a child the seed being broadcast. At harvest time, the sight of the threshing machine belonging to Mr. Henry Wood from north of Tofield was very welcome.

Some of the pioneers of the Bardo district soon made a threshing machine of their own. Some of the ingenious men concerned were Mr. Haugen, Mr.J.Johnson, Mr. Hugh Mitchell and Mr. Lerbekmo.

This machine called the Beaver Lake Chief was manpowered. Six men were required to turn the crank, three on each side. The feeder was just wide enough to receive the strawtied bundles. To a small boy, it was a very wonderful sight. (A model of the Beaver Lake Chief is in the museum of the Tofield Historical Society, a vivid reminder of the ingenuity and determination of the pioneers.)

The pioneers raised cattle for cash sales as well as for meat. Shipping and marketing conditions were vastly different. Once a year, usually in the fall, a cattle buyer came from Wetaskiwin. He made the rounds of the district, buying any available cattle. The going price was $25 for a threeyear-old steer. When about 200 cattle were bought at this munificent price, they were rounded up and driven to Wetaskiwin by the buyer and his helpers.

Hogs were raised, too, but for use locally.

When flour was required, a long trip to the flour mill at Fort Saskatchewan was in order. Each householder kept his own supply of flour, and the storekeepers kept only a small supply on hand. Mr. Coombes recalls that once when their supply of flour ran low, they went to the store operated by Mr. La Fond to get an emergency supply, and all that could be secured was a 50 lb. sack. This would have been fine, except that a can of coal oil had been spilt on it. Since a choice between hunger and coal oil-flavored flour had to be made, the Coombes family ate bread that had a distinctive flavour as long as the fifty pounds of flour lasted.

Edmonton was the trading center for this area when Mr. Coombes was a boy. The long trip took a full week to complete and was accomplished twice a year. In summer the route lay through Fort Saskatchewan, as there was no road through the Beaver Hills.

One of the most dreaded hazards of pioneer life was the incidence of prairie fires. The native grass grew high and luxuriant and provided excellent fuel for windswept flames. Mr. Coombes recalls sitting up most of the night to watch the lurid flames of a prairie fire reddening the eastern sky. The neighbours ploughed fire guards these, except for rain or a change in the wind, were the only defense against the terror of a prairie fire. The worst fire was one that came in from the Beaver Hills. The flames were coming straight for the Coombes house when the Mitchell family came to offer sanctuary in their home which seemed to be out of the path of the holocaust. Fortunately the wind changed and the Coombes' home was saved.

One of the pleasures of pioneer life was the annual Dominion Day celebration. This has been held so long in the Tofield area that it is doubtful if anyone can recall the first celebration. But Canada's birthday was always the occasion of highly enjoyable picnics and sports events.

Mr. Coombes remembers particularly the Dominion Day celebration of 1909. This much anticipated event was held on the site of the present school grounds. Baseball was the order of the day. All the official equipment required was a ball; a bat could be secured from the nearest tree.

Horse races were always a featured event. No special track was required a section of the road cleared of pedestrians was all that was required. A small money prize was awarded, but the glory of owning the fastest horse was probably a reward in itself. On July 1, 1909, the horse belonging to Robert Logan was the winner, recalls Mr. Coombes. The small fry, then as now, enjoyed foot races and jumping contests.

On this particular July 1st, one of the featured events was a race between two oxen teams. Mr. Coombes remembers that the team belonging to Jerry Gallagher was the winner. Of course the days events, which had been sponsored by the town of Tofield, ended with a dance at night.

William Coombes died in 1905 and was buried in the Bardo cemetery. Mrs. Coombes, in 1920, married Mr. Arthur McMullen.

Chester Coombes made an interesting discovery when he was engaged in breaking up the land on the quarter adjacent to his own, known as the "Dick Turner quarter." About six inches underground, the land was found to be white with buffalo bones. This boneyard extended for about a quarter of an acre. When this discovery was made, Mr. Coombes recalled that "old Jeremy" Gladue, uncle of the Mr. Jeremy Gladue who resided near Hastings Lake till his recent death, had told of big buffalo hunts carried on in their area. Near a spring at which the buffalo were accustomed to drink, an Indian buffalo pound had been constructed. Then the Crees drove the buffalo between the ever-narrowing fences which led to the slaughtering place. The abundance of bones proves the efficiency of this method of securing a supply of meat.

One set of bones which arouses Mr. Coombes' curiosity looked very much like the bones of a man. A skull, obviously that of a wolf, has also been found there. Many Indian weapons were found among the bones, as would be expected.

Mr. Coombes also remembers Rev. Finlay, a minister who travelled to this area by horseback or horse and buggy from Vegreville. Services were held in the pioneer homes whenever a minister was in the vicinity. After the Hugh Mitchell family arrived and built their larger house, services were usually held there.

As a young man Chester Coombes worked at Daly's, where Charles J. Kallal now lives. He also worked for Marson and Walker for the munificent wages of $5.00 per month. It took two extra trips, says Mr. Coombes, to collect even that amount.

Working at Oren Daly's brought an extra dividend, in the person of Mr. Daly's sister-in-law, Ida Grovum, who had come with her widowed mother from the Lake of the Woods, Minnesota, enroute to her new home at Ashmont, Alberta. Mrs. Grovum and her family stopped at Tofield to visit Mrs. Oren Daly, her daughter. The younger daughter Ida, remained in this area to work for Mrs. McBeth in what is now the

Ketchamoot district. On February 15, 1915, she became Mrs. Chester Coombes. Mr. and Mrs. Coombes have six children. Harold, the eldest lives at home, Ethel (Mrs. Hugh McColl) at Stony Plain, Esther, (Mrs. Harry Ketchum) at Mulhurst, Gladys (Mrs, Ewald Gabert) in Edmonton. Ronald farms in the Ketchamoot district and Lyle lives in Edmonton.

Mr. and Mrs. Coombes took an active part in the life of the Ketchamoot district. Their family all lived within easy visiting distance, and the grandchildren were a source of abiding interest to Mr. and Mrs. Coombes.

# THE DISERLAIS FAMILY

Miss Madeline Dumont was born in Calgary in 1887. Later that same year, the family moved to Pincher Creek where Mr. Dumont was employed on a horse ranch and where, a few years later, he was killed while breaking horses.

Mrs. Dumont with her family of three small girls and one boy came to Tofield in 1895 where Madeline (one of the small girls) has lived ever since.

Mr. Jack Diserlais was born in Manitoba and in the early 1900's, came west where he homesteaded N.E. ¼ of Sec. 12-52-19-W4th. In 1905 Jack Diserlais and Madeline Dumont were married. The wedding took place at St. Albert; the honeymoon was a trip to Jack's homestead in a buckboard. Jack lived on his homestead until his death in 1948.

While living on his farm, he broke the required number of acres to get his patent but spent much of his time trapping muskrats, weasels, mink and lynx. He also had a sideline which enhanced the family finances: cutting willow pickets and stovewood. Before the gas line came to Tofield, stove wood was much in demand; Jack delivered hundreds of loads of nicely split wood all ready for use. He was a welcome visitor when the woodbox supply was running low.

Madeline Diserlais remained on the farm for some time after her husband's death, but in 1960 moved into Tofield where she still lives.

Madeline and Jack Diserlais had eight children, four boys and four girls, Katherine (Katie) who died in 1967, Sarah of Ryley, Julia of Ardrossan, Myrtle of Edmonton, Pat and Sosi of Tofield, Clifford and John of Stewart Crossing, Yukon.

# THE DUNHAM FAMILY

Around the turn of the century, times were rough in Ontario for tenant farmers. Rents were high, prices low, and the future held no promise. For this reason Mr. and Mrs. John Dunham and six of the nine members of the family left Woodstock, Ontario in the spring of 1905 and came west to Alberta. They travelled by C. P. R. colonist car to Wetaskiwin via Calgary. They then moved by team and wagon to the Tofield district and lived a time with friends until they could get established.

They filed for homestead on all of section 18, in Township 50, Range 19, W4 and as soon as shelter could be erected they took up residence on their homesteads. They never talked much about the hardships they endured but rather of the good times, the social life, and the house dances when friends came many miles by wagon and sleigh and took two or three days for the trip.

In 1906 their daughter Harriet (Mrs. Henry Lee) and her husband and family also came west to settle in the district. In 1908 their eldest daughter (Mrs. Robert Gee) and her husband and family also came in and settled in the Kingman district.

The oldest member of the family (Mr. John Dunham) had left Ontario several years previously, travelling to Seattle and thence to the Yukon to take part in the Gold Rush.

What Stan Dunham remembers best of the early years was the roads or rather lack of them. The road allowances were seldom passable and trails followed the line of least resistance. But even the least resistance was quite formidable in the way of mud holes, sloughs and creeks. The one main east and west trail come through the yard and passed close to the house. As the land became settled the roads were fenced off, and the road allowances opened up, but it was not until the large machines became available for road building that the trails became only a memory.

The problem of getting to school in the early years was formidable. A few rode horseback or drove but most walked. In the winter, if one team had been through, the road was considered open, and blocked roads could not be claimed as a reason for being absent.

Stan Dunham owns and farms his grandparents' homestead and this land has been in the family name for more than sixty years. He also uses the cattle brand that his grandfather used and had registered in his name in 1912.

# MARK FERGUSON

In this, its Diamond Jubilee, the town of Tofield is indeed fortunate in having a living reminder of its early history in the person of Mark Ferguson, one of the original councillors of the town of Tofield.

Mark was born in Granby, Quebec in 1870. When he was twenty-one, he came west to Manitoba. After a return trip to Granby he came to Alberta in 1904 and homesteaded north of the present town of Ryley.

In 1906, he moved to what was to be Tofield. The roadbed for the Grand Trunk Pacific Railway had just been surveyed. It passed near the Post Office of Tofield, one mile east of the present townsite, and here, in the pioneer village were: W.C. Swift's lumber yard, Mr. Mahaffey's restaurant, R.O. Bird's hardware, C.E. Jamieson's Drug Store, Merchants' Bank, Dr. McKinnon's Drug Store, Logan Hotel, Fred McHeffey's Blacksmith Shop, Cress and Harper's General Store, and A.J.H. McCauley's real estate office.

The first town of Tofield soon moved to a site north of the present school due to the fact that Messrs. Lee, Craft and Gallinger had surveyed the new townsite there and had offered a free business location to anyone who would use it. Thirty business places, among them Mark Ferguson's harness shop were soon established there. Incorporation as a village followed in 1907 with G.B. Harper, W.C. Swift and Joshua

Noland as the first councillors and A.J.H. McCauley as secretary.

In 1908, the present townsite was surveyed and the town moved once more this time to its present location. Mark again moved his harness shop and there it stayed until 1918.

On June 20, 1909 the Grand Trunk Pacific Railway reached Tofield, much to the joy of its inhabitants. The population grew rapidly and in October, 1909, Tofield was incorporated as a town.

Mark Ferguson was then a member of the town council, the other members of which were: J.O. Letourneau (Mayor), R.D. Emery, A.F. Fugl, J.B. Harper, and A. Maxwell with A.J.H. McCauley, as secretary.

Mark well remembers the day the new town was officially named. In his own words. The council was gathered in Alex McCauley's office. The name of the town had to be decided. At the suggestion of Mr. Cookson, since the post office east of town had been called Tofield in honour of Dr. J.H. Tofield, pioneer doctor of this area, it was the unanimous choice of the council for the name of the new town. It isn't everyone who can say he was there when the town was named!

Mark remembers vividly the arrival of the G.T.P. in 1909. This was an event of truly great importance to the pioneer settlement. The steel reached Tofield on June 30, giving the inhabitants a special reason for celebrating on July 1st, already the traditional sports day. Mr. Charlie Cress was appointed the first station agent here. Mark served two terms on the town council. He remembers the building of the original covered skating rink in 1910 by Mr. Ben Barkwell and the addition to it which housed first one., and then two, sheets of curling ice. Mark himself was persuaded to take up curling by Frank McCauley, nephew of A.J.H. McCauley. He had been an ardent curler ever since though the past few years he has curled "behind the glass." Only a few years ago, he was on the rink skipped by Thomas Jacobs who won a "first." The resulting trophy sits proudly in his living room. He has been made a life member of the Tofield Curling Club and in 1959 attended, as an honoured guest, the Golden Jubilee Banquet of the Curling Club.

Mark was highly interested in the Tofield's famous "Silver Seven" hockey team and often practised with them.

While not a charter member of Palestine Lodge No. 46, A.F. and A.

M., which was instituted in 1909, Mark joined it in 1916 and has been made a life member.

His reminiscences of life in early Tofield are fascinating. He has seen horses replaced by tractors. He gave up his harness shop in favour of a tractor with which he did breaking and threshing, thus keeping up with the times.

He remembers Tofield's "industrial site" north of the present east railway crossing. Mark also remembers another of Tofield's early industries the brickyard founded by J.W. Robinson on Jack Cookson's land.

Tofield's gas boom of 1912 is also among Mark's recollections. The first gas well was right behind the town hall (south of L.W. Ferguson's present house); the second was drilled in Tofield's "industrial site", the third and most productive, was west of the present Baptist Church. On the strength of the future promised by this gas well, Tofield surveyed town lots for a considerable distance out of town, laid water pipes and prepared for a big future. Mark says two-inch pipe was laid from the gas-producing well to the C.N. station, with 3/4 inch pipes upright at intervals of eight or ten feet. At night, the gas at the ends of the pipes made a Flare Path lighting up main street. Sad to relate, these lights grew dimmer and dimmer and finally flickered out; at last, only mud came up from the gas well. The boom was over. It was to be a long time before water pipes were to be used in Tofield. Probably, Mark thinks, the well might have been kept in production by use of modern techniques.

In 1928, the homesteading urge sent Mark to Athabasca, where he filed on a homestead north of town. Here he stayed until 1935., enjoying the hunting and fishing in this pioneer area.

In 1935 he returned to Tofield to manage the farm of Mrs. T.E. Seale of the Lakeshore district.

In 1951 he moved into Tofield, retiring to a quiet life. He is deeply interested in all that pertains to Tofield. No doubt he often compares our modern town with the one of 1909 of which he was councillor.

In 1968, Mark was the recipient of his 50-year pin from Palestine Lodge.

# THE FRANCIS FAMILY

Jim Francis, pioneer of the Tofield district, and an active member of the community for many years was born in Tofield of a pioneer family.

Both Mr. and Mrs. Daniel Francis, Jim's parents, were born in Mitchell, Ont., where they grew up and obtained their early education. Later, Mr. Francis attended the University of Toronto from which he obtained his B.A. and M.A. degrees. He taught for several years in Ontario before coming to Estevan, Sask. in 1891. Here he homesteaded for three years but found farming conditions somewhat less than ideal. Jim recalls his father's comment on Estevan as being, "If the grain wasn't blown out it was dried out." In 1894, the Francis family left for Edmonton.

In Edmonton, Mr. Francis taught for a year, but July 1895 found the Francis family again on the move. This time they came to the Tofield district and settled on S.E. ¼ of Sec. 34, Tp. 51, R. 19, just across the road (south) from the present residence of Mr. and Mrs. John Wood. On this farm, Jim Francis was born. From here Mr. Francis drove five days a week to teach inthe MacKenzie School No. 234, one of the earliest schools in the province.

In July of 1897 the Francis family again moved; this time the move was to the site of their permanent home, at the south end of Beaver Hill Lake on S.E. ¼ of Sec. 4, Tp. 52, R. 18. Here Mr. and Mrs. Francis spent the remainder of their lives and took an active part in the community affairs. Mrs. Francis was particularly active where in church work the choir, and Ladies' Aid were her special fields of endeavour. Mr. Francis taught in Tofield School for several years. He was also interested in public affairs, and held office in several community organizations. Mr. and Mrs. Francis raised a family of ten children, three of whom are still living: Mrs. Louise Lovell lives at White Rock, B.C., while Arthur and Jim still reside in Tofield.

Gertrude, the eldest of the Francis family, married and moved to England where she spent the rest of her life.

John married Olive Shrigley, who still lives in Edmonton.

Mary married Earl Moore; they had two children, John and Hazel.

John is well known in Tofield for his many years of leadership in the Calf Club and his interest on purebred cattle. He and his wife Evelyn (McRoberts) have three daughters, Marjorie, Teresa (Terri), and Judith (Judy). Hazel (Mrs. Ivan May) lives in Belleville., Ontario. She has two children: Garry and Marilyn. George Francis married Laura Skinner. Two of their sons died while in their youth, but three of their children are still living. Glen and his wife, Iris (Bjornson), and their children, David, Carol Ann, and Ilene live in the Bardo district as do Pauline and her husband, Charles Rude, and their children, Linda, Lois, Brian, Darlene, Shirley and Barry. Sharon, Mrs. Neil Wease, lives in Ontario. Alana, daughter of Alan (deceased) lives with her grandmother.

Louise Francis married W.H. Lovell. Their children were Alfred, Robert, and Jean. The Lovells have lived at White Rock, British Columbia for several years.

Arthur Francis married Irma Shupe. They live just north of the Tofield creamery.

Jim recalls that his first school days beginning in September, 1902, were spent in the log school house which was later used as the Methodist Church. Eventually a new school was built on the S.E. corner of the N.E. ¼ of 36-50-19 which the Francis family attended The next move of classrooms was to the store above the R.O. Bird hardware in Tofield and finally in the fall of 1909, the students moved into the first brick school in Tofield. Here Mr. Jas. A. Younie was principal, whom Jim remembers as a fine person and an excellent teacher. At the age of 13, Jim left school to assist in the work of the farm which included herding sheep. His pioneer blood called Jim in Nov. 1915 to seek a homestead about six miles northwest of the present Dawson Creek, B.C. At that time, the railway reached only as far as Smoky River so to reach his homestead, Jim became involved in a 210 mile walk, via Grande Prairie. This jaunt took six days; with a 40 pound pack and a rifle to carry, Jim welcomed the end of the trail.

Once having reached his homestead, Jim says, I bet the government $10 against a quarter section of land that I could live on it for six months out of each of three years, break thirty acres of ground, and build a suitable dwelling, and I won my bet.

262

World War I was raging during these years and in 1918, Jim was posted to England until September, 1919. On his way home he received his discharge in Ottawa and went to see his Ontario relatives in Mitchell, Ontario. While there he met not only his relatives, but his future wife who at that time was Miss Marie Skinner.

On returning to the west, Jim spent a short time on his homestead and "proved it up" as required by government regulations. In June, 1920, he returned to Tofield where in the fall of 1920, he became a member of the Tofield Agricultural Fair Board.

In 1927 he was elected an elder in the Tofield United Church, an office he has held ever since. In 1933 he helped to form the Tofield Mutual Telephone Co.,for which he was president and "trouble shooter" for several years.

Mr. and Mrs. Francis were married in 1923 and raised a family of six five boys and a girl. The entire family was active in church and community activities.

Children of James Francis family were : Earl, Reed, Keith, Jack, Josephine and Gary. Earl died in his early manhood. Keith married Lorna Hennessey who died shortly after their daughter, Margaret was born. Later, Keith married Ada Burkholder. With their daughters, Cheryl and Heather, they are still residents of Tofield. Jack and his wife, the former Joyce Hill, live in Edmonton. Their children are Dale and Arla. Josephine, now Mrs. Ward Trotter, lives in Ontario. She has one small daughter, Pearl. Reed, his wife Evelyn(Attwell) and children live in the Fort Saskatchewan area. Gary married Adrienne Kirby. They have one son, James.

In 1957, the Francis family left their farm at the South end of Beaverhill Lake and came to live in Tofield where Jim has been engaged in carpentry. He was chairman of the building committee of the Tofield United Church when the congregation decided to build a new church, and it was under his direction that the present Tofield United Church was built. He has taught Sunday School for twenty years and has been its superintendent. He was a charter member of the Tofield Historical Society and has been active in preparing exhibits for its museum. He is also a member of the Co op and the Tofield Community League and the Tofield Curling Club.

On three occasions, he has been a delegate to the General Council of the United Church—in Sackville, N.B., in London, Ontario and Windsor, Ontario.

Recently Mr. and Mrs. Francis have journeyed to Eastern Canada, to Dawson City and to England. On these trips Jim has been able to indulge his hobby of photography, the excellent results of which he is always willing to share with friends. The illustrations in this book are chiefly from his camera.

He was a member of the Jubilee Committee of 1959 which directed the activities of Tofield's Golden Jubilee year; also a member of Tofield's Centennial Committee (1967).

All his life, Jim Francis has been an integral part of the life of the Tofield area. He has always been generous in sharing his talents and energy. Two expressions heard frequently in the Tofield are, Ask Jim Francis; he'll know and Ask Jim Francis, he'll help!

## CLAUDE GALLINGER

*The material for this article has been secured through the kindness of the Glenbow Foundation, Calgary, Alberta, who have willingly made their book "Claude Gallinger" available for use.*

A man who was to achieve international recognition as a cattle breeder, bringing fame to Tofield as the location of his Killearn Farm, migrated to Western Canada as a youth. At eighteen years of age, he arrived in Strathcona via the C.P.R. He had only eighteen dollars in his pocket but he had a job waiting for him. Robert Lee from Gallinger's home town in Ontario, MacDonald's Corner, had entered into partnership with a man named Ross in Edmonton and, business having prospered, Lee needed help. He wrote to Claude, offering "twenty dollars and found" to keep books and do other odd jobs in the office. So, on December 8,1899, young Claude Gallinger, after walking over ice on the North Saskatchewan yet too thin to bear horses, arrived in Edmonton.

Gallinger had come from a working class Presbyterian family. He worked in his father's blacksmith shop learning how much labor went into each earned dollar. This practical education and thorough knowledge of money values was to stand him in good stead in his Alberta years.

Soon Claude Gallinger was working for Ross Bros. Hardware Company, being paid thirty-five dollars a month; out of this munificent sum came fifteen dollars a month for room and board.

Ross Bros. carried wholesale groceries, supplying homesteaders with food and equipment. Roads to the surrounding tracts of land were miry trails. The North Saskatchewan provided the most comfortable as well as the cheapest highway. Barges, scows, and rafts were accepted modes of travel. Scows freighted loads of flour and lumber down the river. In August, 1903, one of the lumber rafts was boarded by Claude Gallinger en route to the Fort Pitt Lloydminster area where he was to collect some overdue bills for his employers. Arriving at Fort Pitt on Sunday after having been on the raft since Wednesday, Claude rode the remaining twenty five miles to the tent-town of Lloydminster and, later a further hundred miles to Battleford. He learned that travel fatigue was a constant companion.

In 1904, Robert Lee, now dealing in real estate, offered Gallinger a share in his land speculation. The immediate objective was to purchase the John Norris farm which lay adjacent to Edmonton. There were to be four partners involved in the transaction: Robert Lee, Claude Gallinger, W.I. Crafts, and J.R. Black. Gallinger's assessed share in the enterprise was to be a down payment of $11,250.00. To raise this amount presented quite a problem, but, by withdrawing his meagre savings from the Merchants' Bank and obtaining a loan from the bank for one thousand dollars, the necessary down payment was secured. The John Norris farm was bought, subdivided and sold; it now forms the residential district of Inglewood in Edmonton.

This successful venture led to a fulltime partnership; the firm was known as "Crafts, Lee and Gallinger Realtors." The firm was concerned with rural holdings and since Sifton's "men in sheepskin coats" were arriving in large numbers, the firm prospered through sales to these immigrants. In the Tofield area the firm sold a great deal of land to Mennonite farmers who had left Nebraska because of the scarcity of land in that area.

Early settlers near Tofield had discovered coal and had mined some for their own use. By 1906, speculative interests noted that, according to surveys, Tofield was on the eastern rim of the coal beds in the Edmonton area. A readymade coal market lay in the vast, treeless plains to the east.

In December, 1906, the Tofield Coal Company was formed with 2500 shares worth $1000 each for sale. Shaft mining was begun in 1907 with the coal being hauled in wagons to the farmers' homes.

With the coming of the G.T.P. in 1909, a rail outlet for the marketable coal was provided; coal could now be shipped to distant markets. When strip mining proved feasible, a railway spur was built right into the mine so the miners could load the coal directly into box cars. Sales expanded as markets were secured in central Saskatchewan, and even southern Manitoba, though, of course, Alberta points took the bulk of the sales. In 1910, Black sold his share of the Tofield Coal Company. Charles Taylor came to manage the mine.

Horses, dump wagons, and an elevating belt grader were used to clear off the overlay in the strip mine. Later, a Ledgerwood dragline was introduced and in 1913 C.H. Taylor, mine manager, returned from a trip to Germany with a $25,000.00 German stripping machine, which was used until 1917. This machine was succeeded by a steam shovel, powered by a donkey engine; finally the job was contracted to owners of Letourneau scoops. The seam of coal was about six feet thick and varied from twelve to eighteen feet below the surface.

After the mining operation was completed the overlay was filled in and the recovered land seeded to grass to prevent erosion and waste. In twenty years, even the bush has returned.

Since Crafts and Lee were primarily interested in Edmonton real estate, Gallinger accepted responsibility for the development of the Tofield coal mine. By 1914, this mine was in a position to compete with Edmonton mines for Edmonton markets. On the opening of the MacDonald Hotel in Edmonton in 1914, the Tofield Coal Co. received the contract to supply coal for heating the new edifice. Costing $2.00 a ton at the mine the coal was delivered at the MacDonald for $3.50 per ton. However, with the coming of natural gas, the market for coal declined and, in 1956 the mine ceased operations.

As well as being a successful business man, Claude Gallinger was an outstanding cattle breeder; his Killearn shorthorns became famous throughout North America. Beginning with a herd of commercial cattle pastured on reclaimed mine land, Gallinger became interested in raising purebreds which, no more expensive to raise than grade cattle, produced more and better beef.

He began with Herefords purchased from Joe Roper at Lacombe. The herd sire was to be a Prince Domino bull from the Caerlon Ranch at Nanton. As his herd increased, Gallinger bought Blanchard Domino 4th from the McIntyre Ranch of Magrath in 1934.

In 1928 or 29, Gallinger bought his first purebred shorthorn from Joe Brown and Barney Creech of Lloydminster. In 1932, he bought a carload of top quality shorthorns, registered from F.M. Rothrack, Spokane, Washington, I.J. Broughton of Dayton, Moscow, Idaho. One cow cost $1,125.00 a fantastic price in the depression era. The herd sire was Danny Boy purchased in Scotland for thirty three guineas.

In 1935, Gallinger decided to concentrate on Shorthorns and in consequence, had his Hereford dispersal sale. In the same year, George Cummings accepted the position of Gallinger's herdsman; the progress at Killearn farm in the following years was in no small part due to Cummings' exceptional ability as manager. By 1937, Gallinger was making a name for himself as a Shorthorn breeder. He adopted the herd name of "Killearn" the name of the Scotch village where his second wife, Jean, had been born.

Gallinger's first wife was the daughter of his partner, W.I. Crafts. They were married in 1908 and had two children, Wilbur (July 17,1909) and Margaret (May 26, 1911). Mrs. Gallinger died in 1924. In 1927 Jean Galbraith of Killearn Scotland, became Mrs.Claude Gallinger. She died in May, 1958.

The first bull sold under the new herd name was Duke of Killearn 9227686. In 1937, as a yearling, he brought $1500.00 a record price to that date. By the time Duke of Killearn died, ten years later, he was noted as a famous herd sire.

Gallinger continued to build up his Killearn herd. By rigid selection, his herd of females was kept at the very highest standard of quality. No female was ever sold; inferior ones were culled and sent for slaughter.

With herd expansion and increasing fame, Gallinger felt the need to increase his farming operations. Across the Saskatchewan River from Edmonton at Clover Bar lay the D.W. Warner estate which was up for sale by Mary Warner whose husband had died some years before. On purchase by Gallinger, this estate became Gold Bar Farm, and on it, the Gallinger family lived. This farm became a show place and the backdrop of the Gallinger "Killearn Shorthorn Production Sale" which was instituted in 1945. It was held in the Sales Pavilion in Edmonton; this sale brought buyers from all over North America.

However, Edmonton's expansion soon reached Gold Bar Farm and Gallinger sold it for $600,000.00 to Maclab Construction Company in 1955. The estate was of course subdivided and sold; it is now the Gold Bar subdivision of Edmonton.

Wilbur Gallinger married Dorothy McGarvey of Edmonton on August 9, 1938. They had three children: Kathryn, who died while still a little girl, Claude and Michael. Both boys have attended the Vermilion School of Agriculture, and still live on the "mine farm". Claude married Betsy-Ann Schultz, daughter of a pioneer family. Michael married Darlene Wells of Marsden, Saskatchewan; they have a small redheaded son, Sean Michael, who was born in Canada's Centennial year.

Wilbur died on April 30, 1966; his widow still lives on the home farm. Miss Margaret Gallinger, long connected with the offices of the Gallinger enterprises, lives in Edmonton.

## THE JEREMY GLADUE FAMILY

When Tofield celebrated its Golden Jubilee in 1959 Mr. Jeremy Gladue, one of Tofield's earliest citizens, was interviewed by the members of the Golden Jubilee Committee. In his fine modern home on Highway 14, opposite Fort Scott, Mr. Gladue welcomed the committee. Still tall, straight, active in body and keen of mind, Mr. Gladue recalled the era before there was a Tofield.

In 1890, Jeremy Gladue came as a boy to Beaverhill Lake country with his father, mother, sisters and brothers. The trip from St. Albert was made with teams and wagons. His uncle, "old" Jeremy Gladue welcomed them and shared his living quarters on the Logan ranch with them. Young Jeremy attended three school terms in Edmonton, to complete the education begun in St. Albert.

Like all young men of those days, he soon filed on a homestead, NW 12-51-19 the land presently owned by D.W. Jacobs. Other homesteaders on this location were Dr. Tofield on the SW quarter; Billy Rowland on the SE quarter and Louis Pruden on the NE quarter.

Farming then was on a strictly horsepower basis. The walking plow and harrow were the chief, if not the only, tillage implements. Mr. Gladue remembered his dad sowing grain by broadcasting it by hand in the age-old way. Later the process was accelerated by strapping tubs of grain to the back of a wagon, and as the horses moved down the field, the men broadcast the grain. Jeremy said the first mechanical broadcast seeder was brought in by John Phillips; Logans owned the first binder and cut grain for everyone. Soon young Jeremy got a binder and did similar custom work. Clarke Bros. from the east shore of Beaver Hill Lake owned a threshing machine whose motive power was provided by 16 horses. Henry Woods owned the first steam powered threshing machine. All the threshing was done from stacks and the grain sacked as it came from the machine. The fields were small, 25 acres being an average size.

Mr. Gladue recalled that in 1896 the Logan Anglican church was built. (This church is officially recorded as "The Church of St. James the Apostle Newton Logan)". The land for the church and the adjacent cemetery was donated by Robt. Logan. It was situated on the land Joe Laarhuis now occupies. Jeremy had good reason to remember this cemetery, as his mother, dad, and two sisters lie there as well as many early settlers, including Mr. and Mrs. Pruden, and Jeremy's brother Alex, killed in World War I.

Jeremy recalled that Chief Ketchamoot after whom the creek and school district were named, spent his last years in a little shack on the land now occupied by Stan Schacher. The Chief is undoubtedly buried along the creek there.

The pioneers had many hardships but they had fun, too. They held picnics by the lake shore and on the land now occupied by the Tofield Schools. Everyone came from far and near to join in the community fun. When asked what they did for amusement Jeremy's eyes twinkled as he said "We played ball. All we needed was the ball we could cut a chunk of willow anywhere for a bat."

Then he told of Tofield's first triumph in the world of sports. When asked if there had been a baseball team, he said "We had a real baseball team after the Woods and Phillips boys came. We went over to Vegreville (Old Vegreville) when their first fair was held. First we won the baseball game. Then came the horse races. Lloyd Wood owned a little buckskin horse named Dennis and we won all the races with him. Then came the foot races. Jim Ackley was fast but (modestly) I was a bit faster. We won all the races. Then I said, 'Now boys, the rest is up to you!' They went ahead and won all the jumps, too".

"As soon as the sports were over I drove to the store with Marion Hayes in our buggy. We bought a new broom and we drove around and around Vegreville (there wasn't much of it) waving the broom and yelling "A clean sweep for Tofield." At the dance which followed we Tofielders had to stick together for fear of reprisal."

Mr. Gladue was married in 1914 to Miss Donald. They had one son, Albert, and three daughters, Corinne (Mrs. Art Rowland), Kathleen (Mrs. Lloyd Grummett) and Bertha (Mrs. A. Lawrence) of Warren, Oregon.

Mr. Gladue died on November 29, 1960.

# THE GRAY FAMILY

Mr. and Mrs. J.L. Gray came to Alberta from Missouri, U.S.A. in 1902 and settled on N.W. 28-50-18 in the area east of Tofield.

Mr. Gray, a gardener, had the proverbial "green thumb" and all his plants flourished. The spruce trees that he planted during his first years on his farm are now a landmark.

Mrs. Gray operated a nursing home for several years. There being no hospital in the district, this nursing home provided a necessary service.

Mrs. Gray was active in the Ladies' Curling Club and in the U.F.W.A. Mr. Gray was a member of the Amisk Creek and, later, of the Ingram School Board. He was also a member of the Tofield Agricultural Society.

The Grays had four children: John, Lucille, Lowell, and Clarence. After service in World War I John farmed in the Tofield area before moving to Summerland, B.C.

Before her marriage to Dr. D.M. Morrison, Lucille operated a beauty parlor in Tofield. Later the Morrisons moved to Edmonton where they raised their three sons.

Lowell, an electrician, worked most of his life in the Palliser Hotel, in Calgary. Clarence died while still a young man.

In July 1924, John and Lowell made a canoe trip into northern Saskatchewan. Having purchased an eighteen-foot trappers' freighting canoe and planned their expedition carefully, they left Tofield on July 10. The canoe loaded with traps, "grub stake," rifles and other necessary equipment was hauled 175 miles to Beaver Crossing arriving there on July 15.

The next day the canoe, loaded with 1800 pounds of freight, was launched. Going down the Beaver River which was low at that season, the Gray brothers struck several sandbars. Shooting numerous rapids was a new and exciting experience. Game was plentiful on the banks of the river.

August third saw them at the junction of Beaver River and Isle a la Crosse. Soon they were navigating Churchill River, which ran out of the east end of the hundred mile long lake. On September first, after several portages, they reached their destination on Sandy Lake.

Here they built a log cabin and prepared for the coming winter. Fish were plentiful; four deer and two moose provided an ample supply of meat.

By the end of October, winter had set in, bringing a foot of snow. A three days' journey on snowshoes was necessary to get within reach of a caribou herd. Foxes and other small fur-bearing animals were trapped by the two men. If available, a good sleigh dog was worth $50.00.

Toward the end of January, the Gray brothers' supplies ran low so, on receiving a good offer for their outfit, they accepted it and set out, on foot, on the 300 mile return trip which took fourteen days.

Their comment that the trip was "priceless" summed up their feelings for their epic journey.

# THE HARRIMAN FAMILY

Mr. and Mrs. Azro Albion Harriman and their son, Clayton C. Harriman, together with his wife and family consisting of Herbert, Jennie, Ronald, Albion, and Aylmer, arrived in the Tofield district in the spring of 1902. With the assistance of Mr. John C. Phillips, a longtime friend who had left Iowa a few years previously to settle in this district, Mr. Harriman Sr. had purchased Section 12-51-19-W4th Meridian and it was to this location that the families moved as soon as buildings could be constructed.

Mr. Harriman Sr. also acquired the N.W. ¼ of Section 32-50-19-W4th Meridian under the provisions of the Homestead Act which permitted grazing of cattle in lieu of performing of other homestead duties. Mr. Harriman was a veteran of the American Civil War.

Mr. C.C. Harriman purchased a parcel of land consisting of 100 acres in the S.E. 12-51-19-W4th Meridian where the family lived for several years before moving to Flat Lake, Alberta, where Herbert Harriman homesteaded. An adopted daughter, Ruth Evelyn May Harriman, born September 27, 1910, was added to the family.

All the family but Herbert returned to Tofield soon, and after several years ran a dairy on the farm of Mr. Harriman, Sr., he having taken up residence in Tofield. Mr. C.C. Harriman also homesteaded a quarter section under the grazing provisions; this was the N.W. ¼ of 36-51-19-W4th.

On February 22, 1922, Mr. C.C. Harriman held his dispersal sale and shortly thereafter, the entire family left Alberta to take up residence in Bellingham, Washington, where Mr. and Mrs. A.A. Harriman had already acquired a small farm and taken up residence.

Mr. Herbert Harriman and his wife, the former Mildred Abernethy, came back to Tofield with their four children in 1926, intending to move back to their farm at Flat Lake, Alberta, but this move was never accomplished. While visiting at the home of Mildred's parents, Mr. and Mrs. Will Abernethy, Herbert and his brother-in-law, Frank Walker, Dorothy Abernethy's husband met an untimely death by drowning in Beaverhill Lake, just offshore from the Walker farm. This sad event took place on April 26, 1926. Mildred and the girls returned to Bellingham where they owned a small house.

Mr. A.A. Harriman had been a member of the I.O.O.F Lodge for many years.

## THE HULL AND BARNES FAMILIES

*The material for this article was contributed by R. H. Barnes.*

Mr. and Mrs. Frank Hull came to Tofield from Gradbrook, Iowa, in 1906, with their three grown children, Clinton, Lois and Edna, who had accompanied them. They settled on a farm in the Ketchamoot district. The entire family participated in community affairs; in addition , Mrs. Hull delighted her neighbours with the oil paintings which demonstrated her artistic ability.

Lois Hull's fiancé, Oscar Barnes, had come from Gilman, Iowa, arriving in Tofield with the Hulls. Married in 1906, Lois and Oscar Barnes lived in the Farmington district for a short period, later returning to the Ketchamoot district where their son, Ralph Hull Barnes, was born in 1908. From Ketchamoot, Oscar Barnes came into Tofield to play baseball, a sport he loved.

Mrs. Hull died in 1930; Mr. Hull in 1949 at 96 years. Oscar Barnes died in 1948; his wife Lois followed in 1961. They are all buried in the Tofield cemetery as is Clinton Hull.

Mr. and Mrs. Ralph Barnes live in Red Deer.

# ISAAC INGRAM FAMILY

Mary Jane Newman was born in Guelph, Ontario, Sept. 24, 1869. At the age of sixteen she went to Park River, North Dakota to visit relatives. It was here she met and later married Isaac Ingram who had arrived from Ireland. For a while they lived in North Dakota but the lure of the West beckoned the young couple, so they started on the trail with their two young sons, George and Will. Their third son, Allen, was born at Emerson, Manitoba but died when only a few days old and was buried along the trail, not far from Emerson. When they arrived in Edmonton, in 1891, which then was only a small town, they filed on a homestead at Clearwater, near Leduc. This area is now known as Beaumont. Mrs. Ingram and the children spent the summer months on the homestead doing the required work to prove up the homestead. Isaac had obtained employment in Edmonton, at $19.00 a month. It was in 1907 that Isaac decided on another move, and made a trip to Tofield. He liked the country and filed on another homestead in Woodlawn district, 7 miles west of Tofield. However, he was not to realize his ambitions for he became ill shortly after and passed away, leaving his widow Mary, three sons, George, Will and Ed; six daughters, Olive, Margaret, Charlotte, Mae, Mary and Victoria.

In the spring Of 1908, Mrs. Ingram decided to make the move her husband had planned on, so she and her son Will, who was a young man of eighteen, came to Tofield. They spent six months on the homestead where they built a loghouse and barn, dug a well, and brushed and broke the required number of acres. While they were gone, the eldest daughter, Olive (known to everyone as Bella) was left in charge of the younger brothers and sisters; she herself was only sixteen years of age then. In 1909, Mrs. Ingram moved her family to Tofield. George remained in Edmonton where he was employed. The Ingram family were again sorrowed in 1911, when George passed away following a sunstroke.

Among the first families the Ingrams were to become acquainted with were the Yagers, O. Johnsons, McGinities, Hendersons and Carlisles. These families established a life long friendship. They also became good friends with the Henry Woods family and though they lived quite a distance apart the young people were often together.

In the early days, during the winter months, house parties were enjoyed by all and they would bundle up warmly with blankets and off they would go with the team and sleigh for an evening of fun and dancing or a card party. In the summer, there were boating and picnics at Beaverhill Lake.

Mrs. Ingram was always willing and ready to help out her neighbors and was called on many times when sickness struck or when a new baby arrived.

In 1917, Olive Ingram was married to Edmund Cookson. For a short time they farmed near Tofield, before selling the farm to E. McClymont and moving to a farm at Lindbrook. In 1925, Edmund died leaving his widow and three children; Lloyd, Margaret and Nola. Following the death of her husband, Olive moved back with her mother. By this time, the other girls had left, Margaret to Victoria where she had married, the others to San Francisco.

Only Will and Ed were at home. Mrs. Ingram died in 1927 following a brief illness. Will went to Chilliwack, B.C. in 1928 and was only there a short while when he became very ill and passed away. Ed stayed with his sister, Olive Cookson, and children until 1929 when he went out to Vancouver. Mrs. Cookson remained on the family homestead until her death on Nov. 13, 1964. Although none of the family is living their farm is owned by Olive's family: Lloyd Cookson of Edmonton, Mrs. Margaret Bruce of Lindbrook, and Mrs.Nola Ferguson of Tofield, grandchildren of Mrs. Isaac Ingram.

# THE INGRAM AND SEARS FAMILIES

Martha Yerks was born in Ingersoll, Ontario, in August, 1859, and since her mother had died in childbirth Martha was adopted. At the age of seventeen she married William Henry Ingram of Ingersoll. After a ten years' residence in Ingersoll, they, with their family of four moved to Tipton, Iowa and later to Prescott, Adams County, Iowa. Here Mr. Ingram died.

So, in the rolling green hills of Iowa, the widowed Mrs. Ingram faced a difficult decision. She had a family of six sons and three daughters and only eighty acres of land. Obviously, something must be done to ensure better living conditions for her family.

Tales had been heard of plentiful areas of land to be had in Western Canada in the Beaverhill Lake area, so Mrs. Ingram decided to send her eldest son, Peter to verify these stories In 1898, Peter left for Western Canada to ascertain whether it would be wise for the family to make another move. He returned in 1899 with glowing reports of the land east of the small city of Edmonton and of the hospitality of the Hugh Mitchell family, in the settlement of Northern (later Bardo). The decision to come to Canada was taken and in 1900, Mrs. Martha Ingram with her sons, Peter, Jim, Tom, Wes, Charlie and Ernie and daughters Carrie, Frances, and Ellen arrived in Calgary with two carloads of settlers' effects. With them was a young neighbor just back from military duty in the Philippine Islands, William Sears, who was later to marry Ellen Ingram.

Travelling in one of the first trains to run over the newlylaid tracks to Edmonton, or rather to Strathcona, the party arrived at the point of departure for their new home. Here they transferred to horse drawn buggies and wagons and proceeded to the Bardo district visited earlier by Peter Ingram; here their dream of owning land was fulfilled.

Mrs. Ingram filed on SW of 305018W4th where, later, Ingram school was built. (In 1967, this farm is the property of John Baerg.) Later she bought the farm owned in 1967 by J. Korobko. Here the youngest member of the family was raised.

The sons also filed on homestead land. Peter filed on S.W. 24-50-19-W4th and later bought S.E. of 24-50-19W4th now (1967) owned by Dave Schmidt; here he opened the first coal mine in the Tofield area. He also operated a real estate business in Tofield. He married Molly Mitchell whose parents had entertained him on his first visit to Alberta.

Wesley Ingram settled on the present (1967) Arnold Johnson farm and married his neighbor's daughter, Theresa Nordhouse. Later, they moved to the land now occupied by their nephew, Bill Ingram (James

Ingram's eldest son) and his wife, Mae (Wiley) and their son, Wesley. Their daughter, Donna, married Lester Prokopczak.

James Ingram filed on a homestead in the winter when the heavy snow gave it a deceptively level appearance; in the spring, the true terrain with its abundance of sloughs, was revealed. James then bought the land on which, in 1967, Jim, the younger Ingram son, and his wife Florence live with their daughters, Beth, Annis and Susan. Their eldest daughter Sharon married Richard Strong. The Strongs and their son, Christopher, reside in Whitehorse, Yukon.

Besides the two boys, Bill and Jim, the James Ingram family had four girls. Anna, the eldest, married T. D. Ferguson and lived in the Lakeshore district until her early death in Dec. 1952. Her husband and two sons, Lloyd and Stewart still farm in the Lakeshore district.

Mildred Ingram, the second daughter, married Wendall Wiley. Their family consisted of Dale, Yvonne (Mrs. Roy Kawinsky), and Linda. The Wiley family lives in Terrace, B.C. Also in Terrace is the former Gertie Ingram, now Mrs. Les Ovelson. The Ovelson children are: Laverne (Mrs. Bernie Dekergameaux), Anne (Mrs. Grant Johnson), Gail (Mrs. Ron McHugh),Joyce (Mrs. Robert Hippsley), Wayne and Wendy.

The youngest Ingram girl, Kathleen, married John Nickerson. Living in Edmonton, the Nickersons have three children; Joanne, Royal, and Brent.

Charlie Ingram, like his brother James, took up his land in the winter. He too, in the spring regretted his choice and bought the farm on which, in 1967, A.W. Sears resides. Here Charlie with his wife, the former Emma Moline of Amisk Creek district, spent the remainder of his life.

Tom Ingram lived in the Tofield area until World War I. On his return to Canada with his English bride he moved to Edmonton.

Ernie Ingram met accidental death in Tofield in 1913. Carrie, the eldest Ingram daughter married G.Wilcox and moved back to Iowa where, in her ninetieth year, she still resides.

Frances Ingram married Guy Owens, son of a pioneer Tofield family. Their family now lives in Edmonton.

Wesley Ingram Sr. now (1967) in his ninety third year lives in Victoria, B.C.

Ellen Ingram married William Sears and lived on the former McDevitt farm, now owned by Pete Dueck. Their family consisted of Charles and Stanley (Pat) and a daughter, Hazel, now Mrs. Dyers of Edmonton. Ellen Sears died in 1968.

Albert, Pat and Charles still farm in the Ketchamoot district; Albert (1967) is still a bachelor; Pat and his wife Jean (McCrea), have two daughters and two sons Patsy, Ruth-Ellen, Bill and John. Charlie and his wife Ruby (McLennan) have eight children: Gary, Gail (now Mrs. Lawrence McGinnis), Duane, Dwight, Laurie, Gwen, Robin, and David.

The Ingram and Sears families participated wholeheartedly in the community activities of the pioneer era. The Ingram and Ketchamoot schools were worked on by James and William Sears in 1906. These men were also trustees of these two rural schools. Wes Ingram ran a pool room and a livery stable in Tofield. Pete Ingram had a real estate business and a coal mine to his credit.

The Sears and Ingram families were always ready to lend a hand to help a neighbour or to aid in any community project or recreation. In 1907, William Sears was a member of the Tofield baseball team. His farm was the picnic ground for the Ketchamoot district for years.

The Ingram and Sears families have helped build, through four generations, the strong community spirit of the Ketchamoot district. As Ellen Ingram Sears' son Pat, comments, "This is due to the firm hand of Martha Ingram, a strong-minded little lady who had the courage to get a a place for her family to live." She wished her family to stay close together and they did.

# THE CHARLES JOSEPH KALLAL FAMILY

*The material for the following article was supplied by Margaret Kallal Dickson.*

Charles Joseph Kallal was born on May 25, 1884, to Joseph and Mary

Jilek-Kallal, one of eleven children. His parents, prominent in the farming and livestock industries, lived in Jersey County, Illinois, where they owned hundreds of acres, raising large numbers of cattle for the Chicago market.

Charles Kallall's early education was obtained in a country school and a business school in St. Louis, Missouri. A good student, he was fluent in three languages. He travelled extensively in Mexico and U.S.A.

An older brother, Edward, who had emigrated to Tofield, Alberta, invited Charles to visit him and in 1910 Charles arrived in Tofield; in 1911 he joined his brother in a real-estate business in pioneer Tofield. The brothers also opened a pool hall. Charles soon became a Canadian citizen.

Shortly, he sent for his bride-to-be, Frances Loretta Hanson from Carrollton, Illinois, who packed her trousseau and ventured forth to Canada to be married. Frances had been born in Green County, Illinois on March 16,1890; she was educated in High Street School. She early learned to drive a Model T Ford owned by Mr. Knight, for whose family she worked. This was before women drivers were common and Frances generated much excitement rolling along dusty country roads on her errands.

Frances met her husband-to-be through one of his cousins; this meeting led to the marriage of Frances Hanson and Charles Kallal on April 15, 1915 in St. Joachim's Catholic Church in Edmonton with Frances attired in traditional bridal finery.

To this union, six sons and three daughters were born. Charles Jr., for many years a Tofield business man, with his wife, Nan, and their four children, James, Linda, Jerry and Vernon, now reside in Edmonton. Joseph with his wife Genevieve and children David, Anne, Bruce Michael, Mary and Evelyn live at Thorhild where Joe feeds commercial cattle. Prior to ranching, Joe worked for twelve years for the Alberta Government, promoting the cattle industry. Paul, his wife Esther and their children Patrick, Edward, Ronald, Theresa and Catherine live northwest of Tofield. He too is a cattle rancher, taking prizes at the Spring Show in Edmonton, though holding a teaching certificate and the Military Medal for gallantry in action in World War II.

Kenneth, still a bachelor, is the welder and mechanic of the family. He ranches with the youngest brother Lawrence, assisting in the raising of purebred Herefords. Constance (Hatherton) a graduate of McTavish Business College and an X-Ray technician from the St. Joseph's Hospital, Toronto, School of Radiography lives with her husband and son Donald in Vancouver. Margaret (Dickson) widowed in 1965 lives in Tofield with her children Robert, Ruth, Rita, and Allan. Margaret was a Sgt. with the C.W.A.C. and is a registered nurse, now employed at the Tofield Hospital. Anthony (Tony) and his wife Jacqueline live in Edmonton with their children Denise, Lawrence, Albert, Bernard, Lorena, Susan and Rosanne. Tony has degrees in Engineering and in Pharmacy. Dorothy (Shewchuk), her husband Louis, and their children Daniel, Louise, Rosemary, BetsyAnne, Michael, Stephen and Sandra live southwest of Tofield. Graingrowing and stockraising are their occupation; Dorothy has artistic pursuits as well. Lawrence, his wife Theresa, and their daughters, Carol, Debra, and Margaret live on the original Kallal ranch where Lawrence raises purebred Herefords; he is the cattleman, also judge and showman of the establishment.

In 1917, Anthony (Tony) Kallal joined his brothers in Tofield; in the same year, he and Charlie bought property on the southeast edge of Beaverhill Lake known then as the Morton and Adams land. This holding was later expanded to include 2000 acres north of Shonts; it bordered on Beaverhill Lake and contained much of Amisk Creek ideal ranching land.

In 1927, the partnership was dissolved; Charlie and his family moved to the site of the present Kallal Ranch; here Charlie both grainfarmed and raised cattle, at first commercial and then purebred. The cattle became of prime importance; between 200 and 300 head were fed each year and in the early '30's, a shipment of choice steers was sold to Scotland for 2½ ¢ per pound.

While her menfolk were building up the ranch, Frances built up her reputation as a rancher's wife, capturing many prizes at the Edmonton Exhibition for her culinary entries.

In spite of the responsibilities belonging to a home and a large family,

Frances found time to be a good neighbor to all and to participate in church and community affairs. She held office in the C.W. L. and the F. W. U. A.

In the 1940's, the Kallal ranch turned from commercial to purebred cattle. In April 1945, Lawrence, then 11 years old, won the Prince of Wales Challenge shield with his baby beef calf which was also judged the best animal at the Edmonton Spring Stock Show. In 1950, C.J. Kallal showed cattle at the Toronto Royal; here too, a Kallal palomino was chosen to compete. This year, the C.J. Kallal family was given the Master Farm Family award which consists of a $1,000.00 cash award, an engraved plaque and a name plate for the farm entrance. The Tofield Community League tendered the Kallals a banquet in recognition of their achievement. Members of the Department of Agriculture, neighbors and friends all participated in honoring the Kallals.

In 1958 Charles was a guest of the Calgary Chamber of Commerce on his return from the Toronto Royal. He was awarded the Canadian Hereford Breeders' and the Canadian Hereford Exhibitors' awards. Once again, the community of Tofield officials of the government, and the Livestock Breeders' Association joined to express thanks to the Kallals for bringing to this district continent wide recognition. In 1961, the Alberta Livestock Breeders Association honored the Alberta winners at the Toronto Royal.

In 1962, the Kallal home was chosen to be one of the stops for the Nash Farm Tour of the United Kingdom. The members of the tour inspected the Kallal farm and enjoyed the hospitality of the C.J. Kallal family.

In 1963 and 1965, members of the Agricultural Department of the U.S.S.R. on a cattlebuying mission, purchased a number of the Kallal Herefords which were shipped to Russia to improve the herds of Russian cattle.

In November, 1962, Charles suffered a stroke while attending the Chicago Livestock Show. Charles Jr. and Margaret flew to Chicago to bring him back to Tofield. At this time he had retired from active farming: the Kallal Hereford Ranch was incorporated with sons Kenneth and Lawrence taking charge. In 1964 Charles and Frances retired to Tofield where, in 1965, they celebrated their Golden Wedding. Later in 1965, Charles Kallal died, his six sons carrying him to his final resting place. Frances Kallal still resides in Tofield maintaining her interest in her family, and her church. Her daughter Margaret with whom she lives, says of her, "Very humble with a heart of gold a real mother and a real friend."

## THE EDWARD ROBERT KALLAL FAMILY

*The material for this article was supplied by Mrs. Malisa Nomeland,, stepdaughter of Edward Kallal.*

The third of eleven children, Edward Robert Kallal was born near Jerseyville, Illinois, to Mr. and Mrs. Joseph Kallal, a Bohemian Catholic Family, on April 11, 1878. He learned to speak three languages: German, the language of the school where he obtained his early education; Bohemian, which was spoken in the home; English, the language of the school where his late education took place.

Until the age of 21, Edward helped his father and brothers on the farm. Then, given an option of $1,000 cash, or a farm as a gift, he chose the cash and travelled through the U.S.A. and Mexico. Canada attracted him; he arrived in Tofield in 1906 but shortly moved to Vegreville where he sold real estate. In 1907, he returned to Tofield, building the first pool hall and bowling alley. In 1908, his building was moved from the old town to the G. T. P. town site. Mule trains were used to move the building.

Edward, who was fond of animals, was given a black bear cub which he raised and trained. Kept in the Pool Hall, it was everyone's pet as it danced or boxed with great gusto and was sadly missed when, after becoming old and cross, it had to be destroyed.

Widowed Mrs. Jennie Harnish, born February 3,1884, came to Tofield with her small daughter Malisa, in 1909. Mrs. Harnish, born of Pennsylvania Dutch mother and an Irish father, had lived on a farm at Lacombe. On coming to Tofield, Jennie Harnish worked at the Queen's

Hotel. Here she met Ed Kallal; they were married in 1911.

Shortly after their marriage, the Kallals moved to Edmonton, where real estate again engaged Ed; later, a pool hall in Evansburg occupied him.

As well as Malisa, the Kallals had three other children; Edward Robert Jr. on April 5, 1912; Joseph Thomas on October 23, 1913; Mary, on December 29, 1916.

After returning to Tofield in 1917, Ed ran a pool hall till 1921 when he returned to farming. For two years, the Kallals farmed what is now the Bill Davison farm; in 1923 they farmed the present Art Francis farm, then known as the Ball place. In 1924, Ed bought 385 acres just south of Tofield; the family moved into a log house with a big kitchen addition on what was known as MacKenzie Hill. Here they remained till 1929.

From here, Malisa recalls, the Kallals ran the first milk delivery in Tofield. Malisa herself was the milkman, covering the route with the help of a democrat and a swayback mare. Before delivery, of course, the handmilking, the watercarrying for cooling the milk, the bottling, all had to be done.

Malisa remembers her childhood pet a pig called Jiggs. Jiggs, a "runt" was raised by Malisa and spoiled by the entire family to the point where he did not accept the fact that he was a pig. He had his own little house but in time grew so big that he could carry it on his back so Ed put him in with the other pigs. Jiggs squealed so loud and long that night that Ed went out to investigate early in the morning where upon he found Jiggs crouching in the corner of the pen terrified of the pigs! His aversion to others of his own kind was so great that, when the time came to ship him, Ed had to lead him on a leash to the shipping point. "Ed", says Malisa, "almost had tears in his eyes when he left Jiggs to his fate."

An avid hunter, Ed delighted in the hunter's paradise around Beaverhill Lake where the geese, ducks, and upland game were to be found in unbelievable quantities.

In 1929, when the family moved to the farm north of Tofield, Joe was old enough to assume much of the field work. A tractor eased the effort of farming 385 acres south of town and 640 acres north of town, but a hired man was necessary as Edward Jr. had a badly damaged heart, the result of rheumatic fever. Joe, the farmer, went to school only in the offseason of farming but managed to get his grades. At 17, he attended the Vermilion Agricultural College from which he graduated with honors and an award. He had also participated in all sports activities at the college.

In 1933, Joe and Helmer Moen won a trip to the Royal Winter Fair in Toronto (as members of the Tofield Beef Club Calf Team) where they won second place in the Dominion finals judging competition. In 1932, Joe concluded two years of Junior Swine Club work by representing the Tofield club in the provincial finals. In 1933, he was runner-up in the grainjudging team representing Alberta at Regina. In 1933, Joe and Ed placed second and third respectively in the Junior wheat class at the Toronto Royal Winter Fair.

On July 29, 1933, the Edmonton Journal reported, "Ed Kallal Sr. helped put the Edmonton district to the fore at the world grain show in Regina. In the Hard Red Spring Wheat 10-bushel class, he won fifth prize ($300) and in the 50-pound sample class won sixteenth ($45). Entering the Chicago World's Grain Show in the 50-pound class, in 1933, Ed won fifth prize.

This prize-winning wheat was grown on a hundred-acre field broken by Joe in 1931, seeded, cut and threshed in 1932 yielding fifty bushels per acre. It was Reward wheat bought from Herman Trelli, who had developed it. The Kallal exhibit weighed 70 pounds to the bushel. The average weight of championship wheat samples was 67-68 pounds per bushel.

Always interested in hograising, Ed. Sr. increased his herd in 1930 to 300 per year. The first in the district to raise purebred Yorkshires, he constantly improved his stock and from 1930-1933 won many prizes, including the Grand Champion Boar at the Edmonton Purebred Yorkshire Show.

In 1928, Ed. Sr. purchased a tiller for the control of weeds by cultivation. This, the first tiller north of Calgary, was of great interest in the community.

Ed. Sr. farmed till 1948. He enjoyed retirement until his death on

November 16,1956. He is buried in St. Joachim's Cemetery, Edmonton. Jennie Kallal died on January 4, 1968, having spent the last five years of her life in Tofield.

# J.O. LETOURNEAU

The first mayor of Tofield was J.O. Letourneau. The following account is an account of his life in Tofield written by his daughter, Mrs. C.C. Spence of Edmonton. His other children were: Oliver Letourneau,, who was killed in a car accident October 22, 1939; John W., who died July 9, 1956 and Mrs. R.H. Woodford on the teaching staff of Baker Sanitorium, Calgary. Mrs. Spence wrote:

"Dad was born at Trois Rivieres (Three Rivers) Quebec on June 10,1860. His schooling gave him a third class certificate for teaching in French and English and he taught a few years in Quebec. Tiring of this he went to the States, ending up in Argyle, Minn. Here he clerked in a general store, was married and became a county sheriff.

In 1892 he, his wife and son Oliver, came to the area that is now Tofield. They spent the first winter with a Mr. Lafond who had a log house and barn on the S.W. ¼ 65118 and built a small log house, dipping into a small reserve of cash to put shingles on the roof. The "picture windows" one on each side and one in each gable were about 12" x 18". The chinks in the logs were filled with mud mixture. Interior decorating was taken care of by papering the walls with newspaper. Bachelors and others leaning back on chairs often cracked this and children put grease and mud spots, so that a touching-up bee was often held and these spots and holes covered. Through the years this became somewhat thick and I suspect these thicknesses helped in the heating problem and also the bedbug problem. The homestead seemed to be on the highway from Edmonton and people often stayed overnight especially when a larger barn was built that could take care of four teams. Women and children slept upstairs and men and boys downstairs, and often hardly enough room to turn over! Once in awhile these visitors had extra baggage they left behind, and in a few days we were being bitten a search found these gruesome little bugs and as the beds were home made they had excellent places to hide. The bedding all went out in the sunshine and was turned and turned, bedframes also went out and were scalded with hot water and lye and left in the sun. This didn't hurt the "finish" on them but it did put in more cracks.

When dry they were dusted with bedbug powder, and so was everything else. The family must have eaten some, I'm sure, besides putting up with the peculiar smell no wonder the bugs curled up! The next poor wayfarers were not-very welcome and when weather permitted they were asked to sleep in the hayloft.

A well was dug that summer-lots of hard water and not too palatable but you grew accustomed to it—also a pole shed was built to hold two horses and a cow. The hay was placed over this and fenced, and before spring had been eaten by the "stock." A small field was broken and this gave the family a few vegetables and oats for the second winter.

In the succeeding years more land was cleared, roots grubbed, and broken for crops. The first fields were enclosed by rail fences very picturesque but not too good at keeping pigs, cows, or horses enclosed. There was always repair work to be done. Later when wire became available humans were the trouble for a while. People objected to prairie trails being fenced off and simply cut the wires, drove through the crop, cut the other side and did no repair work you knew what had happened when you saw the stock in the crop.

Gradually stock was acquired, horses, cattle, pigs, chickens, geese, turkeys. Dad kept improving his horses and cattle, being very interested in Clydesdales and Shorthorns.

Marketing was quite a problem, Edmonton being the nearest town with no road to it and refrigeration only by nature. You carried an axe or two, a shovel and a load and allowed a day at least to rest the team and shop, and two days to return.

Cattle buyers came through and often bought cattle "delivered to Edmonton" and you were paid for the number delivered. If any got away, you lost. Pigs had to be butchered after freezeup. Chickens, geese and turkeys were dressed. Butter was saved in crocks, eggs gathered, held and packed in oats and you hoped for the best. Goose oil was rendered, bottled and sold to the drug store. Wheat was taken in and traded for flour. Bachelors provided the only market as some of them bought butter, eggs and sometimes bread.

In the earlier years, there was plenty of pasture, and hay. Before haying season you "sneaked" out early and cut a swath around the dry slough or patch of prairie, and claimed it for you or caused a local dispute.

As settlers came in and fenced off their places, pasture and hay became harder to obtain and it was a case of getting more land or quitting the homestead. Dad talked of going to the Peace River area, but Mother vetoed that. She had pioneered enough.

The G.T.P. was coming through and the town of Tofield was starting up. They sold the place and Dad started up a furniture store with Joseph Harper (Harper and Letourneau) where the Red and White now stands. Mother started up a millinery store where the former Crown Lumber was located. Sometime later they lost everything in a fire that cleaned nearly the whole block. They rebuilt the millinery store and Dad took over the Tofield buying station of the Edmonton City Dairy, east of the present Bank of Montreal.

He was a keen booster for Tofield and had high hopes for it when the town tried for gas. And when they lit the gas flare at the station they thought they had arrived. Water got in and they lost. Twenty years later his granddaughter sat in a class in Tofield High and heard the teacher say that Tofield had been sunk in debt by an error in judgment of the Mayor and Council of 1912.

Dad was very active in the Oddfellows and Masonic lodges. He passed away in April, 1922.

# ROBERT LOGAN

Robert Logan, born in Winnipeg in 1864, became one of the first settlers on the western shore of Beaverhill Lake. He came here in 1886, having worked, prior to that time, for the Hudson's Bay Company in Edmonton from 1864 to 1874 in partnership with John Norris. In 1886, he sold his share of the business to his partner and came to Beaverhill Lake area where he became widely known as friend and neighbour as well as a storekeeper. As well as operating a trading post, Robert Logan farmed and kept stock.

At one time, he owned thirteen quarters of land which he later sold to G.A. Trent. Moving into Tofield he built two large stores and became a noteworthy pioneer merchant. Later, he retired in Edmonton where he lived until his death. He left to mourn his widow, three sons and three daughters.

His eldest son, John Robert, had been born in Winnipeg in 1874 and had come to Tofield with his parents in 1886. In January, 1897, John Robert Logan married Emma Rowland whose father was an employee of the Hudson's Bay Company from 1864-1875 during which time he worked as a special trader and interpreter. Rowland Road in Edmonton perpetuates the memory of William Rowland who had his home where Alex Taylor school was later built.

John Robert and his bride Emma, drove in a sleigh to the town of St. Paul on their honeymoon. Here John had a small store and a freighting business which operated between St. Paul and Edmonton.

To this marriage was born three girls and six boys. The eldest son, Robert, was killed in April, 1917 at the Battle of Vimy Ridge.

In 1902 the John Logan family returned to the Tofield district settling on a farm in the Summer School district. Here the Logan home became a "stopping place" for the men hauling coal from the Tofield mine to Chipman and Mundare. Frank Saver who used to haul freight, passengers, and sometimes mail also made the Logan home his stopping place. All such travellers carried their bedrolls, consisting of a large warm feather tick, which they spread on the Logan floor for the night.

In 1924, the Logan family entertained an escaped prisoner from the Fort Saskatchewan Jail for a few days. They were quite unaware of their guest's record until they discovered his prison suit hidden in nearby bushes. Somewhere between the Fort and Logan's the escaped prisoner had raided a clothesline and then discarded the evidence of his incarceration.

John Logan worked on the railroad in company with William

Hopgood during a period of 1920's, as well as working at Lake Wabamun. After selling his farm at Tofield, he and his family moved to Camrose and later to Dinant.

John Logan served on the school board of the MacKenzie School District. His family name was frequently used to designate the area north of town where he had lived. Old timers refer to the area between the Lakeshore and Summer School as "Logan". This name was given in the early 1890's to the first post-office north of Tofield.

John Logan died on November 25, 1942, and his wife Emma, followed him on January 22, 1945. One daughter of the pioneer Logan family, Mrs. Myrtle Nerland, still lives in the Tofield district.

# MR. A.S. MAXWELL

A half-century ago, when Tofield was incorporated as a town, Mr. Aquilla Smith Maxwell was a member of the town council. Although, later living near Edson, Alberta, he continued a keen interest in Tofield, partly for old times' sake and partly because it was the home of his son and daughter-in-law, Alan and Bev. Maxwell and their four sons, James, Douglas, Keith and Murray.

Aquilla Smith Maxwell was born in 1874 in Tennessee and always spoke with a faint southern accent. After some time spent in Arkansas, Mr. Maxwell felt the attraction of the Northwest and came to what is now Alberta, in 1901. High River, the centre of the ranching country became the home of the man from Tennessee. Here he worked at what his grandsons no doubt regard as a glamorous occupation that of a cowboy riding the range.

After a few years, Mr. Maxwell moved north to the pioneer town of Vegreville, Alberta. Here he ran a livery stable and then became manager of what is now the Prince Edward Hotel.

In 1908 he married Miss Helen Grosland of Bittern Lake and, in the fall of that year moved to Tofield. He became manager of Ed Kallal's poolroom in which Lem Abbott had his barber shop on the present site of Harold Ferguson's house.

The association was the beginning of an enduring friendship between the Abbotts and the Maxwells. Whenever the Maxwells visited Tofield in later years, they renewed their former acquaintance with the Abbotts and many happy hours of the "Remember when?" variety were shared.

The two families lived side by side for a year just east of the present site of Mrs. Hosler's house. Soon the Maxwell Abbott team decided to move the poolroom and barber shop to Railway Avenue to the present site of the Federal Grain Co.'s house. The move was accomplished in typically pioneer fashion. The poolroom remained open until midnight; it was again open for business as usual in the morning.

In 1909, Mr. Maxwell was one of the members of the council when it decided to perpetuate the name of Dr. Tofield by naming the town after him and become incorporated as a town. In the minutes of the Council meetings of that important year, we find that he was an interested and capable member of the Health and Relief Committee of the Council. The records show his interest in laying the foundations of good health laws for the new town. A Medical Health Officer was secured, collection of garbage arranged for and land bought for a nuisance ground.

In lighter vein, Mr. Maxwell is remembered around Tofield for the pet black bear, "Ole" by name, owned in partnership with Ed. Kallal. He was trained to dance, thereby greatly amusing the local small fry and probably their elders, too. It is said that "Ole" danced especially well to the strains of Lem Abbott's violin. Unfortunately, "Ole" was teased too much by the railway construction workers and became so cross that he had to be destroyed.

Mr. Maxwell had one unforgettable experience. At one time, Robert Logan had a boat on Beaverhill Lake on which he took passengers for pleasure rides. Once when Mr. Maxwell was on board, a severe storm arose. The passengers were mightily alarmed as the ship was making straight for the rocks on the east shore of the lake. In the anxious hours that followed, each passenger acted according to his own lights. Mark Ferguson and Lloyd Wood frantically stoked the boiler with boards torn from the deck of the boat, thus ensuring enough power to get past the rocks. Other passengers did some equally frantic praying. No one was ever sure which method brought the boat safely to shore in a small bay.

The thankful passengers spent the night on board while their friends and relatives worried at home. Mr. George Cookson, Sr., reports in his diary for August 23, 1909:- "Mr. Morton called to get the field glasses, and was going around the lake as there was a party on Logan's boat they think they got caught in a storm. But they had put up at a bay north of Morrison's and were safe."

The passengers returned safely to Tofield, in rented vehicles but Mr. Logan had a repair job to do on the boat.

One of Mrs. Maxwell's experiences illustrates the difficulty of being helpful to a pioneer husband. Mr. Maxwell was engaged in cutting some of the luxuriant slough hay for sale to the railway to feed the horses used in construction work. Mrs. Maxwell went along cooking for the crew.

One morning, just after the large batch of bread was "mixed stiff," Mr. Maxwell announced that the camp would move to the next location. So camp was broken, the bread warmly wrapped in blankets and the stove loaded into the wagon. The trip was long, the day warm, and the bread rose rapidly. With no prospect of a stove to bake it in before evening, Mrs. Maxwell spent the day kneading down the batch of bread. She was very relieved when the new campsite was reached and the stove set up, and the bread finally baking in the oven. The men were ready for it when it came out.

In 1912, the Maxwells left Tofield, to the regret of their pioneer friends and moved to Hinton where they managed a stoppingplace. In 1919 they moved to Coalspur with a general store as their business. Edson was their final stop. Here they ran a general store till 1929, until Mr. Maxwell took over the Ford garage.

In Edson Mr. Maxwell was a charter member and the first president of the Men's Curling Club and a member of the Masonic Lodge. Mrs. Maxwell was also a curler, being one of the first lady skips in Edmonton. In 1934 they 'retired' to a farm in the Bear Lake area.

On April 12, 1958, Mr. and Mrs. Maxwell celebrated their Golden wedding with their sons Allan and Donald and their daughter Mrs. Kathleen Christie, twelve grandchildren and a host of friends present to wish them happiness.

# A.J.H. MCCAULEY

Alexander J.H. McCauley was born in Winnipeg, July 1, 1876. At the age of three, he moved with his parents, by oxcart to Edmonton.

Alex's father, Matthew McCauley was Edmonton's first school trustee and the first mayor of the town of Edmonton. He was a member of the Legislative Council of the NorthWest Territories and later of the Legislative Assembly of Alberta.

Alex, his brother, and sisters grew up in Edmonton attended its first school, skated and curled on its Saskatchewan River in winter, swam and fished it in the summer.

There was work to be done, too, and Alex helped his father with the livery and freighting business and kept books for this thriving pioneer business. He studied music and became an accomplished pianist and organist. He was organist for the First Presbyterian Church until he went to South Africa in 1900 to fight in the Boer War.

Upon his return from South Africa he went to Port Arthur and worked for a time as a bookkeeper for a grain company. He returned to Edmonton in 1906 and in 1907 he moved to Tofield and started his own real estate business. He was the first secretary-treasurer of the Village of Tofield. His first home was near the Creamery on the spot where Art and Irma Francis now live. His brother Frank lived there with him for a time.

Tofield became a town in 1909 and Alex became its first secretary. A month later he married Barbara Ann Sinclair of Yorkton, Saskatchewan (originally from the Orkney Islands). In 1911 they built the house still frequently called "the McCauley" house (now occupied by Mr. and Mrs. Don Shaw). In all the years they lived in Tofield this house remained their home.

In 1911, too, Mrs. McCauley's twin nieces, Clara and Susie Fergus came to live with them. They are still residents of Tofield. Clara became Mrs. E. W. Rogers, and lives with her daughter, Muriel, and son-in-law Don Shaw and their children Philip and Tannis in the McCauley house. Susie became Mrs. Al Innis, and is still a resident of Tofield. Jack, Jean (Mrs. Bernie Chandler) and Joyce (Mrs. Arnold Swift) were the Innis family.

The McCauleys had three children born and brought up in this house and to Helen, Margaret and Bill, it is still home.

To say that Alex McCauley took an active part in the community life of Tofield is an understatement. He was Mayor in 1915, 1916, and 1921-28 inclusive. He was secretary of the town, the school board, Palestine Lodge, of which he was a charter member. Almost any record or minute book of that era contains pages in Mr. McCauley's neat handwriting. He was economical with words, but from his factual accounts a very clear picture of that period emerges.

In his early days in Tofield, Alex played a little football but curling was his real interest in the sporting field. He skipped a rink for many years.

He was always closely associated with the church: first, the Presbyterian Church and, later after the union, the United Church. He was always organist until 1941. During this time he also played for choir practice, weddings, and funerals, frequently closing his office to do so.

The organ he played was quite a fine organ in its day, boasting two manuals and two rows of pedals. Unfortunately, it had to be pumped by hand and for many years Alex paid some child to perform this service. Then when his own children came up, each one had to take a turn at pumping graduating when tall enough to be seen over the top of the organ. Alex was always either an elder in the church or on the board of stewards or both.

Mrs. McCauley was also active in church work. She was a member of the Ladies' Aid and of the Women's Missionary Society. For many years she also taught Sunday School and led a C.G.I.T. group. She was an ardent curler and skipped many winning rinks both at home and at out-of-town bonspiels. She won Grand Challenge in the Northern Alberta Ladies' Bonspiel in Edmonton, in 1931. Her rink, on that occasion, consisted of Mrs. G. Brace, Gertie Chapman and Clara Rogers. She was once president of the Northern Alberta Ladies' Curling Association.

Having been a school teacher herself, Barbara McCauley was always interested in school teachers and in school. Many teachers stayed in the McCauley home over the years. Mrs. McCauley also served a term on the school board.

Teachers and other young people of the town came often to the McCauley home for an evening of music. Everyone gathered around the piano and sang. The small McCauley children used to creep quietly downstairs in their nightgowns and sit, just out of sight on the stairs. It was draughty there but they could hear the accompanying conversations and keep up on the current romances. At the McCauley home on Sunday, if they didn't go for a drive between Sunday School and Church, the children could take a walk, read a book, or write a letter. Both parents were great readers and there were always plenty of good books available. According to the daughter, Margaret, Mr. McCauley had no resistance whatsoever to book salesmen.

The Sunday drives were taken in the family Ford after Old Nell and the buggy were disposed of. The big barn, relic of the days of old, was there (and still is) for the children to play in. Margaret remembers the big loft and the grain chute to slide down, (it was dark and scary in there) and the lean-to on the side which was a playhouse. The only concession made to the car was the garage doors put in at the back.

Margaret says, "Remember the open Fords with the storm curtains to put up if it rained? We had lots of Sunday rides in ours. Sometimes we went as far as Cooking Lake, for a picnic with a few close friends. Father kept an eye on the weather though, because if it should rain, that road back through the hills was not easy to travel. And even if the day were fine, we had to leave in time to get back for church.

"The Jack Cookson's had a horse and buggy and sometimes we could have a ride with Mrs. Cookson when she drove to Sunday School. That was a real treat! Mrs. Cookson taught the primary department of the Sunday School for many years and the many, many children she started in Sunday School remember her with affection, and recall the Sunday School picnic held at her home, complete with big freezers of ice-cream.

Tales of the early days in Tofield before there was a church and student ministers served the district in the summer while living at the Cooksons, delighted the children. The Jack Cooksons had no children of their own but loved all children.

Both Jack and George Cookson loved to sing and we remember their duets, especially "Golden Slippers". They both sang in the first choir. I can remember some of the others were: Mr. Swift, Mr. Jobb, Irene and Roland Murray, the Rowes and Mrs. Firth.

There are happy memories of our neighbours, the Abbots and the Carters next door to them. Across the street were the Tofields. Mrs. Tofield was still living and the Simmons lived with her. Then the Policeman's house; the Swifts; the Bissets; the Pincotts; across the avenue,, the McLaughlins; the John Lees; and on the corner, the Phillips. Many of these families had children we grew up with."

Margaret remembers a father who was strict, but just; shy and reserved, but loving company, conversation and music; who could tell exciting tales of the Boer War or play lullabies till the children went to sleep; who had a quiet, but keen sense of humor.

"He was a person of integrity-so honest he cheated himself. A secret was as safe with him as though in a locked vault. Who were the last to know when a local wedding of interest was to occur? Why, the McCauleys except for Mr. McCauley, who had sold the license days before!

Alex McCauley was for everything that was for the good of the community. Witness the number of times he and other solid citizens signed the Chautauqua guarantee and paid the deficit to bring it back for another year and keep Tofield on the sixday circuit which brought the best programs."

The McCauley children remember their mother as "gentle and loving; entertaining and energetic; and completely unselfish. She could find good in everyone-she just plain loved people. Did anyone ever leave our house without a cup of tea? She was a woman who never raised her voice but had a strong will to do whatever she thought was right. Both Alex and Barbara McCauley had great faith in their fellow men in their country and in their nation."

Tofield appreciated the McCauleys years of service, too. When ill health forced them to retire to Edmonton in 1946, the town honored them with a presentation as it had done years before when Alex retired as mayor.

The McCauley children have pursued widely varied careers with great success. Helen (Mrs. Gemeroy), after teaching for some years, trained for a nurse. In addition to her R.N.,. she has her B.A. degree and is teaching psychiatric nursing in McGill University in Montreal. She has the distinction of being the first nurse to be a member of the Advisory Committee of the Canadian Mental Health Association.

Margaret (Mrs. Rennie Wood), also has her R.N. She and her husband and four children live in Edmonton.

Bill McCauley obtained his Bachelor of Music degree from the Toronto Conservatory of Music and had been for many years Director of the Music for Crawley Films. He was granted leave of absence while studying for his Doctorate of Music on a Canadian Council Scholarship at the Eastman School of Music, Rochester, New York.

Margaret's account of her parents life in Tofield ends: "Alex's only consolation in moving to Edmonton was that, from his home, he could see across the river to where he had lived as a boy. He and mother both enjoyed visits from Tofield friends. He died in 1948, and mother followed in 1951. They are buried in Tofield.

So Alex and Barbara McCauley are back home."

# THE MCHEFFEY FAMILY

The McHeffey family, six boys and two girls, was raised in Gays, Nova Scotia, near the city of Truro. Fred and Murray came to Alberta in 1905. Murray, after working the bush for two years, came to Tofield in 1907 and homesteaded S.E. ¼ 22-51-19-W4th, where he spent his remaining years.

Fred, too, worked for two years before coming to Tofield; after working in Edmonton at his trade of blacksmithing, he was employed on the construction of the Clover Bar railroad bridge. In 1907, on arrival in Tofield, he bought a blacksmith shop from O. Mahaffey, which was situated about where the Wideman sisters now live; a house was built just west of the shop, but it was later moved to its present location, opposite the school bus garage. Fred later bought the Lafond log house, moved it to behind his own house and used it as a shop. Fred was janitor of the Tofield School for many years; he was also an active member of the I.O.O.F. The Fred McHeffeys had two sons Horace and Murray. Murray was accidentally killed while a member of the R.C.A.F. in World War II. Horace is an entertainer and a teacher of various kinds of dancing and has given lessons all over Canada. He also has a museum in the home of his parents who both died in the early 1950's.

Arthur McHeffey, brother of Fred and Murray, came west in 1906 and in 1907 homesteaded S.W. ¼ of 22-51-18-W4th, now owned by Pete Koop. In 1911, his wife and children joined him.

Willard, son of Arthur, married Margaret McKenzie, and to this union, one daughter Agnes, now Mrs. Earl Rose was born, her children are: Conrad, Phyllis, Miles, Linda and Dixie. Willard farmed all his life until his wife died and he remarried, this time to Audrey Warner, widow of Donnelly Warner; they now live in town.

Ina McHeffey married Ronald Harriman moving to the States shortly afterwards. They have two boys and two girls.

Arthur McHeffey known as a good neighbour was also an active member of the I.O.O.F.

William and Walter homesteaded the north half section 20-51-19-W4th now owned by Ed Tiedemann where they lived out their lives. One of the sisters for a short period ran a restaurant in Tofield before she returned to Eastern Canada. Willard and his nephew Horace are now the only remaining members of the McHeffey family.

# THE MCGINITIE FAMILY

*This article was submitted by Raymond Henry McGinitie, grandson of John Maurice McGinitie.*

John Maurice McGinitie was born in Eddyville, Iowa on May 10, 1872. He later moved to Nebraska. He married Mary Elizabeth Likes in Ponca, Nebraska on December 10, 1895.

Their first son, John Maurice Jr. was born on Dec. 22, 1896 in

Beacon District, Dixon County, Nebraska.

They moved to Strathcona, now Edmonton, in 1899. Their second son., Henry Newton, was born there on June 25, 1899.

Mr. McGinitie homesteaded in 1900 on S.W.28-50-19-W4. He built a log house and moved onto the farm in 1901. Their third son, Lloyd Leslie, was born on the farm May 15, 1901.

John Maurice Jr. married Margaret Gratz on November 21, 1925, in Fresno, California, and moved to a farm in the Tofield district, before moving back to the United States.

Henry Newton married Agnes Bruha, April 4, 1923, and farmed on a quartersection one mile from his father's farm.

Lloyd Leslie married Annie Brown, December 1, 1927. He also farmed one mile from his father's farm. He passed away from a heart attack on June 30, 1963.

John McGinitie Sr. had only two horses, with which to go to Edmonton once or twice a year for supplies. It took four days for the round trip. He bought a well boring machine, and for several years bored wells for his neighbors. He was a member of the school board and named the school and district after an Indian Chief called "Ketchamoot." He worked on the first hotel built in Tofield called the Queen's Hotel, and bored the well at the hotel.

He was called to Edmonton several times in the early days for jury duty.

His wife, Mary Elizabeth, died at the age of 57 years on June 13, 1936. Shortly after, he rentedhis farm and lived with his son, Henry until his death on June 29, 1958. He lived a fruitful life and was always able to see the humorous side of things.

The Leslie McGinities had two daughters, Doris (Mrs. Tipper) and Nola (Mrs. Godwin).

The Henry McGinities had three sons, Donnelly, Harvey and Raymond and one daughter, Alice (Mrs. Munkedahl).

Donnelly McGinitie and his wife Opal (Blakely) still live in the Tofield area. Their children are Barbara, Floyd and Darlene. Henry McGinitie died early in 1969.

# THE MCMULLEN FAMILY

The Arthur McMullen family consisting of Mr. and Mrs. McMullen and their four children, Jesse, Viva, Paul, and Harold arrived in the Tofield District April, 1906.

They had left their native Oregon, U.S.A. the previous spring, travelling by team and wagon as far as Kalispell, Montana, where they spent the winter of 1906. This was the Michael Pablo country; buffalo and cattle were seen frequently. The remainder of the journey was made by box car the following spring via Fernie, Frank, McLeod, Calgary and finally, Strathcona, the end of their railway journey.

Team and wagon were again pressed into service on the route over the old baseline trail through the Beaver Hills, stopping at Tom Wesson's en route and finally emerging at the well-developed farm of John C. Phillips on the westerly shores of Beaverhill Lake.

The family camped here for several weeks during which time Mr. McMullen travelled about the district, photographing many of the residents, their homes and their livestock.

Homesteading was the order of the day but the N.W. ¼ of Section 32-51-19-W4th was never much of a success and was sold by Mr. McMullen as soon as he had "proved up". Mr. Robert Logan was the purchaser in 1910 when the McMullens decided to return to their old home in Oregon. However, the call of Canada proved too strong and the following spring found them back in Tofield where Mr. McMullen built a small residence and a commercial establishment on Queen's Avenue, West.

Arthur McMullen conducted a photographic business for a time before renting the studio to Mr. Thomas Whitmore who ran the business up to the time he enlisted in the C.E.F. Mr. McMullen enlisted in the 211th American Legion Battalion of the C.E.F. which was recruited in the Edmonton area. Several local boys served in this regiment, some of whom were: the Turner boys, Jack Letourneau, Big John Lee, E.P. Rowe and Red Montgomery. Of course, the greater number of the Tofield enlistments were with the 49th, the 51st, and other earlier regiments.

On being discharged from the C.E.F., Mr. McMullen bought a quarter of land south of Tofield N.W. 1550-19-W4th where he was living when Mrs. McMullen passed away in 1920. He continued to make his home on the farm until he and his youngest son, Harold were killed in an auto accident while on their way to Tofield on December 1, 1928.

Jesse McMullen was the secretary-treasurer for the town of Tofield for a number of years commencing in 1912. He quit this position to try ranching on the west half of section 19-50-19-W4th in 1918. He left the farm in 1937 to take a position with the Municipal district of Beaver Lake at Ryley and later, with the newly-formed larger district of Beaver until he resigned to seek his fortune on the coast of British Columbia.

Paul McMullen served overseas, having enlisted for Siberian service while with the R.C.M.P. at Peace River.

Never conspicuous in municipal or community affairs Arthur McMullen was nevertheless always ready to lend a helping hand wherever it was needed. He enjoyed the respect and confidence of all who knew him. He was a member of the Tofield Lodge, No. 43, I.O.O.F. for many years.

Two members of the McMullen family survive, Jesse in New Westminster and Paul in Cedar, British Columbia.

## THE MITCHELL FAMILY

Hugh Mitchell was born in the state of Pennsylvania, and was one of the family of four boys. His father was a bridge contractor but died when Hugh was very young. The widowed Mrs. Mitchell felt the Civil War in the U.S.A. was about to break out so she moved her family to Ontario where they lived until the war subsided, then she returned to Tama County.

The future Mrs. Hugh Mitchell had emigrated from Woodstock, Ontario, to keep house for a brother in Tana County, Iowa. Here she met and married Hugh Mitchell, and here five of their six children were born. These were Mary (later Mrs. Peter Ingram), Robert, Elizabeth (later Mrs. James Younie of Edmonton), Jean (Mrs. Dawe of Edmonton), Will of Tofield, Dave the sixth child, was born after the family moved to O'Brien County.

When Dave was about a year old, the family moved to Oregon, in the hope that Mrs. Mitchell's health would be improved. Here they settled at a place called Peoria near Carvallis. After a short interval, the family again moved; this time they travelled across the Wettamett Cakkey to a place called Waterloo. There were rumors that a large woolen mill had been built there.

Mr. Mitchell obtained work on the building of the mill but just as he and his millwright friend, Mr. Carthew had the foundation finished, the project was called off. When, many years later, Dave Mitchell visited the scene, part of the old foundation was visible in the river.

A small town called Shedd was the Mitchell family's next home and here Mr. Mitchell bought a blacksmith shop from Mart Mullen. The tools were all stamped MM; some of them are still in existence.

Mr. Mitchell hired a good blacksmith by the name of Sam Bennett, who had worked for Fish Brothers' Carriage Works in the east. Mr. Miller himself did all the woodwork; the wagon and wheel work were his specialties For two or three years before leaving for Alberta, Mr. Mitchell went up into Washington, around Colfax, to thresh each fall. Here he made better money so was willing to go away and leave the shop in the capable hands of Sam Bennett.

While he was threshing around Colfax he had a man by the name of Sam Stirrett working for him "jigging sacks" to be exact. Sam Stirrett told him of the good land to be had for homesteading in Alberta. His brother Bob, had planned to go to Alberta and have a look at this reputedly rich land.

When Bob had looked at the homestead land, he and the. Fletchers immediately moved to Alberta and took up homesteads. In 1895, Hugh Mitchell and his old friend Carthew followed suit and also acquired homesteads in what was to be the Tofield area. The homestead Hugh Mitchell took had been filed on formerly by a man called Peterson, who had built two shacks on it. Carthew filed on the place known as Francis Point at the south end of Beaverhill Lake, but he never came back, apparently preferring Manitoba where he went after filing on the homestead.

The Mitchell family got settled. Mr. Mitchell had just fifty cents left. He had one very valuable asset. This was a top buggy he had made in Oregon in his spare time. "It was a nice job, and the first one in that district, maybe in Edmonton for that matter, says Dave Mitchell's letter.

Mrs. Roderick MacKenzie saw it and wanted it. She didn't have enough money to purchase it, but finally terms were arranged. It must have been a valuable buggy; for it, Mrs. MacKenzie gave four 2-year-old heifers in calf, four thousand feet of lumber and forty dollars cash.

In the spring, the heifers calved and the Mitchell children had "milk to go with our cracked wheat, which helped to take the wrinkles out of our bellies," says Dave in his letter.

Of course Mr. Mitchell had brought his blacksmith equipment. It was well that he did he had all the blacksmith work to do for the entire district.

Mr. and Mrs. Will Mitchell lived on the Mitchell farm in the Ketchamoot district until they retired to Tofield. Mrs. Mitchell was the former Amanda Henderson who had come with her family in 1895 from Tennessee to Wetaskiwin and thence to Tofield by wagon.

Mr. and Mrs. Mitchell have vivid memories of pioneer days. These include sod houses, whose roofs leaked for days after every rain. The roads were so bad, recalls Mr. Mitchell, that he got stuck many times with an empty wagon on the road to Tofield. Supplies were brought in, at long intervals, from Edmonton or Fort Saskatchewan. The neighbours took turns making these arduous trips—each family's turn came about once a year.

Mr. Mitchell, then an 11-year-old boy, spent his first year in the Tofield area being chore-boy for Dr. J. H. Tofield, pioneer doctor, after whom the town was named. Dr. Tofield lived where the Krystal family now reside.

Mr. and Mrs. Mitchell recall that the pioneers did a great amount of visiting whole families went for a day's visit, and were joyfully received.

Mr. and Mrs. Mitchell have a son and daughter. Their son Bill, is a fire ranger in the forestry service near Edson. Their daughter is Mrs. Andy Jalbert.

Mr. and Mrs. Mitchell are enjoying their retirement. Frequent visits from their son, daughter and grandchildren are thoroughly happy occasions. The Mitchells have taken an active part in the United Church activities and are keenly interested in the welfare of Tofield and district even though their retirement has taken them to Edmonton.

# THE CHRIS MOOS FAMILY

Chris Moos came from Denmark to South Dakota and established a hog farm. But after his hogs got cholera and all but one died, he decided to try his luck in Alberta. In 1906 he filed on a homestead in the Vegreville area but gave this land up soon after because Mrs. Moos, coming to a pioneer area, wanted to live near her relatives the Bowicks and Lotts. They were on the S.W. and N.W. quarters of section 12-59-19-W4th in the Logan district north of Tofield. Mr. Moos bought the N.E.¼ of 12 and built a log house with a sod roof. Living in this house wasn't easy at times because after a rainstorm it continued to rain in the house for many hours and everything and everyone got damp.

Mrs. Moos and Matie, who was then a year and nine months old, arrived in Chipman on May 24, 1907. Chris met them with a team of horses and a buggy, and drove through drifts to their new Alberta pioneer home. Verlyn was born in this same log house on October 30, 1907. Marguerite was born December 18, 1909 in Dakota, where Mrs. Moos had gone, at that time, to visit her family.

Chris hauled freight from Chipman to Tofield with horses and a wagon for a number of years. The Logan post office was in the Moos home so there were always neighbours dropping in.

The Bowicks and Lotts, wanting to move nearer Tofield sold their land to Mr. and Mrs. Moos. Chris had a steam engine and threshing machine and did threshing for many from Chipman to Ryley. He also had a saw mill and in 1909 had lumber to build in 1914. Near neighbors were the Roberge, McKenzie, Logan and Henry Wood families.

Since Chris Moos was able to speak six languages anyone coming from Europe and unable to speak English was sent to the Moos home. All were taken in until they could learn enough English to be understood. This created many problems and much work for Mrs.

Moos, who could speak only English.

The children got their elementary education at the McKenzie School.

Chris Moos passed away in 1931. Mrs. Moos continued to live on the farm until 1965 when she moved to Tofield to live with Marguerite and then to the Good Samaritan Auxiliary Hospital in Edmonton. Matie continues to live on the home farm. Marguerite works in Edmonton. Her son-in-law and daughter, Mr. and Mrs. Douglas Murray live south of town; their children are Dennis and Janice.

# THE MORTON FAMILY

John W. Morton was born March 29,1870, in southern Illinois. At an early age, he moved with his parents to Kansas, where in 1890, he married Flora Mahaffey. The young couple, lured by the Oklahoma land rush, set up housekeeping on land later designed as Pawnee. Amy, their only child was born in Kansas.

In 1904, the Mortons arrived in Edmonton where John ran a butcher shop for two years before he moved to Tofield. Here, he and his partner, Harvey Adams, started the first general store in Tofield Number One, which was not even a village just a Post Office.Their business was moved to the site of the second Tofield, and again, to Tofield's present location. In 1910 Morton and Adams sold their business to Rogers Brothers.

Always ready for a "horse trade," John Morton enjoyed farming and cattleraising o n the east side of Beaverhill Lake until he enlisted in the Canadian Army in World War I from which he returned with the rank of Sgt.

Resuming farming, the Mortons moved to the Ingram district. Interested in community organizations, Mrs. Morton won local fame for her "fancy work" crocheting, and embroidery.

When the Mortons left the Ingram district, they came to live very close to the location of their original store; in 1940, they bought a house in South Edmonton. Mrs. Morton eventually resided in a nursing home in Camrose while Mr. Morton ended his days in the Veterans' home at the former Goverment House in Edmonton, passing away in October, 1961. Amy, the Morton's daughter, is now Mrs. Amy Walter of Oakland, California; her son resides in Edmonton.

# THE NEAL FAMILY

William Henry Harrison Neal, his wife (Sarah Anne Elizabeth Rolston), and their son Harry came to the Tofield area in 1894. They had come to Canada from Auburn and Lincoln, Nebraska.

Mr. W.H.H. Neal and his son Harry filed on homesteads south of Tofield near the quarter homesteaded by the late Mr. Peter Lee.

This land was later given up and the family moved to another homestead situated about half a mile west of the land until recently occupied and owned by Jim Francis family. The Harry Neal quarter is now owned by Mr. J. Kauffman. The W. H. Neal quarter was directly across the road from this to the south.

Harry Neal married Tealy Lena Rickner on April 10, 1901. This marriage united two very early pioneer families. Mrs. Neal was the eldest daughter of Mrs. Nettie Rickner, a lady of truly pioneer qualities. Mrs. Rickner had been left a widow with a large family to raise. She did this successfully and also became a respected, beloved pioneer neighbour.

From the marriage of Harry Neal and Tealy Rickner are five living children: Mrs. Dorothy Calvert of Vancouver; Mrs. T.E. Seale (Bertha), of Toronto; Ralph of Los Angeles; Mrs. C.A. Everitt (Edith), of Edmonton; Mrs. S.B. Yakabuski (Nettie) of Edmonton.

Mrs. W.H.H. Neal passed away in 1907 following a lengthy illness; Mr. Harry Neal in 1909; Mr. W.H.H. Neal in 1921.

Mrs. Harry Neal later married Mr. J.S. Munro. There are three living children from this marriage: Fred, of Los Angeles; Archie and Kenneth, of Vancouver. Jessie (Mrs. Bennie Hobson), passed away in June 1951; also a baby died in 1921.

Lester Edward.

Mrs. J.S. Munro passed on in December, 1934. Of the pioneer Neal family, there are thirteen grandchildren and eight greatgrandchildren. Mrs. Seale, Mrs. Everitt and Mrs. Yakabuski frequently visit in Tofield, renewing old acquaintances, and visiting their aunt, Mrs. Jack Appleby, the former Vena Rickner.

This material was made available by Mrs. T.E. Seale.

# THE JOSHUA NOLAND FAMILY

*Thelma Noland Wallis*

Joshua M. Noland was born in Madrid, Iowa, in 1861. In 1887, he married Lida Luella Nelson; to this union were born two daughters, Ethel (Urquhart) and Thelma (Wallis).

Coming to Tofield in 1902, Mr. Noland settled on a homestead five miles north of what is now Tofield. In March, 1903, he brought his family to Alberta, landing in Edmonton. Until the freight and stock arrived, the Nolands stayed at the Strathcona hotel where they were met by Mr. Henry Wood of Tofield who assisted them on their journey to Tofield.

While living on the homestead, Mrs. Noland was Postmistress of the Logan Post Office which served not only the Mackenzie District, but also outlying districts.

In 1907 the Noland family moved to the old town of Tofield but when their home burned, moved to the present town of Tofield where they built the cottage directly opposite the United Church.

Mr. Noland was one of the original councillors of the Village of Tofield on its incorporation in 1907. For many years he also ran a livery stable and delivered mail in rural areas. He was one of the early road builders of the district, putting the first graded road through the Blackfoot Reserve now known as Highway 16. Mrs. Noland often accompanied her husband on road building trips, cooking for the crew.

Mr. Noland died on September 2, 1939, Mrs. Nolad on March 24, 1958, just prior to her ninetieth birthday. Their daughter Thelma married Rev. A. Wallis (now Canon Wallis). They now live in Victoria, B.C.

# NATHANIEL NOLAND FAMILY

*Rachel (Noland) Schultz*

Nathaniel Noland was born in Madrid, Iowa. He married Lenora Biggs and they farmed until 1902 when having heard of free homesteads in Canada, Nathaniel and his brother Joshua came to investigate the possibility of filing on land. While looking over the land around Tofield, they stayed with Henry Wood and his family. They returned to Iowa, loaded their equipment and livestock into colonists' cars, and returned, arriving in Strathcona, in March, 1903. Here everything was packed in two sleighs and the family consisting of Nathaniel and Lenora Noland and their three children, Rachel, Clillie, and Lester, set out for the Tofield area. One day was not sufficient for the trip, so a stop was made at Gladues for the night. There, on a bed of hay in the big barn, the Noland family spent the night.

Arriving in Tofield, the Nolands stayed with the Prudens who had several log houses and would accommodate homesteaders. Jordie Norris and family were living in one house so the Nolands moved in with Grandma Pruden or "Kookum" as she was known, who let the Nolands have part of the small house where she and her granddaughter, Annie, lived. This was just west of the Bethel farm. Here on April 27, a month after arrival of the Nolands, a baby boy, Everitt, was born.

That summer, Nathaniel filed on N.W. ¼ of 36-51-19-W4th; his brother Joshua filed on the S.W. ¼ of the same section. The other two quarters were owned by Clayt Harriman and Sam Bethel. With Nathaniel cutting logs, and Joe Norn dovetailing them, the Nolands' log house was built.

The Noland family lived in this house for many years as did the George Francis family who later owned the land. Logs cut by Nathaniel and sawed at Henry Wood's sawmill were used in further building as were the loads of slabs that sixteen-year-old Rachel hauled.

Unfamiliar with the severe winters, the Nolands found themselves short of food when potatoes stored in an outdoor pit froze solid. On discovering this calamity Nathaniel, Rachel remembers, cried because the potatoes were to have been the mainstay of the family diet.

"So," says Rachel, "that left us with frozen potatoes and rabbits for the rest of the winter."

The school attended by the Noland children was four miles south near the Phillips' farm; Mr. Whillans was the teacher. Six miles north was Robert Logan's trading post where supplies were available. To eke out the family income, Nathaniel hauled freight and when Henry Wood's first threshing machine arrived in Edmonton, Nathaniel helped bring it home. Bringing the machine to Tofield by way of Fort Saskatchewan, the men did some threshing jobs en route.

In the pioneer district, with distances great and doctors few, Mrs. Noland served the area as midwife.

Nathaniel, and his neighbor, Sam Bethel, were both fond of good horses. Their imported stallions were much in demand. Nathaniel drove in a buggy and led "Old Perch," a fine Percheron; Sam Bethel rode "Dibbie," his Punch. There was great rivalry between these two owners at local fairs.

Roads were only trails and Rachel well remembers driving the six miles to the Logan Store for supplies and having a balky team which lay right down in one of the many mudholes. Rachel crawled out of the back of the wagon, walked to her Uncle Josh's to get his hired man, Pete Gaets, to come and help Mrs. Noland in her predicament. Pete came, unhitched the horses, got them up, rehitched the horses to the wagon and pulled the wagon out. The trip was then resumed.

In 1917, Nathaniel became ill and was operated on for an ulcer an unheard of operation at that time, in the Mayo Clinic at Rochester, Minnesota. After seven days in the hospital he became impatient to be home so he invented a tale of serious illness having struck his wife. The hospital staff sympathetically allowed him to go home.

Through all of the hardships of pioneering, Nathaniel and Lenora never wanted to go back to the States. However, on retirement they moved back to Eugene, Oregon to be near their youngest daughter, Flo. Nathaniel died at 86; Lenora then returned to live in Alberta, until she died at 92.

# THE PHILLIPS FAMILY

Born in Guelph, Ontario, John Phillips moved to the U.S.A. when a young man; here he married Viola Ackley, of Pennsylvania. They lived in Webb, Buena Vista County, Iowa, until 1901 when, with his wife and family, John Phillips returned to Canada.

Leaving the train at Wetaskiwin where they were met by Henry Wood and Marion Hays of what is now Tofield, the family secured wagons to continue the journey to their new home north of Tofield on N.E. ¼ of 25-51-19-W4th. Their house, situated as it was on the old Edmonton trail, became one of the stopping houses so necessary to the travellers of the era who needed a place where both they and their horses could rest overnight, before proceeding on their journey. Here the family grew up.

Dave, the eldest son, married Ethel Rule; Anne married Ed Hill; Linnet married Grover Van Buskirk; Hiram married Pearl Rule. Another daughter Jane came with her husband, Halbert Eaton, in 1906. Rueben married Zoe Plants, daughter of the pioneer Plants family of Tofield; Roenza married Bertha Wolfe, living on the quarter north of the home place till 1947; Emery married Elizabeth Donnel and lived at Hastings Lake till retiring in Edmonton.

After the death of his first wife, John married Bessie Bowd. They built the house in Tofield now occupied by Mr. and Mrs. Bruce Warner.

Jane and Halbert Eaton had four children, Freda, (Mrs. Fry); Curtis and Gladice (who died very young) and Owen.

Owen married Ellen Campbell of Lamont, and farmed S.W. 35-51-19-W4th. Owen died in 1961. The eldest Eaton son, Walter, lives with his wife Evelyn and their children Brenda, Donnie, Kevin, Brian and Karen in Seba Beach. LeRoy, the second son and his wife Shirley and children Margie and Ronnie live in Leduc. The only daughter, Rita (Mrs. Herb Niemetz), her husband and two daughters, Linda and Sherry, reside in Ancaster, Ontario.

Rueben C. Phillips, his wife Zoe and their three sons, Neil, Lynn and Donald lived on the home place till 1928 when they moved to their new home on S.E.35-51-19-W4th. R.C. Phillips was a member of the Lakeshore School Board for many years; his wife, Zoe, though in indifferent health, took an active interest in the Ladies' Aid and the F.W.U.A. until her death in 1936. In 1939 Mr. Phillips married Mrs. Minnie McConnell. His death occurred in 1945. The eldest son Neil and his wife, Grace(McKinnon) live on S.E. ¼ 23-51-19-W4th, and are active community workers. Their two daughters, Barbara ( Mrs.Harold Conquest) and Sandra, both live in Edmonton.

Lynn Phillips was a member of the Loyal Edmonton Regiment in World War II. He married Doris Light, R.N. from Saskatchewan. His wife and children Barrie, Lynda and Kenny survive him.

Donald Phillips and his wife, Yvonne (Tough), and children, Jack, Donna, Colleen and Sherry live in Edmonton. Don has two sons, Larry and Ronnie, by a previous marriage to Marie Graham.

Roenza (Roe) Phillips and his wife Bertha live near Kingman; they have raised seven children, Patrick (Mike) now lives at Ponoka; Calvin (Bob) and Gilbert both live in Edmonton; Eileen (Mrs. Conrad Simonson) in Kingman, Angeline (Mrs. Peter Laskoski) in Holden, Eugene in the R.C.N., and Shirley (Mrs. Hierlihy).Edmonton.

Roe recalls Chief Meechum who, with his band of Crees, lived on what is now the Blackfoot Forest Reserve. Meechum had very dark skin and features, Negroid rather than Indian.

Travelling in a caravan of approximately twenty-five wagons, the band made frequent, leisurely trips to Tofield, returning late at night with the effects of the "firewater" obtained who-knows-where plainly audible. By the time Ketchamoot Creek was reached, the supply of liquor now depleted, was boosted by the addition of creek water. The same procedure was followed at Hastings and Maskawan Creeks. The dilution of the liquor did not diminish the whooping of the band as the caravan wended its way homeward.

Neighbours of the Phillips family in the early days, recalls Roe, were: Halbergs, Herndons, Bill Bloss, Van Buskirks, Bob Logan, Atkinsons, Lennies, Savers, Andersons, James Pruden, Ed, Frank, Mrs. Norn, Mrs. Jones, Mrs. Fraser (whose husband was a furbuyer for McDougall and Secord and who once owned the land where the

H. B.C.'s Edmonton store now stands), the Gladues, Augustine and Jeremy, Sr., Jeremy Jr. and Jerome, Roderick McKenzie, Billie Hopgood and the Thompson family.

While living north of Tofield, Roe purchased a pair of tamed Canada Geese from C. Oulton. This pair increased over the years to a flock of forty and were an unusual sight in a farmyard. They liked water, and the creek being dry, they flew to a slough on the Neil Phillips' farm. Though Roe promptly clipped their wings they refused to stay home they walked back in single file the mile to the slough. Eventually after 15-18 years, they became annoyed at cattle being fed too near and flew away.

Roe recalls the trials of early travel, the poor roads, the log bridges. He also remembers (with more pleasure) the baseball games, the dances, the coyote hunts engaged in by the pioneers.

Roenza and Emery Phillips are the only two survivors of the original Phillips family.

## THE PLANTS FAMILY

Charles Plants and his wife, the former Effie MacPherson, were born and raised in the small community of Winnfield, Iowa. Charles was born in 1867, the year of Canadian Confederation.

A few years after their marriage they drove in a covered wagon to the State of Oklahoma, where a tract of land known as the Cherokee Strip was being opened for settlement. After living near the town of Pawnee for six or seven years, they came to Alberta.

So in the year 1906 the couple and their four children arrived at the town of Wetaskiwin, Alberta, after a tedious train trip of two weeks. Shortly after that they moved to what is now the city of Camrose but which at that time was only a small community.

Charles Plants was a carpenter and helped build some of the earliest structures in Camrose, but in 1907 the family moved again, this time to Tofield, which had only then been declared a village. Again, Charles Plants helped construct some of the earliest buildings of the village, including the old Queen's Hotel.

In 1909, the family moved to a homestead southwest of Tofield in the Woodlawn district. Charles, however, continued his carpenter work and had a hand in the construction of many of the older (as well as the later) buildings in the town and surrounding district.

Altogether, the Plants family consisted of four sons and one daughter, the youngest son being born after the family arrived in Alberta. One son, Gerald, was killed in action duty in France, with the 50th battalion of the Canadian Infantry to which he had been transferred from the "202's". Two other sons, Arlo and Irvin died while in their early manhood. The daughter, Zoe, married R.C. Phillips, the son of another early pioneer family of the Tofield district. She and her husband raised three sons, but she, too, passed on while a comparatively young woman.

Mrs. Plants lived to the age of seventy-six and was quite active till shortly before her death. Charles Plants lived to be eighty-seven and continued active work until a few years before his death. The youngest son, Clifford, died early in 1968.

## THE PRUDEN FAMILY

*The material for this account is taken from a family history compiled by James M. Reed of Toronto in 1955. Mr. Reed is a descendant of the Prudens.*

John Peter Pruden, the greatgrandfather of Mrs. Herman Tiedemann and Mrs. Frank Kortzman was born in Edmonton, Middlesex, England in 1778. (Pruden's birthplace, Edmonton, is now part of greater London). When he came to Canada he brought with him the name for the future capital of Alberta that of his own birthplace.

Pruden entered the service of the Hudson's Bay Company in 1791 as an apprentice; later, at York Factory he became a writer for the Hudson's Bay Company.

In 1795 he was clerk for George Sutherland, the factor at the H.B.C.

post on the banks of the North Saskatchewan. In 1807, this fort was destroyed by fire, but in 1808, it was rebuilt twenty miles downstream from its original site. Here it was to grow into the City of Edmonton, a name suggested by Pruden to the Chief Factor.

From 1808-1824, Pruden was in charge of Carlton House where, in 1821, he was made Chief Trader. In 1825-1826 he was placed in charge of Norway House but later returned to Carlton House where he was promoted to Chief Factor in 1836. In 1837, Pruden retired and lived in the Red River Settlement where he served for a time as a member of the Council of Assiniboia. He died on May 30, 1868, at the age of ninety.

John Peter Pruden had seven children: William, Charlotte, Peter, James, Cornelius, John and Caroline.

The third son, James, the grandfather of Mrs. Tiedemann and Mrs. Kortzman, was born in the Northwest Territories in 1820. He married a woman from the Peace River district who is recorded as Geneve; she was born in 1821 and died in 1914 at the age of ninety-three.

James Pruden left for the Oregon Territory early in the 1850's with a group from the Red River Settlement, led by James Sinclair but later returned to the Edmonton district where he filed on a homestead on the west side of Beaverhill Lake, thus becoming one of the first settlers in the Tofield area. James Pruden died on January 13, 1902 and was buried in the St. James, the Apostle-Newton-Logan cemetery seven miles northwest of Tofield. This was the Anglican cemetery usually referred to as the Logan cemetery; the land for the cemetery had been donated to the Anglican Church by Mr. Pruden.

James Pruden had ten children: The oldest boy John Edward, was born June 3, 1852. He married Eliza Rowland and they had nine children Flora (Mrs. Kortzman); Bill, who died during the 1918 influenza epidemic; Ned, killed in action in World War I; Archibald, who died in 1958, leaving a reputation as a boxer during his service in the Armed Forces; Carrie; Walter also killed in World War I, Emma; John and Joe.

Charles, another son of James Pruden, was born Feb. 7, 1856. He had four children: One of his daughters, Annie, married Lawrence MacKenzie of Tofield.

Maria, James Pruden's daughter, was born Nov. 22, 1857 and died in 1955, aged 98 years. Married to George Kennedy, she lived in the H.B.C. house in Edmonton, near the site of the Legislative Buildings in Edmonton.

A news item from the Winnipeg Free Press of Monday Nov.3, 1935, states:

"Edmonton pioneer traces her roots back to another Edmonton, Fort Edmonton was named after her grandfather's birthplace in England. Her husband named Grand Prairie. Her home may be the oldest dwelling in Edmonton. It was built 68 years ago by her husband, the late George Kennedy. This pioneer of pioneers is 97 years old."

Another of James Pruden's daughters was Margaret Ann, born Dec.31,1859. She married Henry Fraser, fur trader for the H.B.C.; she died April 16, 1956, aged ninety-six.

A third daughter, Elizabeth Jane, (born Dec. 18, 1861, died July 13, 1952) married Joseph Norn (1862—1914). They had five children: Adeline who married Roy Foss in the little St. JamesNewton-Logan Church on Oct 31, 1907, Frank, and Sophia, who married Steve Hafner; Alice who married Martin Hafner, and Lily who married Herman Tiedemann. The Tiedemanns had five sons, Walter, James, Marvin, Joe and Floyd.

Another son, Frank, born May 1, 1865, married Annie MacKenzie and had four children: Olive, Marvin, Ivy and Holden.

The fourth daughter of James Pruden, Caroline, born April 25, 1869, married George Pace Jones, a former member of the R.N.W.M.P. They had nine children: Harry, Lillian; Mary; Albert (Bert) who farmed north of Tofield until his death a few years ago; Maude; Grace; Maggie, Elsie; and Vernie.

Still another daughter, Sophia Maria, born Sept.15, 1871, married George Norris. Their five children were: James, Henry, Rose, Beatrice and Clara. Frederick, the youngest son of James Pruden, was born June 1, 1876 and died at the age of twelve.

# THE RAY FAMILY

Frank H. Ray left Boston with the intention of joining the Gold Rush. Landing in Camrose in 1902, he met Mr. Wildman, a surveyor and a brother-in-law of Amanda Mitchell, who told him of some wonderful land near Tofield. This appealed to the traveller who was very weary and felt he had travelled far enough. In 1904, accompanied by his wife, he came to Tofield and "squatted" on land next to Mr. Wildman; soon he filed on this land as his homestead. He also hauled freight from Camrose to Tofield for several years. Later he clerked in Morton and Adams General Store. The children of Mr. and Mrs. Ray were: Milton, Roger, Franklin, and Grace, (later Mrs. Mitchell). Frank Ray also worked in the L.C. Hay store before retiring to the farm.

Still farming here are: Oliver Ray (Roger's Son), Charlie Ray (Milton's son); Bruce Ray (Roger's son), and Harold Ray.

# THE RICKNERS

In the year 1893, on September 27, the Rickner family left Colfax,Washington, by way of the Mullen trail. It was a bright sunny morning when they departed from that good country to get a taste of pioneer life in Sunny Alberta. Their reason for leaving Washington was their inability to buy land of their own.

They had a family of seven, two boys aged 14 and 8; the girls ranged from 10 years to 3 months. They travelled all the way on two covered wagons. Mrs. Rickner and her eight year old son managed one wagon while Mr. Rickner and the eldest son managed the second wagon as well as the band of extra horses. Mrs. Rickner commented "This was not a pleasure trip. "

Some of the trails were dangerous; more than one stream had to be forded and this meant that the belongings of the wagon were frequently soaked. Even the crossings on the ferries were at times nervewracking. Camping along the trail was the order of things most nights but the occasional night was spent in deserted houses along the way.

The roaring of a mountain lion was frequently heard but fortunately for their peace of mind, the Rickners could not identify the animal at the time. When they were told later, it was too late to be alarmed, but they understood why their horses had come into camp from the grazing area.

Other circumstances made travel slow and difficult. Several times the horses strayed away at night causing the travellers to fear that their means of transportation had gone back to Washington. The horses got sore feet, too, and this caused delays in travel as did illness among the children.

Mr. Rickner occasionally sold some of the horses and though he got poor prices for them, the extra cash was welcome. Horse trading was also carried on; not always to the Rickners' benefit. Mrs. Rickner commented, "I shall never forget the day that a stranger led away our surefooted Creamy and left us that pretty, but worthless black, and how the boys longed to have our own lovely beast back again."

The Rickners arrived at Lethbridge in a blizzard on November 3 and had considerable trouble finding shelter. During the winter Mr. Rickner and the boys worked in the mines; Mr. Rickner's health was failing, and he could work only spasmodically.

Next September saw the Rickner family again on the move, this time to Edmonton. They lived for two years ten miles out of the city during which time Mr. Rickner filed his claim on a homestead in the Tofield area. On this homestead, Mr. Rickner and the two boys with the help of the kind neighbors laboriously constructed a log house. Finally, shortly before Christmas in 1896 the Rickners made ready to move to the Tofield homestead but Mr. Rickner fell seriously ill and died on January 23, 1897. On February 11 of that same year, Mrs. Rickner and her bereaved family arrived at the log home, ready to begin the hard life of homesteaders. Of such stuff were the pioneers of this area!

It was, needless to say, hard going with this young family. As soon as possible, the boys prepared some land and raised what grain they could.

Even though in the wet years the grain was usually frozen, it was always good for feed. The season of 1898 was exceptionally dry and the crop yielded only enough for the next year's seed, but the quality of the grain made up to some extent for the low yield. At no time did the Rickners experience a complete crop failure. Even when the grain was completely lodged by a heavy snowstorm, the boys mowed it and stacked it like hay.

A good garden was a necessity for the Rickner household as was a supply of milk and butter. In summer, when butter was more plentiful, Mrs. Rickner packed the excess supply into crocks until winter when she then made it into prints which she then took to Edmonton, the nearest market, for sale. In winter, butter was worth twenty cents per pound rather than the 12 1/2 to 15 cents obtained for it in summer. Mrs. Rickner thus made a little extra cash for her family. In addition to butter, Mrs. Rickner sold dressed chickens at ten cents a pound.

Supplying meat for the table was a recurrent pioneer problem. Prairie chickens were often on the table as were rabbits in various guises. Dinner fare was plain but hearty and no one needed to go hungry. Mrs. Rickner had a high opinion of bread and milk as components of children's diets. She maintained "if all children liked bread and milk as well as mine, there would be fewer cases of appendicitis."

Soon the Rickner boys were old enough to work away from home and add their wages to the family coffers. When seasonal help was required, in turn, by the Rickners, some kind neighbors were always available. The Rickner family reciprocated this kindness in traditional pioneer fashion.

Mrs. Rickner was a thrifty, capable housewife. She sewed for her own family and for the neighbours. She took the raw, sheared wool, carded it, spun it, and knitted it into mitts, stockings and socks. Working by coal oil if possible, by tallow candle if necessary, Mrs. Rickner ensured her family a supply of warm winter clothing

A homemade loom produced, under Mrs. Rickner's hands, yards of carpeting which made the house warmer.

Mrs. Rickner's service to her neighbors included nursing. Doctors were not always available so a skilled nurse for confinements, serious illnesses and accidents was always eagerly sought for. Mrs. Rickner was apparently a successful nurse; she said, "I can thank the Lord for my success."

Any money the Rickner family could earn was solely needed to buy the necessities of life. She commented, "When I bought dry goods for the family, there were no silk and fancy broadcloths, or silk stockings included, in supplies. More material was needed for skirts then; we didn't see so much hosiery then."

Travel was no pleasure for the Rickners. Edmonton, the nearest market, was 40 miles away in winter; in summer, the poor roads forced travellers into a circuitous route which was much farther. Thus summer trips, especially in wet years were avoided at all costs. If a summer trip became urgent, several families would go together thus ensuring help in getting out of the ever present mudholes and up the steep, slippery hills.

Mrs. Rickner had particularly vivid memories of one summer trip. Leaving Edmonton, she found the ferry inoperative due to the dangerously high Saskatchewan. She was forced to wait there three days for the river to subside! "Three days might not seem like much to some people but it seemed to me when my purse was so flat and I was so anxious knowing four girls under 14 years were home under a sod roof. Sure enough, when I got home, they told me that the barn had been a better shelter than the house. Soon after that, we got a board roof."

If, when on a journey, a stopping house could not be reached, travellers were forced to camp by the trail. Once when Mrs. Rickner and her fourteen year old son were in this predicament, a bear smelled the dressed chickens Mrs. Rickner had placed on the seat of the wagon to keep cool during the night. Mr. Bear was so entranced by the smell that he came right up to the wagon, frightening the horses badly, and, needless to say, preventing the Rickner mother and son from completing their needed night's rest.

While keeping up a brave front for her family's sake Mrs. Rickner, in her own words, "could have died of homesickness the first two years on the homestead." After she lost her husband, Mrs. Rickner's sister offered to finance her return to her old home in Missouri; but she always felt that if she could just hold out a little longer, she would win. In this new country, each new quarter of land obtained was a jewel beyond price.

Soon conditions became easier for the Rickner household. A saw mill not far away made lumber from the logs cut by the Rickner boys. Soon a comfortable five room frame house took some of the hardships from pioneering. Economy was still a necessary practice, but eventually the house was comfortably furnished. No purchases were made on credit; what the Rickners couldn't pay for, they did without.

A better market and local stores made life more pleasant. More milk cows, more hogs for market, more grain to sell, all increased the Rickners' income. In 1904 the railroad came in; this was a great asset to the country. Shortly, Tofield became a town and in 1912 a gas boom raised land values. Mrs. Rickner sold her homestead for $150 per acre. Unfortunately the gas boom did not last. Soon she repossessed her homestead which she later resold when she acquired more land.

Pleasures of pioneer life, said Mrs. Rickner, included attending church and the Union Sunday School. Her greatest pleasure was in seeing her family grow up."There is always a laugh where there is a family of jolly children," she said.

As the Rickner family grew up, they took an active interest in the affairs of the community, especially in those of the church. At one time four of the Rickner girls sang in the choir.

The eldest son, Perl, returned to the U.S.A. Though he is dead, his wife still lives there in 1967. The eldest daughter, Tealy, married Harry Neal; of the marriage, five children were born (Bertha, Mrs. T.E. Seale), Dorothy (Mrs. Bert Calbert), Ralph, Edith, (Mrs. C.A. Everitt), Nettie,(Mrs. Stan Yakabuski). Mrs. Neal became a widow and later married Jack Munro; the Munro family consisted of Frederick, Archie, Kenneth and Jessie. One son died in infancy. Lillie, Mrs. R. Hazelhurst, is, in 1967, living in Merritt., B.C.; Oma (Mrs. C.McKeoun) is in Calgary. Venah (Mrs. J. Appleby) and her husband live near Tofield; Fannie (Mrs. D. Munro) is deceased as is the other brother Marvin.

The Appleby families are all active in community and church work. Clifford and Barbara have four children; Kenneth, Leslie, Nettie and Susan. Keith, the youngest son, died in 1967, leaving his wife Elsie and four children: Robert, Heather, Donald and Dale.

# THE ROBERGE FAMILY

Mr. and Mrs. C.C. Roberge were married in Armand, Ontario on April 24, 1872. They came to the west in 1890 and were residents of Edmonton for three years before they took up residence on their homestead north of Tofield in what is now the Ross Creek district. Mrs. Roberge, coming west to join Mr. Roberge, was a passenger on the first passenger train that went over the steel from Red Deer to Edmonton.

The Ross Creek district at that time was nearly all bush; only about four acres on the Roberge homestead were available for breaking. For some years, Mr. Roberge worked as a carpenter in Edmonton and Mrs. Roberge and children were alone on the homestead.

Edmonton was the nearest trading point and it took a three-day journey to reach it and another three days to return to Tofield. These journeys held no terror for Mrs. Roberge even though they involved sleeping under the sleigh when the temperature registered as low as 30 or 40 degrees below zero.

For some time Mrs. Roberge and Mrs. Daniel Francis were the only two white women in the area; the rest of the population consisted of Indians and Metis.

To these neighbours, Mrs. Roberge paid fine tribute, stating that they had always treated her like a lady.

Mrs. Roberge was friends not only with the Indians but with Mr. and Mrs. Frank Oliver and felt that no man had done so much for the west as Frank Oliver, former Minister of the Interior and original editor of The Edmonton Bulletin. Mrs. Roberge was proud to declare that she had always taken the Tofield paper and The Edmonton Bulletin "Ever since it was a small 6" by 9" sheet."

The Roberge family endured the pioneer hardships common to the era. Oxen were the motive power of travel for the first eighteen years of Mrs. Roberge's life in the West; later, horses became valued possessions.

Mr. and Mrs. Roberge endured all the hardships which were part of the pioneering era, not the least of which was the impassible condition of the roads, if indeed the vaguely defined trails through the bush could be called roads. On one occasion while driving cattle to Edmonton Mr. Roberge and his two sons.,William and Albert, were lost for several days, the last four of which they were without food.

Mr. and Mrs. Roberge were charter members of the First Baptist Church in Edmonton and their names, among others are under the cornerstone of that ediface.

During the winters of the early years, Mrs. Roberge lived in Edmonton to enable her children to go to school and it was thus possible for her to continue her active work in the church. She was an active worker in the church. She was an active member of the Mission Circle and the W.C.T.U.

On June 24, 1924, the Jubilee of the Mission Circle was celebrated and Mrs. Roberge was presented with a gold pin to commemorate her work as a member of that organization. The following letter which was sent to her shows how highly her work was regarded and the difficulties which she overcame to do her work in the church which to her came next in importance to caring for her family.

"As one of the Baptist trail blazers, we feel you are in a class quite by yourself, for we are sure there never was another woman who drove an ox team fifty miles to attend church. As a financier, too, you have surpassed us all, for even Mrs. Bellamy, who, in olden days, could get blood out of a stone, never wheeled a team of stubborn oxen freighting for storekeepers and neighbours. You freighted your way to church. The fact that you could drive a team of oxen at all and keep your religion proves you to be a Christian, worthy of lasting tribute.

We are not unmindful of your courage in sickness and trouble, neither hard work nor trouble has ever daunted your efforts to render aid.

For such labor, selfsacrifice and not least, for the happy, loving spirit you have always brought with you, we are grateful. We wish you every blessing and many years of wear this Jubilee pin. On behalf of the Mission Circle,

signed, President, Mrs. H. H. Hall

Secretary, Mrs. K.E. Meades."

In 1922,Mr. and Mrs. Roberge celebrated their golden wedding.

They were honored by gifts from organizations in the community. In the evening for their golden wedding day, a large crowd danced in the home of Mr. and Mrs. Roberge.

The Roberges had three sons, Austin, Albert and William, and two daughters who later became Mrs. Cameron and Mrs. Harris. Two sons, Edward and Charles, died while still young.

Until his death in 1967, Charles Roberge, son of William and grandson of the pioneer Roberge family, lived in Tofield. His wife, Mary, and his two sons, Kevin and Brendan remain in Tofield in 1967; his two daughters Georgina and Patricia are married and no longer live in the area in which their great-grandparents, Mr. and Mrs. C.C. Roberge were pioneers.

# THE ROBINSONS

Long connected with the industrial activities of Tofield, Mr. J.W. Robinson came to Tofield in 1913 from St. Anthony's, near Newcastle, in Northumberland, England. He and his brother Christopher started a brickyard in Tofield. For twenty-four years Mr. Robinson was a steam engineer with the Tofield Coal Co. During World War II, he spent four years at Coal Valley as engineer. In 1947, he helped to construct the Tofield Municipal Hospital before working for two years in the Northwestern Utilities' shop in Tofield. In 1951 and 1952, he supervised the building of St. James' Church, Edmonton; in 1953 he performed the same service for the Tofield United Church.

He has been connected with Holy Trinity Church, Tofield since April 20, 1913, holding the offices of People's Warden, Minister's Warden, Secretary, Lay Reader, and Choir member. Mr. Robinson was also a member of the Tofield School Board, as well as its chairman for many years.

Mrs. Robinson (nee Isabel Bundy) graduated from Portsmouth College, Portsmouth, England in 1909. Coming to Canada that fall, she taught near Leduc and Wetaskiwin. While visiting Rev. J.P. Mason and his wife at Tofield, Miss Bundy met her future husband. They were married July 21, 1917 in All Saints' Cathedral, Edmonton.

Mrs. Robinson has taken an active part in work for the Red Cross, the Bible Society, the Musical Festival, and Sunday School services. Both Mr. and Mrs. Robinson have been faithful visitors to the sick and the shut-ins of this community. They have two daughters, Mrs. J. A. Smith, and Mrs. J. Brickman and one granddaughter Edith Mary Smith.

## THE ROWLAND FAMILY

The Rowland family is one of the earliest in the Tofield area. William Rowland was a trader for the Hudson's Bay Company. William's son, Billie, and his wife were Tofield residents. Their children were: Jim, Charlie (who was killed overseas), Edith, George and Ellen. Ellen is now Mrs. Giffin of Washington, U.S.A.

Cousins of the Billie Rowland family, Art Rowland and Russel Rowland are still living in the Tofield district. Art Rowland is the maintenance man for the Town of Tofield.

## THE SCHULTZ FAMILY

Charles L. Schultz, widower, from Sioux City, Iowa, arrived at Strathcona, on September 3, 1901. With him came his three sons, three horses and a carload of settlers' effects. Charles and the three boys, Walter, Otto and Tom were all in search of land to homestead.

Their first winter in Alberta was spent a few miles south of Strathcona. They did not live in luxury; part of their shelter was a dugout on a hillside.

1901 was an open winter, at least in its early months, and Otto and Tom journeyed on horseback east and north of Beaverhill Lake to Vegreville. They then went southeast around the lake to Northern (later Bardo), on to Wetaskiwin and back to Strathcona. This was really a scouting expedition as the boys were searching for homesteads.

On October 30, 1901, Otto obtained his first job. Working for

McCauley, he cut wood for the ten-horse-power-steamer. This steamer was an upright model and took sticks of wood two and a half feet long. It operated in the Blackfoot Reserve on the east side of Beaverhill Lake.

In the spring of 1902, Otto and Tom again headed east from Clover Bar to the north end of the Beaverhill Lake. Here they were amazed to see the amount of water covering the land. A small river, Beaver Creek, ran out of the north end of the lake. The horses had to swim part way across this river.

The Schultz brothers decided, after travelling around the lake, to take up land in the Tofield area and in the next few months all had filed claims on homesteads. Charles Schultz' homestead was N.W. 34-50-19-W4th, the home for the father and the three boys.

In the summer of 1902, another Schultz boy, Alfred, came to visit his father and brothers. He had come from Chicago and felt he was a long way north when he reached Tofield.

Al Schultz had been a construction worker in the U.S.A. a long time. He was assigned to help move the world's first Ferris Wheel. The Chicago World's Fair in 1893 saw this gigantic wheel put into operation for the first time. It cost $350,000; the problems of construction were enormous. The axle was 45' 6" long, 33' in diameter, weighed 46.5 tons and was the largest single piece of steel ever forged in America up to that time. The passenger cars were 24' long, 13' wide, 10' high. Each car carried 38 passengers to look out both sides of the car.

After ten years of successful operation in Chicago this gigantic structure was dismantled to be moved to St. Louis for the Louisiana Exposition. It was at this time that Al Schultz was engaged in helping move the Ferris Wheel. Harold Schultz., Alfred's son still has his Father's "Workman pass" to the Exposition and a picture of his father among a gang of men who were engaged in dismantling the huge wheel.

Twenty flatcars were required to transport this structure; the cost of the move was $265,000.00. Later, because no further large fairs were in sight, the World's first Ferris Wheel was dynamited and sold for scrap.

Before returning home from Alberta to Iowa, Alfred bought land in the Didsbury area. On his return to Alberta in 1906, he purchased land in the Ketchamoot area. This was S.W. 10-50-19-W4th. (the James Ingram homestead) and S.E. 10-50-19 (previously owned by Doug Black). Here Al Schultz farmed until his retirement. After the death of his first wife, Margaret (Appleby), he married Miss Frances Fawcett who cared for the four Schultz children Russel, Harold, Alvin and Helen (now Mrs. Jack of Edmonton.)

Alvin died in 1954 leaving three children: Robert, Alfred and Babs. Mrs. Jack has one daughter, Dawn (Mrs. Haug); Russel, now of Edmonton has two children, Duane and Lana.

The original Alfred Schultz land in 1967 is the home of Harold Schultz and his wife Lily (Haugen) who have four children: BetsyAnn (Mrs. Claude Gallinger), Frances, Brian and David.

In the winter of 1902, both Otto and Tom worked for McCauley's mill on the shores of Island Lake. The mill ran on a twenty-four hour basis in two twelve-hour shifts.

The men were paid one dollar for each twelve hour shift they worked. When the mill was shut down in April, Tom worked as a horsewrangler, breaking horses for Mr. McCauley.

In the spring of 1904, Otto again worked at the mill which was then located two miles east of Hasting Lake on Hastings Creek. It had been hoped to float the cut logs down Hastings Creek but had constant trouble due to the sharp turns in the creek. J. McGinitie was hired with his team of oxen to pull the logs out of the creek. For his services and those of his team he was paid $1.50 per day. Mark Ferguson, later a member of the Town of Tofield's first council, was also a member of this crew of log floaters.

In the spring on 1903, Tom and Otto trapped 2,000 muskrats in the area between the north end of Miquelon Lake and the present Highway 14. They "camped out " using a canvas canopy over a wide sleigh as a portable home. Here they slept, dried furs beside the light metal stove which was used for heating and cooking. This mobile home was shifted from place to place by prearrangement with homesteaders. Once an area was "trapped out," a move must be made to a new site. The pelts were sold in Edmonton for 11 cents each.

All four of the Schultz boys engaged in mixed farming in the Tofield area. With the coming of the railroad, Otto worked on subcontracts, running an outfit consisting of 25 teams, 7 dumpwagons, 10 wheelers and an elevating grader.

Two sisters, Minnie and Doris, visited their father and brothers from time to time, taking back stories of Alberta pioneer experiences to their home in the States.

Minnie became Mrs. George McConnel and some years after her husband's death, married R.C. Phillips. She died in 1965.

## THE SHUPE FAMILY

Frank Shupe's family homesteaded in the Tofield area before Frank and Mary were married in Pawnee, Oklahoma on April 9, 1911. After living in Pawnee for a year, Frank and Mary came to the Tofield district where they lived with Frank's folks for a year. Then they moved to the town of Tofield where Frank did team work hauling coal, etc.

On April 2, 1913, their first child was born; she passed away February 8, 1917. Their second daughter, Irma, was born February 6, 1918. Irma is now Mrs. Arthur Francis.

In the spring of 1918, the Shupes started farming and continued until 1943 when they moved to the acreage west of Tofield which had formerly been owned by Frank Pruden who had hauled water to the town for many years.

In 1963, the Shupes retired and moved into town.

## MRS. PETRA STAUFFER

Mrs. Petra Stauffer, a member of the Bardo Norwegian community for the earlier part of her life and now a resident of Tofield, wrote the following account of her life. It was written for the celebration of the Golden Jubilee of the Bardo Lutheran Church several years ago but it is equally valuable in the year of the Diamond Anniversary of the Town of Tofield.

Mrs. Stauffer says:

"I was born here in Alberta on the bank of the Amisk Creek in a log house with a sodroof built by my father. I was ushered into the world by the kindly competent neighbor ladies. There were no doctors or trained nurses available in those days.

No doubt we had rain then, too, for mama used to tell me that the only place she could protect me from the leaky sod roof was in my cradle under the table.

It was a friendly peaceful country I grew up in. Everyone was a neighbour and a friend, willing to help each other whenever and wherever needed. There was no class distinction.

There were only two things we feared: the dreaded forest fires and a few Indians who travelled along the trails. The only reason we feared the Indians was because we had no common language. We spoke only Norwegian at first so could not understand even the limited English the Indians knew.

I'm sure our folks faced many difficulties and hardships but they did not despair. They lived for each other and looked forward to the future of their family.

Looking back over the past fifty years, I feel I have so many things to be thankful for. I'm thankful for being here today celebrating our Golden Jubilee Thanksgiving among friends and neighbours. I'm thankful to have been born and raised in Alberta where we are free to think as we like. We have never known fear and persecution as have so many other lands. I'm thankful to have been born in a new country and to have seen its growth from the beginning until now.

Fifty years ago, I was rather small and had just barely started school; I was not so thankful for the many things at that time for instance, walking to school. We walked three miles to the school which was opposite the Bardo cemetery. There were no school buses nor any cars, so walking was the only way to go if you had no horse.

Our school days were limited. We started at eight years and went until we were fourteen, but if, at anytime we were needed at home, we could stay out. Our school year was six months to begin with, then eight, and since it is now ten months, we must have all been very clever!

Most of our parents were very poor; they came as emptyhanded immigrants. We were all needed at home so very few of us could go on through high school.

Our roads were only trails and we had a lot of rain with the inevitable mudholes on the trails making travel difficult. When our first roads were built we were so thankful more thankful than we are now for our paved highways. We were grateful to be able to ride in wagons and when buggies came in, we were really well away! We went many a mile with horses and wagon; today, we often consider a similar journey too far by car.

Speaking of journeys by wagon reminds me of a teacher we had who went to a neighbourhood picnic in a wagon.

She was dressed in a nice white dress and when the horses splashed mud on it she was 'put out' about it. During the day when 'Canada the Land of the Maple' was being sung, she was heard to murmur, 'It may be the Land of the Maple to some, but to me, it's the Land of the Mudhole.'

We surely did not have the material things that the children of today have but maybe we learned, through lack of them, to appreciate things when we got them. I remember Mother making our summer dresses of flour sacks. When Christmas came., she would dye them and we were so happy to have new dresses for Christmas!

Our shoes were homemade for a long time. My father was the shoemaker for the entire commnity, and a very fine one too; the shoes he made lasted a long time -too long it seemed. So I really treasured my first pair of "boughten" shoes. Walking to school, I stopped every few yards to dust them.

My first train ride was taken from Bardo siding to Kingman in company with Inga Johnson with whom I walked to Bardo to take the train.

We had been told that riding on trains made some people seasick; so after riding a few minutes I asked her "Do you feel anything?" "No," was the answer. After a while she asked me "Do you feel anything?" I, too said "No" and we felt we were very lucky indeed not to get sick on a train ride.

My first trip to Edmonton was an event. I was sixteen years old and was thrilled to get my ticket and fiftycents spending money for the three days I would be gone. I accompanied Agnes Haukedal to visit her cousins. It was really an occasion; out of my fifty-cents, I came home with thirty-five cents. Could we do that now?

One time my father and my Uncle Haugen took their steers to Edmonton on foot, walking all the way. After a few days journey through the Beaver Hills and around the lakes, they arrived in Edmonton and Uncle Haugen left his there, feeling that he had chased them far enough.

Our mothers were hardy too. The district stretched from Tofield to Round Hill and from Kingman to Ryley. Once when Ladies' Aid was being held at Mrs. Hunt's (now the Jack Appleby home), I remember the mothers skiing all the way, some of them even carrying their little ones on their backs.

Thinking of these difficult years makes me very grateful for the progress which has taken place in our community. It seems that God has blessed us and our country most wonderfully. From walking behind the plough and tilling our soil the hard way, we have advanced to sitting in comfort on tractors which pull modern machinery. We have new cars, modern homes, new schools and churches and we ought to be thankful indeed.

I've enjoyed wonderful health and a nice home. I am thankful to be living among my children with so many lovely neighbours and friends."

Thus ends Mrs. Stauffer's account of her life but it is by no means complete. For several years, she drove one of the County of Beaver school buses. She decided to leave her farm home and so built a lovely modern home in Tofield, doing much of the work herself. Her son Leonard and his wife, Evelyne, and their sons, Kenny and Warren, live in the Bardo district; now in Edmonton but until recently in Tofield, were Mrs.Stauffer's daughter, Mrs. Norman Stauffer, her son-in-law, Norman, and the grandchildren, Sylvia, Duane and Patricia.

Petra is still an active member of the community. In the Centennial year, she was chosen by the mayor of Tofield, Dr. Freebury, to be the Centennial Queen, a post which she fulfilled with charm and dignity.

As well as presiding at all official functions, Petra visited the Senior Citizens' homes and the hospitals both in Tofield and Camrose, bringing pleasure to the residents of both institutions. She was also instrumental in the construction of the Tofield Centennial Park, on the main street of the town; in fact, due to the interest she had in the park and the work she put into it, the park is frequently spoken of as "Petra's Park."

## THE W.C. SWIFT FAMILY

*The material for the following article was kindly sent by Mrs. W.C. Swift, longtime resident of Tofield., later of Edmonton.*

Mr. Swift was on the council of the village of Tofield in 1907, two years before the date of incorporation as a town. Before coming to Tofield Mr. Swift worked for four years for Revillon Freres in Edmonton.

"November 1906, we left Edmonton for Chipman by Canadian Northern Railway now the Canadian National. After spending the night there, we were driven by bobsled, I think, by Jeremie Gladue. We had very heavy going because of the deep snow. When we reached Ross Creek., we stopped at the home of Mr. and Mrs. John Logan. Here we had dinner and rested the horses.

We arrived at the hamlet of Tofield (named after Dr. J. H. Tofield) at 6 p.m. We were welcomed by Mr. and Mrs. Cress. Mr. Cress later became the first station agent for the Grand Trunk Pacific Railway in Tofield.

The hamlet was situated on the farm of Mr. George Cookson Sr. where the Rempel family now live. The post office was on the Cookson farm, too, just a little east of Mr. Cookson's home. Mail came once a month at first but soon came every fortnight. Mr. Cookson was the Postmaster.

Like most pioneers of that day, the Swifts lived in a small two-roomed shack and also operated the newly established business from it. Mr. Swift established his lumber yard that year (1906). The following merchants were also in business then: Mr. Robert Logan, with a general store one mile north, C. Cress and J. Harper with general stores at the townsite; Morton and Adams had a butcher shop; Mr. R.O. Bird had a hardware; Mr. Omar Mahaffey had a blacksmith shop; Mr. and Mrs. James Mahaffey had a stopping place. When the noon meal was ready at the stopping place, Mr. Mahaffey played a tune on a huge metal triangle. Dr. McKinnon had a dispensary. The two resident ministers, Rev. Bradley (Presbyterian) and Rev. Laidman (Methodist), held services in the school house, a mile north of the hamlet.

In 1907, Crafts, Lee and Gallinger had the quarter section where the school now stands surveyed and gave free lots to anyone who would build a home or place of business there. So the town was moved to a site just west of the present school. The Presbyterian congregation brought the Presbyterian church from a site just north of Mr. John Thompson's present residence to a site just north of the Methodist Church.

Mr. Swift, following the general exodus to the new townsite, built a larger house in that locality. The front room served as office by day, as a living room by night, and as a church on Sunday.

As the village moved to its present site, the Swifts followed suit. The house of Mr. Swift's partner, Mr. Emery was, Mrs. Swift tells us, the first house in the new townsite. This house (in 1967) is now occupied by the F. Shupe family. Mr. Swift built the house now owned by Earl Moore in 1910. In 1917, the Swift family moved to the Nickelson house now owned by the Leo Bauer family, and finally in 1923 to the Stewart Hall house (now the John Wall home). Here they remained until they moved to Edmonton in 1947, where Mr. Swift still resides.

The partnership of Swift and Emery began in 1907 and continued until 1934, though Mr. Emery died in 1934 and his interest was taken over by Mrs. Emery. In 1915, the business became lumber and implements. This paved the way for the Ford garage which Mr. Swift ran until 1947.

Mr. Swift served Tofield well. He was on the Council in 1907 and was mayor of the town for sixteen years in 1917-18, 1929-32 and 1937-46. He was councillor for fourteen years. He was an early member of the School Board; he was on the Official Board of the United Church and Sunday School Superintendent for many years.

Mr. Swift was a member of the Palestine Lodge No. 46, AF & AM and an ardent curler. Chess was his recreation.

Mrs. Swift shared her husband's interest in church work. She taught a class in the primary department of the United Church Sunday School for many years and was also treasurer of the W. M. S. of the United Church for many terms. She also shared the family interest in curling. Knitting and crocheting were her hobbies at home.

Mr. and Mrs. Swift have four children. The eldest Dr. W.H. Swift, B. Ed., MA., Ph. D., has climaxed his career by becoming Alberta's Deputy Minister of Education. Mrs. English (Ann), R.N. was also a teacher and now lives in Edmonton. John Swift, B.Sc., is plant superintendent with C.M. & S. in Calgary. Arnold carries on the family business as well as the family traditions in Tofield, for he is an ardent curler, a member of the Town Council and an active member of the Palestine Lodge AF & AM. Arnold's wife, Joyce, is active in church and community work and also adds to the family curling trophies. Arnold and Joyce have two children Shirley and Donald. A third generation of Swifts calls Tofield home.

## MR. AND MRS. WILLIAM THOMPSON

Mr. and Mrs. William Thompson both came to Canada from Scotland. They met in British Columbia where he had a position as a "setter" in a sawmill. They were married in the spring of 1898, and two years later, moved to Tofield where he had proved up on his homestead and built a small house on the N.E. 24, Twp. 50, Rge. 19, W.4. All their possessions were loaded into the wagon in which they travelled, driving one team and leading the other, and driving their cattle. The first three summers Mr. Thompson went back to his job at the saw mill as soon as the crop was in, returning in time to take it off in the fall.

Coal was found under part of this farm, and dug out for fuel. About 1906, Mr. Thompson and Peter Ingram Sr. opened the "Pioneer Coal Mine" on the farm now owned by David Schmidt, at that time owned by Pete Ingram, who owned the coal rights. Work was underground, using pick and shovel. Coal was sold to settlers as far away as Vegreville, who came with teams, across the lake in winter, and around it during the threshing season when the steam engines were fired with coal whenever possible. Several teamsters came together for company, planning to spend the night, but bringing food for themselves and horses to last several days in case they had to wait for coal to be dug or a storm to pass. The Thompson home was often filled to overflowing with these men sleeping on the floor or anywhere they could find a place. Mrs. Thompson had many a laugh when she recalled being asked for permission to play cards to pass the long hours. She agreed to their playing but would have no gambling in her house. With a loud laugh one replied, 'Missus, we have no money to gamble; we'll be lucky to find enough to pay for our coal."Mining regulations were becoming stricter, and the two owners, Ingram and Thompson were finding the business getting too big for them to handle, so in 1908 the Pioneer mine was leased to J.J. McDevitt, a qualified miner.

One of the first community projects undertaken was building the Presbyterian church, which was first located across the road from the N. W. corner of the Thompson farm, with the understanding it was to be moved to town when it was decided where the town site should be. Trees for the rough lumber were cut on the farm recently owned by Mr. Lancaster, a portable sawmill was rented from Matthew McCauley and operated by Mr. Thompson, with Asa Erickson in charge of the steam engine, and Otto Schultz hauling the water. Alex Kellner hauled the finished lumber to the building site Also assisting were J. McGinitie, H. Mitchell, J. Henderson and probably others. Mr. Wilcox was the carpenter, while the finer work was done by a Frenchman with a name like Kazee, who installed the Gothic windows, possibly even making them. The women served the meals and took a turn with the hammer when needed. This church was moved to town by Chas. Bowick's steam engine in 1908, to cross the grade before the steel was laid for the railroad.

Mr. Thompson was one of the organizers and the first Secretary of the Local Improvement District # 25P4 and when it was replaced by the Cornhill Municipality he served as councillor and for many years as Reeve.

The Ingram School was burned, and when a new one was built in 1916, William Thompson was voted in as secretary. For the next 18 years he was never off the board, as trustee, secretary, or chairman.

Both Mr. and Mrs. Thompson, with a group of neighbors were organizers and charter members of the Tofield Agricultural Society and served as directors for several years. These first members backed a note to borrow $1600.00 to buy the present Fair Grounds from the Grand Trunk Co. and they paid off the loan before turning the Society over to younger people.

Mrs. Thompson, too, served her community in the Church, the Women's Institute, and later the Farm Women's organizations and the Red Cross. She had the honor of placing the first call from a rural phone into the Tofield switchboard in June 1910. The family was four daughters, and one son, John.

John and his wife—the former Dorothy Baptist, still live on the original Thompson farm. Their two sons, David and Donald are in Edmonton; their daughter, Kathleen (Mrs. Norman McLellan) lives in Grande Prairie.

Three of the Thompson girls live in the Tofield area in 1967. Mary (Mrs. Earl Moore) has two daughters, Audrey (Mrs. Peterson) and Louise of Vancouver as well as two sons, Glenn of Edmonton and Wayne of Tofield. Dolina (Mrs. Carl Blake) has four daughters: Mrs. Evelyn Blakesman, Miss Enid, Mrs. Yvonne Jans all of Edmonton and Mrs. Jean Richardson of New Westminister. Mabel (Mrs. Russel Ferguson) has one daughter, Ellen (Mrs.Hoflin of Edmonton) and three sons, Leonard, Willard and Clifford of Tofield.

# THE TOFIELD FAMILY

Dr. J. H. Tofield, pioneer doctor of this area and after whom the town was named was born in Yorkshire, England and educated at Oxford. Here he obtained two degrees, one in medicine, and one in engineering.

He went to India as an army doctor. Here he learned to speak

Hindustani as well as the other five languages in which he was proficient.

After seeing various parts of the Canadian west, he came to Edmonton in 1882 and served as doctor among the Cree Indians. During the Riel Rebellion of 1885 he served as an army doctor.

In 1894, Dr. Tofield, along with Dr. J. D. Harrison, Dr. E. A. Braithwaite, Dr. H. C. Wilson, Dr. T. S. Royal and Dr. H. McInnes made a request to the Roman Catholic Bishop of St. Albert for the construction of a hospital in Edmonton. This request was granted and Edmonton's first hospital, now the General Hospital was completed in 1895 and staffed by the Grey Nuns of the Sisters of Charity. The hospital bought the whole block where it now stands 46 lots, for $2300.

While in Edmonton at this time, Dr. Tofield's buckboard broke through the ice on the Saskatchewan River at the Walters' Ferry. It was extricated with considerable difficulty and his passengers, Mrs. Bannerman and her child narrowly escaped a severe wetting.

In 1896, he and Mrs. Tofield and their family, Florence (later Mrs. A. B. Clutterham); Edith (later Mrs. H. E. Rogers) and Mae (Mrs. Tofield's daughter from a previous marriage) came to Tofield and lived for a time on the Pruden place, now the site of the local cemetery.

Doctors being desperately needed in the Northwest Territories, Dr. Tofield was persuaded to use his degree in medicine rather than his degree in engineering. (This original licence to practice medicine is in the possession of his daughter, Mrs. H.E. Rogers of Tofield).

After a short time in Tofield, the family moved to Agricola near Fort Saskatchewan where they remained until 1903 at which time they returned to Tofield, homesteading the land now (1968) occupied by the Krystals. To move back to Tofield entailed several trips with horse and buggy and the children's saddle ponies. The travellers were glad to break their journey at the John Phillips' stopping house.

The Tofield girls now went East to complete their education; Edith, to Owen Sound; Florence, to Montreal. Mrs. Tofield, a nurse by profession, was privileged to make the acquaintance of Lord Beaverbrook and Lord Strathcona when she was acting in her professional capacity to the C.P.R.

construction crews during the building of that railway.

About the time the G.T.P. reached Tofield, Dr. and Mrs. Tofield moved into town and built the house where Ray Henriksons now live. The Tofield girls, returned from their schools, held many parties for the engineers working on the G. T. P.

Dr. Tofield maintained his own dispensary even after J.E. Jamieson, a druggist, came to town. He also had his own scale of fees. One patient with a fractured jaw and broken teeth resulting from a kick by a horse went to Dr. Tofield for attention. The teeth were extracted. the jaw wired, the man was boarded and nursed by Mrs. Tofield for ten days for the sum of ten dollars. Another man had his broken arm set and splinted for $1.50.

In "Pioneer Days in Bardo, Alberta", the story is told of how Dr. Tofield, in a pioneer home without the aid of modern equipment, performed a remarkable operation on a man who had been in a coma for two days. After shaving the man's head, he sawed out a piece of the skull, removing the projection which was pressing on the man's brain. Then he cleaned off the cut piece, put it back in place in the skull and bandaged it. Two hours later, the man regained consciousness and was able to speak. Eventually he recovered completely.

In 1896, according to a record by Mr. John Cookson there was agitation for a government school. The school was started in a building rented from Billie Rowland with Miss Harriet McCallum as teacher. Dr. Tofield was secretary.

When a post office was established in this area, it was called "Tofield" in recognition of Dr. Tofield's services. When the village in 1907, and then the town in 1909, became incorporated the same name was chosen unanimously by the councillors.

His journeys to aid the ill took Dr. Tofield far afield. He was called to Pakan during a smallpox epidemic. He forded swollen creeks nonchalantly assuring his daughters who accompanied him that he would not let them drown. Even the odd bear met in the course of his travels did not faze him.

Pioneer days had compensations for their hardships. Visiting, says Edith Tofield Rogers, made never to be forgotten occasions, especially when made to the Rickner family who lived near Beaverhill Lake. Dancing, parties, baseball, hockey, and swimming were all enjoyed by the Tofields.

Dr. Tofield was a great hockey fan as his picture taken with the E.A.H.L. Champions in 1909 testifies. He was also interested in the Silver Seven who made hockey history a few years later.

Dr. Tofield never did "retire."He was always busy. When he died in 1918, the town mourned. Some, who are now mature men remember "waiting in the horsedrawn buggy for mother and father to come from the funeral" of Tofield's honored pioneer doctor.

Remembered by his daughter as "a kind wonderful man," by a neighbor as "the most interesting man to talk to," the most vivid memories of Dr. Tofield are held by those he served in the pioneer era of this community.

## THE WEATHERILL FAMILY

John Weatherill was born in Toronto on January 31, 1854. His father, a blacksmith and wheelwright, owned a shop on Yonge Street where he made wagons.

He left school at the age of fourteen to apprentice in a lawyer's office where he had the job of looking after the books of a county close to Toronto.

After completing his apprenticeship he went to New York to work, but it wasn't long till the urge to go west got the best of him and he set out for Edmonton, North West Territories, Canada.

After journeying to Winnipeg, which was the end of the steel at that time, he purchased a pony and a Red River cart and started out.

Seven miles west of Brandon the cart broke down and he decided to settle there so he filed on a homestead. When local government was organized around Brandon, John Weatherill got the job as secretary and drove to Brandon with pony and buggy every day. By sleeping on the homestead, he fulfilled his obligations as a homesteader.

At that time there was a young family of two brothers and two sisters from Lancashire who operated the first hotel in Brandon. John Weatherill courted and married the youngest sister, Betsy Pilling.

About this time the Yukon gold rush was in full swing. Some of the young men left Brandon to take part in this rush; one of them by the name of McGregor a former rival for Betsy's hand, who operated the livery barn in Brandon at that time, did quite well. He returned to Brandon and later became LieutenantGovernor of Manitoba.

A short time later, there was another gold rush, this time to British Columbia. Unable to resist the temptation to show Betsy that he, too, was a moneymaker, John sold his farm, sent his young wife and baby to Ontario, and set forth! Two years later, Betsy sent John her two years' savings that he might return home to Ontario! A grocery store occupied them for a short while.

From Ontario they moved to Peoria, Illinois, where their second son was born. From Peoria they moved to Chicago where John worked for McCormick Farm Implement for fifteen years. By this time the family had grown to include four boys.

In 1906 a big depression hit the U.S.A .so the eldest son, J.P. Weatherill headed for Canada and finally filed on a homestead near what is now Deville, Alberta. Johnny Dunn is now farming the place.

J.P. Weatherill returned to Chicago for the winter of 1906 and 1907. In the spring of 1907 the whole family decided to move to Canada. Betsy and the two younger boys stopped off at Brandon while John and the two older boys came to Edmonton to build a home for the family.

This was the spring following a very hard winter. They mentioned seeing many dead cattle along the CPR between Calgary and Edmonton. The dead fish were piled on the shores of Hastings Lake like huge snow drifts.

John Weatherill filed on the N.W. of 16-51-20-W4th and built a house overlooking Hastings Lake, just east of what is now Weslake Beach.

The main winter road between Edmonton and Tofield went over Hastings Lake and many freighters lost at night headed for the light on the hill, where they took shelter for the night. One young Englishman by the name of George Weslake came to the door with his hands badly frozen. He probably would have perished had it not been for the light on the hill.

The second son, George Weatherill, filed on the S.E. 23-13-0, one mile west of Lindbrook hall. He built a home and lived there until 1928.

Betsy and the two small boys came to Edmonton in November of 1907 and were met by George, with a team of cayuses and a lumber wagon. It was a long day's trip over corduroy trails. There were no spring seats on the wagon and Betsy and the boys sat on trunks which bounced continuously. The youngest boy cried with pain from the "stitch in his side" so the pauses were made to walk for short stretches. About two miles from home one of the cayuses balked on a slippery hill. When Betsy saw a light close by, she and the small boys went to investigate and found themselves at the door of a house, which proved to be that of family by the name of Rowland. They were busy skinning and stretching the hides of rats. One two-year-old by the name of Art had one by the tail and was galloping around the room.

The small group had to walk the rest of the way, with the owls hooting and coyotes howling; it gave the city raised children quite a thrill.

After the novelty of the new house wore off, the young boys missed their playmates and the youngest boy went to Betsy crying, "I don't like it here." Betsy sat down and started to cry too, and said "I don't like it here either."

On one trip to Edmonton for supplies John was delayed longer than usual and the little family had nothing to eat but flour and water. When the local auctioneer, Shorty Carter, came along with a team and buggy, he put his horses in the stable and came to the door where Betsy met him saying she was sorry but they had nothing but boiled flour to offer him. "Oh," said Shorty, " I just stopped to rest my horses" and he went and got a lunch from his buggy and left it on the table for the children.

When spring came the number of the wild ducks was tremendous and many swans floated on the lake. The Beaver Hills were a hunter's paradise at that time and with the help of the Ward children, who taught the young Weatherills to set a trap and to skin a rat, and

Augustus Gladue who bought their furs and didn't complain that the first ones that weren't stretched or fleshed too well, the young boys were able to adapt themselves to the pioneer life quite well.

John took an active part in trying to organize a school district, but with no success at that time as the bachelor neighbours outvoted those with families. He attended the meeting that organized the Lindbrook school district and chose the name Lindbrook from two pioneer family names; Lindberg who lived south of Hastings Creek and Sherbrook who lived north of Hastings Creek.

But John Weatherill was a misfit as a homesteader so his wife, Betsy, didn't have too much trouble persuading him to leave the homestead after four years, to move to Edmonton.

In Edmonton he had difficulty at his age competing with the young Englishmen, who were coming to Canada in large numbers at that time to do office work. However about this time the Rural Municipality of Cornhill was formed and they were having trouble keeping a secretary Mr. T.J.Glenn, the reeve at that time, advised John to apply for the position. He did and was accepted at the salary of $60 per month. So in the spring of 1915 the family moved to Tofield where the office of Cornhill Municipality was located.

By this time there was only one boy left home, Charley, the third boy, having gone back to the States. Harold, the youngest, received most of his education in Tofield and still farms north of town. He and his wife Margaret (Bates) have one son Laurie. Harold raises purebred Herefords on his "Dlorah" farm.

In March 1928 John Weatherill died at the age of 74.

# GEORGE WESLAKE

George Weslake was born in Exeter, England, where, during his years in school he was very active in sport being especially proficient in football.

Being an adventuresome chap who didn't care much for city life, George, at the age of nineteen sailed for Canada and a new life in the Canadian West. Arriving in March 1907, he filed on a homestead in the Beaver Hills northwest of Tofield; this area later became known as the Weslake District, north of Lindbrook.

The first years were hard for the city boy engaged in clearing and breaking the land. Soon he became the proud owner of a yoke of oxen with which, of course, came a new vocabulary. To supplement his meagre income, he worked part time on the railway construction gangs as the railway was built through this area. George also added to his coffers by trapping muskrats.

Travel in those days was mainly accomplished on foot; George often walked to Tofield, Chipman, or Edmonton for supplies and for recreation. This recreation was the sport of football at which he excelled. He was a valued member of Tofield's football team.

In 1909, George Weslake returned to England to marry his childhood sweetheart Miss Elsie Tett. The next year saw the Weslakes back in Edmonton via C.P.R. where they hired a livery team to carry them and their belongings to George's homestead.

Here the English bride made the acquaintance of her neighbors. Women were scarce in this pioneer district but bachelors were plentiful. Bill Harres, Clint Frary Mike Hahn Corbett Caniels, Mr. Mercier, the Morrows, the Sherbrooks, the Gladues, the Donalds, and many others soon became friends of the newly arrived English couple

Four children were born to George and Elsie Weslake: Dolly, (Mrs. Walter Griesson), Edmonton; Pat, Hastings Lake; Hazel, (Mrs. Herb Reynar), Leduc; and George, (married to Cora Broen) still living on the original homestead in 1967.

His growing family provided an incentive for George Weslake to be instrumental in organizing the school district which bore his name. He was chairman of the Weslake School Board through almost all of its existence. Until 1934, the Weslakes lived and worked in the Hastings Lake district where they lived until George Weslake's death in 1961. His widow, now (1967) in her eighties, still resides at the lake with her son, Pat, during the summer months.

## THE WHILLANS FAMILY

The Whillans family came originally from Roxburghshire, although several generations lived in the parish of Southdean at Chester, whose name is derived from the Roman word "camp". Some of the family also lived in Castleton Parish which adjoins Southdean but which is drained in the opposite direction, west, by the Liddel and the Esk. When Sir Walter Scott visited Liddesdale to collect ancient ballads, he found it without roads; his was the first wheeled vehicle ever seen there.

It is believed that the name Whillans was originally Quheillands or Whilland.(Que in Scotland was pronounced as "W").This name originated from the lands near the Wheel Kirk, situated on the spring (the word for which was Quelle with 'Qu' pronounced as "W") which forms the headwaters of the Liddel River. So the name Whillans means "owner of the spring lands". Wheel Causeway, following an old Roman road, passes near Wheel Kirk as does an earthwork called the Catrail which is said to have been built by the Picts. Edward I visited Wheel Kirk on May 24, 1296.

William Whillans was born in Southdean parish in 1779. He traced, documented and recorded the Whillans' family tree, beginning with his grandfather, James Whillans, who was born in the parish of Jedburgh in 1688 and died in 1783.

William Whillans and his family emigrated to Canada and settled near London, Ontario, in 1837. His brother Robert, settled at the same time at Hurdman's Bridge near Ottawa. Robert's eldest son became the Rev. Robert Whillans M.A, a competent Greek scholar, and the grandfather of Roy Whillans of the Ketchamoot district south of Tofield. The youngest son became the Rev. George Whillans, D.D. a minister and minister emeritus of the Presbyterian Church in Quebec. George's brother John, living in Calgary, celebrated his hundredth birthday by walking to church.

Another famous member of the Whillans family was "Big Jack Whillans" who was reputed to be the strongest man on the Ottawa. Standing 6'3", weighing 275 lbs. he had no difficulty in maintaining this reputation.

Rev. Robert Whillans of Ottawa had nine children, Wally and Wardy, who died in World War I; Allan; Harry, who became a doctor; Charlie (father of Roy Whillans); Carie, a nurse; Mary, Winnifred and Lina.

Charlie Whillans came to Alberta from Ottawa as a young lad of seventeen. He worked on a farm north of Tofield until he had saved enough money to make a down payment on a homestead south of the present Bardo elevator. He started his farming operations with a team of oxen named Tom and Jerry of which he was very proud. One ox being smaller than the other, had less endurance and thus preferred to quit early in the day When the oxen died, their horns were mounted and now hang in the Tofield Museum.

Charlie soon tired of "batching"and began courting Clara Sheperd who had come to Alberta with her parents from Barrie, Ontario, to a farm at Round Iill. Albin Anderson, an old timer of the Kingman district recalls that Charlie drove a pretty snappy team and cutter the winter he was courting Clara. He wore an old cap with the ear flaps pulled down against the winter's chill until he approached Clara's home at which time, he made a fast change to a hat. So when he arrived at the door, he was a dapper young suitor.

Charlie and Clara were married in March,1907. By 1918, the little log house was so crowded with a growing family that a new eight-roomed house was erected. The children born to Charlie and Clara were Gordon, Roy, Ralph, Lloyd, Marguerite, Neil and Joyce.

Every Sunday found the entire Whillans family in church first at Bardo Methodist services and then at Ketchamoot United Church.

When Mrs.Whillans took a few days' much needed holiday, the children received a treat when father cooked plum pudding for them. Roy recalls that the first two puddings were horribly sweet but later ones were greeted with joy by seven hungry youngsters.

Charlie passed away in July 29, 1961, at the age of 76 years. He had lived for a few months in Tofield after retiring from the farm. Clara lived quietly in a nursing home in Edmonton where she passed away on March 14, 1966.

Roy is the only one of the family remaining in the Ketchamoot district where he still farms. He married Dorothy Ovelson of the Kingman district in 1938. To this union were born four sons: Jerald, Vernon, LeRoy, and Barry.

Jerald married Sylvia Grace Kettletz of New Sarepta. Their children are Marlin and Marleen. Vernon married Lorraine Redford of Edmonton; Tracy and Todd are their children. In 1968,Vernon and his family are stationed with the Armed Services in Germany. LeRoy and Barry are students in the Tofield School in Grade XII and Grade IX respectively.

Gordon Whillans resides in Tofield. His children are Donald, Dennis and Karen.

# HENRY WOOD FAMILY

*The material for this article was supplied by Mrs Esther (Wood) Majakey of Edmonton.*

Henry Wood was born in Yellow Springs, Ohio in 1859. He was the eldest of the family and when he was three years old his father joined the Union Army of the Civil War. Thinking of this as a winter's adventure and a means of earning a little money, he left his family on the farm. Instead, the war lasted four years. Soldiers' dependants received no allowance and had no contact with their families for months at a time. Mrs. Wood was forced to return to her family and Henry was sent to live with an uncle until the war was over. He grew up in Ohio and then moved with his parents to Lewton, Kansas, where in 1888 he married Louella Patton, the daughter of a former Methodist minister. They settled for a time on a farm near Newton and then moved to Western Kansas. This was done by driving over land in two covered wagons, the mother driving one team and the father the other. One of Mrs. Wood's exciting stories was of swimming her team across the Cimarron River, and not knowing if they would ever make the other bank.

This venture was not as successful as the young couple had expected and they returned to Newton. Here the talk of the time was the opening of the Cherokee Strip of the Indian Territory of Oklahoma. The method of land granting was most exciting. One registered at the land office and was given a place in a long line formed by all the competitors. At the appointed time a gun was shot and the race was on. There were no restrictions as to the rype of conveyance. Buggies, wagons and even men on foot were all in evidence. The first one to reach the quarter section of his choice staked it, and it belonged to him.

Mr. Wood had an excellent horse and the spirit of adventure so once again those covered wagons with all the Woods' effects plus three children set out across to Perry, Oklahoma, to take part in the great run. The origin of this fast horse was always vague. Good horses were always Mr. Woods' greatest pride. A noted Sire was being brought to Newton and it was Mr. Wood's greatest desire to own a horse of this lineage; so, taking his prize mare, he proceeded to town. But the fee was exorbitant so he put his mare up at the livery stable and went away to spend the night, a ,very disappointed young man. The next spring, much to his surprise, along came a beautiful black colt. It was rumored that the attendants at the livery stable just couldn't see a young man so disappointed. With this horse, Henry Wood outdistanced all the competitors and got a good farm with a creek on it, something much desired in Oklahoma. The horse ran for several miles with no trouble; a picture of him hung on the Wood's front room wall to commemorate the events.

After seven successful years in Oklahoma neighbors by the name of Mason returned from the North West Territories in Canada with glowing stories of a new country that was opening up. Once again the spirit of adventure was aroused and this time a colonist car was secured and everything the family owned, cattle,horses, and machinery, were loaded and the long trip to Wetaskiwin was started. Henry's brother William Wood and his family, a cousin Iva, later Mrs. Pete Logan, and many young men of the district joined the group.By this time there were seven children in the Wood family, the youngest being twins. At one point, Ardis, one of the twins was missing. Later she was found under a seat by Sam Bethel who was also one of the colonists coming to Wetaskiwin.

On reaching Wetaskiwin, they unloaded their car and drove by team over the trails to what is now Tofield. They had to cross the Pipestone Creek and even though it was September the water was so high the wagons were taken over by raft; the livestock swam.

They were met by Mr. Mason, the man who influenced their

coming, and stayed with him, while Henry Wood looked for a house for his family. Mr. Mason lived on the farm that now belongs to J. C. Warner. After a few days a log house was found for the family on the farm of James Pruden. This farm was directly across from the Bethel farm. The Jordy Norris family also had a house there.

The Wood family settled on the S.W.quarter of 8-51-18-W4th, now (in 1968) part of the Dodds farm. After a few years he sold it to Mathew McCauley, and bought the north half of 1-51-19-W4th which was to became Tofield No. 2. He sold this property to Crafts & Lee who subdivided it into town lots. The next move the Wood family made was to the west half of 35-51-19-W4th where Mrs. M.C. Wood and her son Donald and his wife Phyllis (Rose) now reside.

In 1903 Henry Wood purchased one of the first steam engines and ran a sawmill on his farm, during the winter. Most of the logs came from what is now known as the Cooking Lake Forest Reserve. The settlers hauled their own logs and if they were able, they paid, but mostly he took lumber in trade. In 1906 he built what was then a large house, hauling most of the lumber for it from Edmonton. One summer he made twenty-two trips. The flies and mosquitoes were very bad and he had rather fancy fly nets for the horses.

This house had no basement as Mrs. Wood had not forgotten her days in Oklahoma and was still afraid of cyclones. As was the custom there the family had a sort of root cellar in the yard where you could take refuge from the twisters.

While the Wood family did not run a stopping house this was the last place on the old base line to Edmonton, and travellers were never turned away. In those days people carried their own bedding and were glad of any place to put up for the night. One time when Henry Wood was on one of his trips to Edmonton, a man came requesting a place to stay. Bill and John were making a bit of money looking after someone's horses and the barn was full so the traveller was told he would have to put his team in the shed. This he refused to do and when the boys refused to move their horses he became hostile and said, very well, he would go on to the next place. The boys gleefully told him to GO, neglecting to tell him that it was twenty-five miles to the Watson stopping house at

Ardrossan. The man drove all night and when he arrived weary and worn and was asked why he had come so far he said he would have stayed at the last place but there were two such sassy kids there and they hadn't told him how far it was. Unfortunately Henry Wood was one of the travellers at the Watsons and such treatment wasn't his idea of hospitality as the boys found out when he arrived home.

As the settlers began raising crops, the need of a threshing machine arose and as Henry Wood already had the engine he bought a grain separator. This was for many years the only threshing machine in the country and the district was from Chipman to Ryley. The crew started in the fall and were lucky to be home by the new year. The last farmers stacked their grain and the time of the threshing didn't make much difference. Threshing in those days was a big undertaking. The farmer supplied the fuel, usually wood, for the 140 lb. pressure engine. A crew consisted of ten teams and there were spikepitchers, field pitchers and grain wagons. Jack and Charlie Bowick were the engineers for many years until Lloyd Wood took over. The crew carried their own bed rolls and usually slept in the hayloft of the barn. Henry Wood was always sympathetic to the farm women, who, he said did more work than anybody, cooking for up to twenty-seven men and vying with each other to serve the best meals. In later years this same steam engine was used to break the land on many of the farms around the district and even after gasoline tractors became popular it was unequalled in pulling the stumps of the large poplar trees that grew on much of the land.

The Woods family were very community-minded, helping in any way they could to make life better for them selves and their neighbors. They raised nine children, two of whom are still living. Lloyd will be remembered by the old timers as the member of the Tofield ball team. In later years he served as a councillor on the Cornhill Municipal Council and as a member of the Lakeshore school board. Bill was known for his marksmanship with a rifle and would entertain the young fry who gathered at the Wood home by throwing up a nickel and shooting a hole in it before it hit the ground. Pat and Mel promoted the Lakeshore Stampede which was held for several years at the home place. Those who were around in the early twenties will remember names like

Ritland, Sizer and Dumont and our own young bronco busters, Owen Eaton, the Friegen boys and the Donalds. Many of the hearts of the now not-so-young girls, will beat the faster at the memory of the gala barn dance which was held at the end of the day in Tommy Jones' big barn.

Maggie, the eldest of the girls was loved by all who knew her, always working in her quiet and unselfish way to help others. One early settler said, "If it hadn't been for Maggie's kindness I never would have had the courage to face another Alberta winter." Nina, as a young girl, was an active participant in the horse racing at the local fairs. After her marriage she lived at Viking for twenty-seven years where she gave so unstintingly of her time and talent that when they formed a chapter of the Order of the Eastern Star they named it the Nina Chapter in her memory. Ardis trained as a nurse and served the district as a private nurse for Dr. Frank Law where more often than not her winter transportation was the front runner of the bobsled and her patient shared the living room with the rest of the family. She went on to become matron of the Viking and Macleod hospitals and then returned to Tofield as the nurse in Dr. Freebury's office. Melville, the youngest son, won the Master Farmer award in 1958 and lived on the farm which Henry Wood homesteaded in 1903, and where all of the family grew up. John farms north of Tofield and lives on the farm which Lloyd homesteaded and Esther Majakey lives in Edmonton.

Mel and Ethel Wood had a son, Donald, and a daughter Margaret, now Mrs. Lorne Berrecloth, who has two children, David and Sherry.

John and Mary Wood had four daughters, Lorene (Mrs. Jim Francis); Louella (Mrs. Robert Goubault); Evelyn (Mrs. Vic Halwa); Kathleen; the one son, John, married Gloria Miller. They have two children.

Mr. and Mrs. Majakey have one son, Vernon.

Of this large family who did so much in building up our local history, six are buried in the Tofield Cemetery.

# Afterword

## TOFIELD"S GOLDEN JUBILEE

1959 was the Golden Jubilee of the incorporation of the town of Tofield, and in honour of this anniversary a year-long series of events was planned and consummated under the direction of Dr. W.H. Freebury, Mayor of Tofield and chairman of the Golden Jubilee Committee.

Dr. Freebury issued a proclamation of the Jubilee Year celebrations, which the Tofield Mercury published in the January 29 and February 5 issues. The slogan for the year was "A Proud Heritage – A Courageous Future."

In 1959 two of Tofield's original councillors, Mr. Mark Ferguson and Mr. A. Maxwell, were still available for comment. Mr. Ferguson lived here and Mr. Maxwell frequently visited his son and family. The councillors of 1959 were: Dr. Freebury (mayor), James Graham Allan, Allan Herndon, D.L. Jefferson, Charles Kallal, Conrad Patterson and Arnold Swift. Secretary Treasurer was J. Edwin Stinson.

During the year special events were held by many organizations. The Curling Club held its Golden Jubilee Bonspiel; the Lions opened their Natural History Museum and the children's playground with Al Oeming as guest speaker; the churches had special services; the Legion Hall was officially opened with Dick Mutlow as president and Major Frank Fane as guest speaker; biographies of pioneers and histories of pioneer organizations were gathered by Mrs. Grace Phillips and published weekly in the Mercury; the annual Dominion Day sports day organized by the Community League under its president, Norman Glover, was the most successful ever held up to that time; the League's Christmas Carol Festival was an outstanding event. To close the year's festivities, a pot-luck supper under the chairmanship of Rev. S. Bell was held in the Community Hall to welcome all newcomers to the area. H.A. Pike, Superintendent of Schools for Beaver County, spoke on behalf of the new residents. A large cast of school children presented a pageant, written and directed by Grace Phillips, which gave a light-hearted account of Tofield's history.

The huge birthday cake made by Mrs. Mabel Boyles was cut by Edith Rogers, daughter of Dr. Tofield for whom the town was named.

Another Jubilee event was the production by C.F. Annis of "The Late Christopher Bean" under the sponsorship of Holy Trinity W.A.

The University of Alberta Mixed Chorus visited Tofield in Jubilee Year.

Early in Jubilee Year, Mr. R.H. Harris, principal of Tofield School, conducted a competition of his art class for the creation of a distinctive crest suitable for use in Jubilee Year. The winner of the competition was Ray Pittet; runners-up were Anton Tomko and Floyd Taylor. The crests were stamped on T-shirts for all ages; the Tofield stores sponsored the sale of these shirts.

Tofield High School, using "Golden Moments" as its theme, conducted spring graduation ceremonies for: Elvera Baerg, Elsie Baergen, Louis Baergen, Helmet Dueck, Clayton Everitt, Allan Henderson, Shirley Harris, Bertha Johnson, Lydia Mierau, Bruce McFadzean, Erna Neufeld, Linda Neufeld, Art Rempel, Vera Tiedemann, June Foyd, Barbara Sware and Joanne Belcourt.

A well-attended Civic Thanksgiving Service was held in the Community Centre with representatives of all local churches participating.

The Jubilee Committee consisted of Dr. Freebury, Howard Watson, Dick Mutlow, Norman Glover, Graham Allan, Mabel Boyles, Bill Worton, Grace Phillips and Vince Bates.

J.E. Stinson, secretary of the town of Tofield, was also secretary of the Jubilee Committee.

# TOFIELD'S CENTENNIAL YEAR

Tofield's Centennial program was launched on January 23, 1967, at a meeting of interested citizens called by Mayor Freebury. A committee to co-ordinate the year-long program was named, consisting of Dr. W.H. Freebury, Mrs. Marie Worton, Gabe Pittet, Jim Francis, Father Scriven, Larry Willson, Bill Christensen, Rev. W. Hammett, Mrs. Mabel Boyles, Mrs. Petra Stauffer, Mrs. Grace Phillips, Thomas Jacobs, David Halvorson and Andy Heiberg, with Miss Chimko as secretary.

Dr. Freebury appointed Mrs. Petra Stauffer as Tofield's Centennial Queen, an office she filled with charm and dignity.

The whole district entered enthusiastically into Centennial plans. Centennial flags flew from most buildings on Main Street; old-fashioned costumes were worn in the streets and in business places every weekend; teas were held which Queen Petra honoured with her presence.

At a "family night" in April, Queen Petra received her crown from Dr. Freebury. A variety program featuring adults and children of all ages was arranged by Marie Worton.

An "ethnic night" of folk dances, followed by old time dancing arranged by Ruth Kraus and Harold Schultz was held later in the spring with a huge crowd participating.

The Lions Club held a winter carnival, complete with ski-doo races and parachute jumps.

Souvenirs were bought by Mrs. Boyles and sold in Robinson's Store by the kindness of C. Blacklock. A Centennial doll dressed by Mrs. Boyles was raffled.

Mrs. Joan Dunham staged "The Passing Parade," a program well received by its large audience as it followed the fine arts down through the years.

The Tofield High School published a Centennial Yearbook – a pictorial record of Tofield in 1967. The Tofield Historical Society planned and prepared to produce this history, "Tales of Tofield." They also sponsored a visit by Lieutenant-Governor J. Grant MacEwan who spoke to an audience in the Community Centre.

Special church services and carol festivals were participated in by all the local churches. Almost every organization held special events where Centennial costumes were featured and at which Queen Petra was an honoured guest.

A large bulletin board was place on Main Street by Bill Christensen and Thomas Jacobs. On it were announced Centennial events. The Ladies' Bowling Club donated benches to be placed on Main Street.

A park, "Tofield's Centennial Park," was Queen Petra's special project. Aided by the town council and interested citizens, this park is now a reality on Main Street. Its opening by Bud Salloum of the Alberta Centennial Committee was followed by an ethnic supper in the Community Centre late in the fall.

July first was Centennial-oriented. Special attractions such as the fashion show, the large parade, the jumping horses, and the 21-gun salute by the Tofield Gun Club all made the day something to remember.

Bill Bakschaat was chosen by a group of clergymen as Citizen of the Year, and presented with a scroll as a symbol of community appreciation of his services during the years he has worked at the Tofield Hospital.

Queen Petra entertained her "subjects" at a garden party at her home in August.

Exactly a year after it had been appointed, the Centennial Committee held its final meeting. The money in the treasury was divided among the Tofield Library, the Tofield Community League and the Youth Sports Committee.

The committee, having been asked to recommend possible candidates for Centennial awards, did so. In due time these Centennial Achievement Awards were received by Dr. W.H. Freebury, "Queen" Petra Stauffer, and Grace Phillips.

# L'ENVOI

The committee in charge of the preparation of this history of the Tofield community is all too well aware that, in spite of our vigilance, we have "done those things which we ought not to have done, and have left undone those things which we ought to have done." For any such errors or omissions we ask the reader's indulgence; to the best of our knowledge at the time of writing the information contained herein is correct and complete.

We are happy to have been instrumental in preserving for future generations the history of Tofield.

Grace A. Phillips

# AFTERWORD

Later generations are indeed grateful for the foresight and efforts of the Tofield Historical Society who originally published Tales of Tofield. This book has allowed us to appreciate the hardships, share the joys, and value the contributions of those who have gone before.

Re-publication was greatly facilitated by the work of Elizabeth Hubbard of the Tofield Municipal Library, the technological skills of the late Ed Ludwig, and support from members of the present Tofield Historical Society.

Although minor changes in format have been made, the original text has not been altered.

Barbara (Phillips) Conquest
Tofield, Alberta 2004

ISBN 141202872-8